The Complete Egyptian Cookbook

Authentic Quick, Easy and Delicious Food Recipes for Traditional Egyptian Cooking

BY: ANDREA G. BOSCO

TABLE OF CONTENTS

The Complete Egyptian Cookbook..i

1. Koshari:...8
2. Ful Medames:..8
3. Egyptian Lentil Soup:..8
4. Egyptian Rice Pudding:...9
5. Feteer Meshaltet:..9
6. Shakshuka:...10
7. Mahshi:..10
8. Ta'ameya (Egyptian Falafel):...................................10
9. Basbousa:..11
10. Egyptian Flatbread (Aish Baladi):..........................11
11. Alexandrian Liver:..12
12. Kushari Casserole:...12
13. Egyptian Okra Stew:...12
14. Hawawshi Bread:..13
15. Egyptian Stuffed Grape Leaves:............................13
16. Molokhia...14
17. Hawawshi...14
18. Umm Ali...14
19. Egyptian Tomato Salad..15
20. Mulukhiyah Soup...15
21. Bamya Bil Lahmeh...16
22. Egyptian Fish Tagine..16
23. Egyptian Fattoush Salad..16
24. Egyptian Stuffed Eggplant.....................................17
25. Egyptian Chicken and Rice....................................17
26. Baladi Bread..18
27. Egyptian Lentil and Rice Pilaf.................................18
28. Konafa..19
29. Mahalabiya..19
30. Egyptian Stuffed Bell Peppers...............................19
31. Mulukhiyah with Chicken:......................................20
32. Egyptian Spiced Tea:...20
33. Egyptian Bean Salad:..21
34. Egyptian Beef Kebabs:..21
35. Rice-Stuffed Pigeon:...21
36. Egyptian Beetroot Salad:......................................22
37. Basboosa Bil Nisrina:..22
38. Egyptian Grilled Fish:..22
39. Kushari Pizza:...23
40. Egyptian Carrot Salad:..23
41. Egyptian Spinach and Cheese Pastry....................24
42. Egyptian Fish Soup...24
43. Egyptian Lemonade...24
44. Egyptian Sweet Rice with Nuts..............................25
45. Egyptian Meat Stew..25
46. Egyptian Pumpkin Soup..26
47. Egyptian Chicken Molokhia...................................26
48. Egyptian Cheese Pie...27
49. Egyptian Shrimp and Rice....................................27
50. Egyptian Cucumber Yogurt Salad.........................28
51. Egyptian Meatballs...28
52. Egyptian Bread Pudding.......................................28
53. Egyptian Roasted Chicken:..................................29
54. Egyptian Chickpea Salad:....................................29
55. Egyptian Lamb Kofta:...29
56. Egyptian Phyllo Meat Pie:....................................30
57. Egyptian Coconut Cookies:..................................30
58. Egyptian Spiced Rice:..31
59. Egyptian Egg Salad:...31
60. Egyptian Beef and Potato Stew:..........................31
61. Egyptian Lentil Salad:..32
62. Egyptian Stuffed Zucchini:...................................32
63. Egyptian Shish Kebabs:.......................................32
64. Egyptian Date Cookies:..33
65. Egyptian Okra and Lamb Stew.............................33
55. Egyptian Yogurt with Honey.................................33
56. Egyptian Lamb and Rice......................................34
57. Egyptian Cabbage Salad......................................34
58. Egyptian Lamb Chops...35
59. Egyptian Spinach Stew...35
60. Egyptian Chicken Shawarma................................35
61. Egyptian Breaded Fish..36
62. Egyptian Sesame Cookies....................................36

63. Egyptian Tomato and Cucumber Salad 37
64. Egyptian Lamb and Potato Stew 37
65. Egyptian Lentil and Vegetable Stew 38
66. Egyptian Stuffed Artichokes: 38
67. Egyptian Beef Shawarma: 39
68. Egyptian Semolina Cake: 39
69. Egyptian Roasted Vegetables: 39
70. Egyptian Lamb and Eggplant Stew: 40
71. Egyptian Bulgur Salad: 40
72. Egyptian Lamb Kebabs: 40
73. Egyptian Green Bean Stew: 41
74. Egyptian Chicken and Vegetable Tagine: 41
75. Egyptian Rice and Lentil Soup: 42
76. Egyptian Stuffed Onions: 42
77. Egyptian Lamb Curry: 42
78. Egyptian Rice and Chicken Soup 43
79. Egyptian Stuffed Mushrooms....................................43
80. Egyptian Lamb and Potato Curry 43
81. Egyptian Spinach and Lentil Soup 44
82. Egyptian Chicken and Potato Tagine 44
83. Egyptian Rice and Vermicelli Pilaf 45
84. Egyptian Okra and Tomato Stew: 45
85. Egyptian Chicken Fatta: 45
86. Egyptian Fava Bean Salad: 46
87. Egyptian Lamb and Spinach Tagine 46
88. Egyptian Rice Pudding with Rosewater......................47
89. Egyptian Stuffed Squash 47
90. Egyptian Lamb and Egg Tagine................................47
91. Egyptian Lentil and Chickpea Salad 48
92. Egyptian Lamb and Green Bean Stew 48
93. Egyptian Lamb and Chickpea Stew 49
94. Egyptian Stuffed Cabbage Rolls 49
95. Egyptian Lamb Tagine with Prunes 50
96. Egyptian Stuffed Tomatoes 50
97. Egyptian Lamb and Okra Stew 51
98. Egyptian Quinoa Salad 51
99. Egyptian Chicken and Okra Tagine: 52
100. Egyptian Rice and Beef Soup: 52
101. Egyptian Stuffed Peppers with Rice: 52
102. Egyptian Lamb and Cauliflower Curry: 53
103. Egyptian Spinach and Chickpea Soup: 53
104. Egyptian Chicken and Eggplant Tagine: 53
105. Egyptian Rice and Lentil Pilaf with Caramelized Onions: 54
106. Egyptian Stuffed Cabbage Leaves with Rice and Beef: 54
107. Egyptian Lamb Tagine with Artichokes and Olives: ...55
108. Egyptian Rice and Chicken Stuffed Grape Leaves: 55
109. Egyptian Stuffed Bell Peppers with Rice and Lamb: ..56
110. Egyptian Egg and Tomato Tagine: 56
111. Egyptian Rice and Vermicelli Soup: 56
112. Egyptian Stuffed Eggplant with Rice and Ground Beef: 57
113. Egyptian Lamb and Okra Tagine with Tomatoes: 57
114. Egyptian Lentil and Bulgur Salad: 58
115. Egyptian Chicken and Spinach Tagine with Chickpeas 58
116. Egyptian Rice and Milk Pudding with Cinnamon........59
117. Egyptian Stuffed Zucchini with Rice and Lamb 59
118. Egyptian Lamb and Potato Tagine with Green Peas .59
119. Egyptian Spinach and Lentil Salad............................60
120. Egyptian Chicken and Okra Stew with Tomatoes 60
121. Egyptian Spinach and Chickpea Salad: 61
122. Egyptian Chicken and Egg Tagine with Potatoes: 61
123. Egyptian Rice and Vermicelli Pilaf with Chickpeas: 61
124. Egyptian Stuffed Bell Peppers with Rice and Vegetables: 62
125. Egyptian Lamb Tagine with Olives and Lemon: 62
126. Egyptian Rice and Chicken Stuffed Grape Leaves with Mint: 63
127. Egyptian Rice and Chicken Stuffed Bell Peppers: 63
128. Egyptian Stuffed Grape Leaves with Rice and Vegetables: 63
129. Egyptian Lamb Tagine with Prunes and Almonds: 64
130. Egyptian Rice and Beef Stuffed Cabbage Leaves: 64
131. Egyptian Stuffed Eggplant with Rice and Chickpeas: .65
132. Egyptian Lamb and Cauliflower Tagine with Chickpeas: 65
133. Egyptian Stuffed Zucchini with Rice and Chickpeas ..65

134. Egyptian Lamb and Potato Tagine with Green Beans 66
135. Egyptian Spinach and Lentil Soup with Lemon 67
136. Egyptian Chicken and Okra Stew with Potatoes 67
138. Egyptian Rice and Milk Pudding with Pistachios 68
139. Egyptian Stuffed Eggplant with Rice and Lentils 68
140. Egyptian Lamb and Cauliflower Tagine with Tomatoes 69
141. Egyptian Spinach and Chickpea Soup with Cumin 69
142. Egyptian Chicken and Egg Tagine with Green Peas ...69
143. Egyptian Rice and Vermicelli Soup with Cilantro 70
144. Egyptian Stuffed Bell Peppers with Rice and Lentils ..70
145. Egyptian Lamb Tagine with Almonds and Raisins 71
146. Egyptian Stuffed Zucchini with Rice 71
147. Egyptian Lamb and Cauliflower Tagine with Potatoes 71
148. Egyptian Spinach and Chickpea Salad with Tahini Dressing 72
149. Egyptian Chicken and Egg Tagine with Bell Peppers ..72
150. Egyptian Rice and Vermicelli Pilaf with Raisins and Pine Nuts 73
151. Egyptian Stuffed Bell Peppers with Rice and Spinach 73
152. Egyptian Rice and Beef Stuffed Cabbage Leaves with Tomato Sauce 74
153. Egyptian Stuffed Eggplant with Rice and Spinach 74
154. Egyptian Lamb and Potato Tagine with Carrots 75
155. Egyptian Spinach and Lentil Salad with Mint 75
156. Egyptian Chicken and Okra Stew with Lemon 75
157. Egyptian Rice and Chicken Stuffed Grape Leaves with Dill 76
158. Egyptian Lamb Tagine with Dates and Apricots 76
159. Egyptian Rice and Beef Stuffed Cabbage Leaves with Garlic Sauce 77
160. Egyptian Stuffed Eggplant with Rice and Mushrooms 77
161. Egyptian Lamb and Potato Tagine with Onions 78
162. Egyptian Spinach and Lentil Soup with Cumin and Coriander 78
163. Egyptian Chicken and Okra Stew with Cilantro 79
164. Egyptian Rice and Chicken Stuffed Grape Leaves with Yogurt Sauce: 79
165. Egyptian Stuffed Zucchini with Rice and Lentils: 80
166. Egyptian Lamb and Cauliflower Tagine with Chickpeas and Tomatoes: 80
167. Egyptian Spinach and Chickpea Soup with Turmeric and Ginger: 81
168. Egyptian Chicken and Egg Tagine with Moroccan Spices: 81
169. Egyptian Rice and Vermicelli Soup with Mint and Lemon: 82
170. Egyptian Chicken and Okra Stew with Garlic and Paprika: 82
171. Egyptian Rice and Chicken Stuffed Grape Leaves with Dill-Yogurt Sauce: 83
172. Egyptian Stuffed Zucchini with Rice and Chickpeas in Tomato Sauce: 83
173. Egyptian Lamb and Cauliflower Tagine with Turmeric and Cardamom: 84
174. Egyptian Spinach and Chickpea Soup with Harissa and Cilantro: 84
175. Egyptian Chicken and Egg Tagine with Preserved Lemon and Olives: 84
176. Egyptian Stuffed Bell Peppers with Rice and Feta Cheese 85
177. Egyptian Lamb Tagine with Prunes and Cinnamon ...86
178. Egyptian Rice and Beef Stuffed Cabbage Leaves with Tomato-Pepper Sauce 86
179. Egyptian Stuffed Eggplant with Rice and Peas 86
180. Egyptian Lamb and Potato Tagine with Carrots and Cumin 87
181. Egyptian Spinach and Lentil Salad with Lemon-Tahini Dressing 87
182. Egyptian Spinach and Lentil Salad with Pomegranate Dressing: 88
183. Egyptian Chicken and Okra Stew with Turmeric and Coriander: 88
184. Egyptian Rice and Chicken Stuffed Grape Leaves with Mint-Yogurt Sauce: 89
185. Egyptian Rice and Vermicelli Pilaf with Pistachios and Saffron 89
186. Egyptian Stuffed Bell Peppers with Rice and Herbs ..90
187. Egyptian Lamb Tagine with Almonds and Ras el Hanout 90
188. Egyptian Rice and Beef Stuffed Cabbage Leaves with Tamarind Sauce 90

189. Egyptian Stuffed Eggplant with Rice and Tomato-Herb Sauce 91

190. Egyptian Lamb and Potato Tagine with Prunes and Ginger 92

191. Egyptian Stuffed Zucchini with Rice and Dill in Lemon Sauce 92

192. Egyptian Lamb and Cauliflower Tagine with Saffron and Cinnamon 93

193. Egyptian Spinach and Chickpea Soup with Lemon and Cumin 93

194. Egyptian Chicken and Egg Tagine with Harissa and Paprika 94

195. Egyptian Rice and Vermicelli Soup with Chickpeas and Parsley 94

196. Egyptian Stuffed Bell Peppers with Rice and Tomato-Pepper Sauce 94

197. Egyptian Lamb Tagine with Apricots and Ras el Hanout 95

198. Egyptian Rice and Beef Stuffed Cabbage Leaves with Mint-Yogurt Sauce 95

199. Egyptian Stuffed Eggplant with Rice and Chickpeas in Herb Sauce 96

200. Egyptian Lamb and Potato Tagine with Turmeric and Cumin 97

201. Egyptian Spinach and Lentil Salad with Orange Dressing 97

202. Egyptian Chicken and Okra Stew with Tomato and Coriander 97

203. Egyptian Rice and Chicken Stuffed Grape Leaves with Tzatziki Sauce 98

204. Egyptian Stuffed Zucchini with Rice and Tomato-Herb Sauce 98

205. Egyptian Spinach and Chickpea Soup with Ginger and Turmeric 99

206. Egyptian Chicken and Egg Tagine with Cumin and Paprika 99

207. Egyptian Rice and Vermicelli Pilaf with Pine Nuts and Saffron 100

208. Egyptian Stuffed Bell Peppers with Rice and Lentils in Spicy Sauce 100

209. Egyptian Lamb Tagine with Almonds and Moroccan Spices 101

210. Egyptian Chicken and Okra Stew with Cilantro and Garlic 101

211. Egyptian Rice and Chicken Stuffed Grape Leaves with Tomato-Herb Sauce 102

212. Egyptian Stuffed Zucchini with Rice and Chickpeas in Garlic Sauce 102

213. Egyptian Lamb and Cauliflower Tagine with Turmeric and Cardamom 103

214. Egyptian Spinach and Chickpea Soup with Harissa and Lemon 103

215. Egyptian Lamb and Potato Tagine with Turmeric and Cumin 104

216. Egyptian Rice and Beef Stuffed Cabbage Leaves with Lemon-Tahini Sauce 104

217. Egyptian Stuffed Eggplant with Rice and Peppers in Tomato Sauce 105

218. Egyptian Lamb and Potato Tagine with Carrots and Ras el Hanout 105

219. Egyptian Spinach and Lentil Salad with Yogurt Dressing and Mint 106

220. Egyptian Chicken and Egg Tagine with Preserved Lemon and Paprika 106

221. Egyptian Rice and Vermicelli Soup with Mint and Chickpeas 107

222. Egyptian Stuffed Bell Peppers with Rice and Herbs in Spicy Sauce 107

223. Egyptian Lamb Tagine with Prunes and Cinnamon-Saffron Sauce 107

224. Egyptian Rice and Beef Stuffed Cabbage Leaves with Tomato-Garlic Sauce 108

225. Egyptian Stuffed Eggplant with Rice and Tomato-Pepper Sauce 108

226. Egyptian Lamb and Potato Tagine with Carrots and Moroccan Spices 109

227. Egyptian Spinach and Lentil Salad with Lemon-Tahini Dressing and Pomegranate 109

228. Egyptian Chicken and Okra Stew with Garlic and Paprika 110

229. Egyptian Rice and Chicken Stuffed Grape Leaves with Dill-Yogurt Sauce 110

230. Egyptian Stuffed Zucchini with Rice and Chickpeas in Tomato-Herb Sauce 111

231. Egyptian Lamb and Cauliflower Tagine with Turmeric and Cardamom 111

132. Egyptian Stuffed Eggplant with Rice and Tomato-Herb Sauce 112

- 233. Egyptian Lamb and Potato Tagine with Prunes and Ginger 112
- 234. Egyptian Spinach and Lentil Salad with Pomegranate Dressing 113
- 235. Egyptian Chicken and Okra Stew with Turmeric and Coriander 113
- 236. Kushari (Egyptian Rice and Lentil Dish) 113
- 237. Molokhia Soup (Jute Leaf Soup) 114
- 238. Egyptian Spinach and Chickpea Soup with Harissa and Cilantro 115
- 239. Egyptian Chicken and Egg Tagine with Preserved Lemon and Olives 115
- 240. Egyptian Rice and Vermicelli Pilaf with Pistachios and Saffron 116
- 241. Egyptian Stuffed Bell Peppers with Rice and Herbs 116
- 242. Egyptian Lamb Tagine with Almonds and Ras el Hanout 117
- 243. Egyptian Rice and Beef Stuffed Cabbage Leaves with Tamarind Sauce 117
- 244. Foul Medames (Egyptian Fava Beans): 118
- 145. Koshari Pizza (Egyptian Street Food Pizza): 118
- 246. Hawawshi (Egyptian Meat Pie): 119
- 247. Mahshi (Stuffed Vegetables) 119
- 248. Ful Wa Ta'meya (Fava Bean and Falafel Wraps) 119
- 249. Shakshuka (Egyptian Style) 120
- 250. Kofta (Spiced Ground Meat Skewers) 121
- 251. Fiteer Meshaltet (Egyptian Pastry) 121
- 252. Sayadeya (Fish Pilaf) 121
- 153. Kabab Wa Kofta (Combined Grill) 122
- 254. Sambousek (Savory Pastry) 122
- 255. Basbousa (Semolina Cake with Syrup): 123
- 256. Umm Ali (Egyptian Bread Pudding): 123
- 257. Bamia (Okra Stew): 124
- 158. Roz Bil Laban (Egyptian Rice Pudding): 124
- 259. Mulukhiyah with Chicken (Jute Leaf Stew): 125
- 260. Samak Mafroum (Stuffed Baked Fish): 125
- 261. Roz Maa'amar (Egyptian Spiced Rice) 125
- 262. Kofta Bil Saniyah (Baked Meatballs) 126
- 263. Fatteh (Layered Bread and Rice Dish) 126
- 264. Basbousa Bil Laban (Semolina Dessert with Milk) .. 127
- 265. Fattoush (Combined Vegetable Salad) 127
- 266. Koshari Bites (Egyptian Rice and Lentil Appetizers) 128
- 267. Hawawshi Sandwich (Egyptian Meat Sandwich) 128
- 268. Molokhia Salad (Jute Leaf Salad) 129
- 269. Bamia Bil Lahm (Okra with Meat) 129
- 270. Konafa (Sweet Pastry with Cheese) 129
- 271. Fasulia (Green Bean Stew) 130
- 272. Salata Baladi (Egyptian Tomato and Cucumber Salad) 130
- 273. Hawawshi Burger (Egyptian Meat Burger) 131
- 274. Roz Bel Shaban (Rice Pudding with Rosewater) 131
- 275. Ful Medames Dip (Fava Bean Dip) 131
- 276. Fatteh Bil Lahm (Meat and Bread Casserole) 132
- 277. Basbousa Bil Ashta (Semolina Dessert with Cream) 132
- 278. Kushari Salad (Egyptian Rice and Lentil Salad) 133
- 279. Kofta Tagine (Spiced Meat Stew) 133
- 280. Shakshuka with Feta Cheese (Egyptian Style) 134
- 281. Mulukhiyah with Lamb (Jute Leaf Stew with Lamb) 134
- 282. Alexandrian Liver (Egyptian Liver Dish) 135
- 283. Basbousa Bil Pistachio (Semolina Dessert with Pistachios) 135
- 284. Fiteer with Nutella (Egyptian Pastry with Nutella) .. 136
- 285. Bamia Bil Dajaaj (Okra with Chicken) 136
- 286. Mahshi Warak Enab (Stuffed Grape Leaves) 137
- 288. Chicken Fatta 137
- 289. Basbousa Bil Koktail (Semolina Dessert with Fruit Cocktail) 138
- 290. Eggah (Egyptian Omelette) 138
- 291. Hawawshi Sliders (Egyptian Meat Sliders) 139
- 292. Ful Medames Hummus (Fava Bean Hummus) 139
- 293. Basbousa with Rosewater (Semolina Dessert with Rosewater) 139
- 294. Buckwheat and Vegetable Pilaf (Griby s Grechkoy) . 140
- 295. Russian Egg Salad (Mimoza) 140
- 296. Buckwheat and Mushroom Stuffed Tomatoes (Griby s Grechkoy) 141
- 297. Mushroom and Cucumber Salad (Gribnoy Salat): ... 141
- 298. Russian Potato Salad (Olivier): 141
- 299. Mushroom and Tomato Salad (Gribnoy Salat): 141
- 300. Buckwheat and Vegetable Pilaf (Griby s Grechkoy) 142
- 301. Russian Egg Salad (Mimoza) 142

RECIPES

1. Koshari:

Time: 45 mins

Servings: 4

Ingredients:

- 1 cup of rice
- 1 cup of brown lentils
- 1 cup of cooked chickpeas
- 1 cup of macaroni
- 1 Big onion, thinly split
- 4 cloves garlic, chop-up
- 2 tbsp vegetable oil
- 2 tbsp white vinegar
- 1 can (400g) crushed tomatoes
- 1 tsp ground cumin
- Salt and pepper as needed
- Fried onions for garnish

Instructions:

1. Separately prepare the rice, lentils, and macaroni per the directions on the packaging. Place aside.
2. Vegetable oil Must be heated in a sizable pan over medium heat. Split onions Must be added and cooked up to golden and caramelized.
3. Half of the caramelized onions Must be slice off and reserved for garnish.
4. Add the chop-up garlic to the pan and heat for an additional min.
5. Crushed tomatoes, cumin, salt, and pepper Must all be added to the pan. Stir thoroughly, then simmer for ten mins.
6. Layer the rice, lentils, macaroni, and cooked chickpeas in a serving dish.
7. Gently combine after adding the tomato sauce over the layers.
8. Add the fried and caramelized onions that were set aside on top.
9. Serving hot, please.

Nutrition (per serving):
Cals: 480
Carbs: 85g
Protein: 19g
Fat: 7g
Fiber: 11g

2. Ful Medames:

Time: Overnight soaking + 1 hr cooking

Servings: 6

Ingredients:

- 2 cups of dried fava beans
- 4 cloves garlic, chop-up
- 1/4 cup of olive oil
- Juice of 1 lemon
- Salt as needed
- Chop-up parsley for garnish
- Non-compulsory toppings: diced tomatoes, chop-up onions, chop-up cucumbers, tahini sauce

Instructions:

1. The dried fava beans Must be rinsed before being put in a big bowl. Put them in a cover of water and soak them all night.
2. Fava beans that have been soaked Must be drained and added to a big pot. A 2 inch layer of water Must be added to the beans.
3. Once the water has reveryed a rolling boil, turn down the heat and simmer the beans for approximately an hr, or up to they are soft.
4. Olive oil Must be heated in a separate, little pan over medium heat. Cook the garlic up to it is aromatic and browned after being added.
5. Utilizing a fork or potato masher, mash some of the cooked fava beans while leaving some whole.
6. Salt, lemon juice, and the garlic-infused olive oil Must all be added to the pot. Five more mins of simmering after a thorough stir.
7. Serve the hot full medames with chop-up parsley as a garnish. If desired, you can also use diced tomatoes, chop-up onions, split cucumbers, and tahini sauce.

Nutrition (per serving):
Cals: 280
Carbs: 34g
Protein: 14g
Fat: 10g
Fiber: 11g

3. Egyptian Lentil Soup:

Time: 40 mins

Servings: 4

Ingredients:

- 1 cup of red lentils

- 1 onion, chop-up
- 2 cloves garlic, chop-up
- 2 carrots, chop-up
- 2 celery stalks, chop-up
- 4 cups of vegetable broth
- 1 tsp ground cumin
- 1/2 tsp ground turmeric
- Salt and pepper as needed
- Juice of 1 lemon
- Chop-up fresh parsley for garnish

Instructions:

1. Red lentils Must be rinsed in cold water and kept aside.
2. Heat some oil in a big saucepan on a medium heat. Cook up to melted after adding the chop-up garlic and diced onion.
3. When ready, stir in the chop-up carrots and celery and cook for a further few mins.
4. Cumin, turmeric, salt, pepper, red lentils, vegetable broth, and cumin to the pot. To blend, thoroughly stir.
5. The soup Must be brought to a boil, then simmered for 25 to 30 mins, or up to the lentils are done and soft.
6. Puree the soup in a normal or immersion blender up to it is silky and creamy.
7. Add the lemon juice and, if necessary, taste and adjust the seasoning.
8. Serve the hot Egyptian lentil soup with fresh parsley that has been slice on top.

Nutrition (per serving):
Cals: 220
Carbs: 38g
Protein: 14g
Fat: 1g
Fiber: 15g

4. Egyptian Rice Pudding:

Time: 1 hr
Servings: 4

Ingredients:

- 1/2 cup of short-grain rice
- 4 cups of whole milk
- 1/2 cup of sugar
- 1 tsp vanilla extract
- Ground cinnamon (for garnish)

Instructions:

1. Rice Must be thoroughly rinsed in cold water up to the water is clear.
2. Rice, milk, and sugar Must all be combined in a medium saucepan.
3. Cook for 45 to 50 mins, stirring regularly, over medium heat, up to the rice is cooked and the stew has thickened.
4. Add vanilla extract after turning the heat off.
5. Place the cinnamon powder on top of the rice pudding before serving.
6. Prior to serving, let it cool somewhat. Serve hot or cold.

NUTRITION INFO: (per serving)
Cals: 250
Protein: 8g
Fat: 4g
Carbs: 45g
Fiber: 1g

5. Feteer Meshaltet:

Time: 2 hrs
Servings: 6-8

Ingredients:

- 3 cups of all-purpose flour
- 1/2 tsp salt
- 1 cup of unsalted butter, dilute
- 1 cup of warm water
- 1/4 cup of sesame seeds (non-compulsory, for topping)
- Honey (non-compulsory, for serving)

Instructions:

1. In a Big bowl, combine the flour and salt. Gradually add the dilute butter while combining.
2. Add the warm water gradually while kneading the dough up to it is elastic and smooth.
3. The dough Must be slice up into 4 equal pieces, and every Must rest for 15 mins.
4. Set the oven's temperature to 400°F (200°C).
5. Every piece of dough is rolled out into an extremely thin rectangular sheet.
6. As you stack the sheets, spread dilute butter over the bottom sheet before adding the next one on top.
7. Starting at one end, tightly roll the laminated sheets into a log.

8. Place the spiralized log on a baking sheet that has been buttered.
9. Dilute butter Must be brushed on top, and sesame seeds can be added if preferred.
10. 30 to 40 mins of baking, or up to golden brown.
11. Take it out of the oven, then let it to cool a little. If preferred, serve warm with honey.

NUTRITION INFO: (per serving)
Cals: 360
Protein: 6g
Fat: 23g
Carbs: 32g
Fiber: 1g

6. Shakshuka:

Time: 30 mins
Servings: 4

Ingredients:

- 2 tbsp olive oil
- 1 onion, diced
- 1 red bell pepper, diced
- 2 cloves garlic, chop-up
- 1 tsp ground cumin
- 1 tsp ground paprika
- 1/2 tsp ground cayenne pepper (non-compulsory)
- 1 can (400g) crushed tomatoes
- Salt and pepper as needed
- 4-6 Big eggs
- Fresh parsley, chop-up (for garnish)

Instructions:

1. A big skillet with medium heat is used to heat the olive oil.
2. Add the diced bell pepper and onion. Sauté up to they are transparent and supple.
3. Add the ground cumin, paprika, cayenne pepper, and chop-up garlic. one more min of cooking.
4. Add the smashed tomatoes and salt and pepper as needed. around ten mins, simmer.
5. Crack the eggs into every of the mini wells you've created in the sauce.
6. When the whites are set but the yolks are still runny, cover the skillet and simmer the eggs for about 5-7 mins.
7. Before serving, top with fresh parsley. Serve warm alongside crusty bread.

NUTRITION INFO: (per serving)
Cals: 230
Protein: 10g
Fat: 16g
Carbs: 15g
Fiber: 4g

7. Mahshi:

Time: 1 hr 30 mins
Servings: 6

Ingredients:

- 6 Big zucchini or bell peppers
- 1 cup of rice
- 1 onion, lightly chop-up
- 2 tomatoes, lightly chop-up
- 1/4 cup of fresh parsley, chop-up
- 1/4 cup of fresh dill, chop-up
- 2 tbsp olive oil
- 2 tbsp tomato paste
- Salt and pepper as needed
- Water

Instructions:

1. Hollow out the zucchini or bell peppers after Cutting off their tops. Hold onto the tops.
2. Rice, tomatoes, onions, parsley, dill, olive oil, tomato paste, salt, and pepper Must all be combined in a bowl. Combine thoroughly.
3. Place every zucchini or bell pepper in a big pot after stuffing it with the rice Mixture.
4. Place the stuffed vegetables on top of the saved tops.
5. Fill the pot with water so that it covers the vegetables.
6. Bring to a boil while the pot is covered. Once the rice is done and the vegetables are soft, lower the heat and let the Mixture simmer for 45 to 60 mins.
7. Before serving, take it off the fire and let it cool somewhat. Whether hot or cool, serve.

NUTRITION INFO: (per serving)
Cals: 200 (for zucchini), 160 (for bell pepper)
Protein: 4g
Fat: 5g
Carbs: 35g
Fiber: 4g

8. Ta'ameya (Egyptian Falafel):

Time: 45 mins

Servings: 4-6

Ingredients:

- 2 cups of dried fava beans
- 1 mini onion, roughly chop-up
- 3 cloves garlic
- 1/2 cup of fresh parsley, chop-up
- 1/2 cup of fresh cilantro, chop-up
- 1 tsp ground cumin
- 1 tsp ground coriander
- 1 tsp salt
- 1/2 tsp baking powder
- Vegetable oil (for frying)

Instructions:

1. Overnight, soak the dried fava beans in water. Rinse and drain.
2. The fava beans, onion, garlic, parsley, cilantro, cumin, coriander, salt, and baking powder Must be processed into a coarse Mixture in a mixer.
3. The Mixture Must be transferred to a bowl, covered, and chilled for 30 mins.
4. Mini patties made from the ingredients Must be heated in a deep skillet or pan with vegetable oil.
5. Falafel patties Must be fried in batches up to crisp and browned on all sides.
6. Take out from the oil and set on a plate covered with paper towels to absorb any extra oil.
7. Tahini sauce, pita bread, and your preferred toppings Must be served hot.

NUTRITION INFO: (per serving)

Cals: 250

Protein: 12g

Fat: 8g

Carbs: 35g

Fiber: 10g

9. Basbousa:

Time: 1 hr

Servings: 8-10

Ingredients:

- 2 cups of semolina
- 1 cup of desiccated coconut
- 1 cup of sugar
- 1 cup of plain yogurt
- 1/2 cup of dilute butter
- 1 tsp vanilla extract
- 1 tsp baking powder
- 1/4 cup of split almonds (for topping)
- Syrup:
- 1 cup of sugar
- 1 cup of water
- 1 tsp lemon juice
- Rosewater or orange blossom water (non-compulsory)

Instructions:

1. Grease a baking dish and preheat the oven to 350°F (175°C).
2. Semolina, desiccated coconut, sugar, yogurt, dilute butter, vanilla extract, and baking powder Must all be thoroughly blended in a Big dish.
3. Spread the Mixture evenly after pouring it into the oiled baking dish.
4. With a sharp knife, slice the Mixture's surface into diamond or square shapes, and then top every one with an almond slice.
5. A toothpick inserted in the center of the cake Must come out clean after baking for about 30 to 40 mins, or up to golden brown.
6. Make the syrup while the basbousa is baking. Lemon juice, water, and sugar Must all be combined in a pot. To slightly thicken the syrup, simmer for 10 to 15 mins after bringing to a boil. Add a few drops of orange blossom or rosewater for flavor, if desired.
7. After taking the basbousa out of the oven, immediately cover it with the hot syrup.
8. Before Cutting and serving, let the basbousa cool completely in the baking dish.

NUTRITION INFO: (per serving)

Cals: 320

Protein: 4g

Fat: 15g

Carbs: 45g

Fiber: 2g

10. Egyptian Flatbread (Aish Baladi):

Time: 1 hr 30 mins

Servings: 8 breads

Ingredients:

- 4 cups of whole wheat flour
- 2 tsp active dry yeast
- 2 tsp salt
- 2 cups of warm water

Instructions:

1. Flour, yeast, and salt Must all be combined in a sizable combining dish.
2. As you combine the ingredients, gradually add warm water up to a soft dough forms.
3. The dough Must be smooth and elastic after about 10 mins of kneading on a floured surface.
4. The dough Must be placed in a greased bowl, covered with a moist cloth, and leted to rise for an hr.
5. Griddle or skillet Must be preheated to medium-high heat.
6. Form the dough into balls by dividing it into 8 equal pieces.
7. Every ball is rolled out into a circle that is flat and 1/4 inch thick.
8. For about 2 mins on every side, or up to golden brown spots emerge, cook the bread in the heated skillet.
9. Your favorite Egyptian foods go well with the Aish Baladi when served warm.

11. Alexandrian Liver:

Time: 30 mins
Servings: 4

Ingredients:

- 1 lb beef liver, split
- 2 tbsp vegetable oil
- 1 Big onion, thinly split
- 1 tsp ground cumin
- 1 tsp ground coriander
- Salt and pepper as needed
- Juice of 1 lemon
- Chop-up parsley for garnish

Instructions:

1. Over medium heat, warm the vegetable oil in a skillet.
2. Once the onions are added, sauté them up to they are transparent.
3. Stirring occasionally, add the liver slices to the skillet and simmer for about 5 mins.
4. Over the liver, season with salt, pepper, cumin, and coriander.
5. Cook the liver for a further five mins, or up to it is thoroughly done.
6. Stir the liver with the lemon juice after squeezing it over it.
7. Add chop-up parsley as a garnish after removing from the heat.
8. Hot rice or flatbread Must be served with the Alexandrian Liver.

12. Kushari Casserole:

Time: 1 hr
Servings: 6

Ingredients:

- 1 cup of rice
- 1 cup of elbow macaroni
- 1 cup of brown lentils
- 2 tbsp vegetable oil
- 1 Big onion, thinly split
- 2 cloves garlic, chop-up
- 1 can (14 ozs) diced tomatoes
- 2 tbsp tomato paste
- 1 tsp ground cumin
- Salt and pepper as needed
- Crispy fried onions for garnish

Instructions:

1. Separately, prepare the rice, macaroni, and lentils per the directions on the packaging.
2. Vegetable oil Must be heated in a sizable skillet over medium heat.
3. To the skillet, add the chop-up garlic and onion slices, and sauté up to golden.
4. To the skillet, add the diced tomatoes, tomato paste, cumin, salt, and pepper.
5. While stirring occasionally, cook the tomato Mixture for about 10 mins.
6. Layer the cooked rice, macaroni, lentils, and tomato sauce in a sizable casserole dish.
7. Once all the components have been utilized, repeat the layering process, finishing with the tomato Mixture on top.
8. Bake the casserole dish at 350°F (175°C) for 30 mins with the foil covering it.
9. To slightly brown the top, bake for an additional 10 mins after removing the foil.
10. Before serving, top the Kushari Casserole with crispy fried onions.

13. Egyptian Okra Stew:

Time: 1 hr 15 mins
Servings: 4

Ingredients:

- 1 lb okra, trimmed and halved lengthwise
- 2 tbsp vegetable oil
- 1 Big onion, lightly chop-up
- 2 cloves garlic, chop-up
- 2 cups of diced tomatoes
- 1 tbsp tomato paste
- 1 tsp ground cumin
- 1 tsp ground coriander
- Salt and pepper as needed
- Juice of 1 lemon
- Chop-up fresh cilantro for garnish

Instructions:

1. Over medium heat, warm the vegetable oil in a saucepan.
2. Cook the onion in the pot with the chop-up garlic up to the onion is transparent.
3. While stirring occasionally, add the okra to the stew and cook for about 5 mins.
4. Add the tomato paste, cumin, coriander, salt, and pepper along with the diced tomatoes.
5. For 45 mins, or up to the okra is cooked, boil the stew with the lid on.
6. Cook for a further five mins after adding the lemon juice.
7. Before serving, garnish the Egyptian okra stew with lightly chop-up fresh cilantro.

14. Hawawshi Bread:

Time: 1 hr 30 mins

Servings: 4

Ingredients:

- 1 lb ground beef or lamb
- 1 Big onion, lightly chop-up
- 2 cloves garlic, chop-up
- 2 tbsp vegetable oil
- 1 tsp ground cumin
- 1 tsp ground coriander
- Salt and pepper as needed
- 4 pita breads

Instructions:

1. Over medium heat, warm the vegetable oil in a skillet.
2. Cook the chop-up onion in the skillet with the chop-up garlic up to the onion is transparent.
3. Cook the lamb or beef ground in a skillet till browned.
4. Add the salt, pepper, cumin, and coriander by stirring.
5. After 5 more mins of cooking, turn off the heat and take out the meat Mixture.
6. To create pockets, slice the pita breads open.
7. Put a fair amount of the meat Mixture inside every pita pocket.
8. Heat a pan on the stovetop or a grill to medium heat.
9. The stuffed pitas Must be cooked on the grill or in a skillet for about 2 mins on every side, or up to crispy and heated through.
10. With tahini sauce or any other preferred dipping sauce, serve the hawawshi bread hot.

15. Egyptian Stuffed Grape Leaves:

Time: 1 hr 30 mins

Servings: 6

Ingredients:

- 1 jar (16 ozs) grape leaves in brine, drained
- 1 cup of short-grain rice
- 1/2 cup of lightly chop-up fresh parsley
- 1/2 cup of lightly chop-up fresh dill
- 1/2 cup of lightly chop-up fresh mint
- 1/4 cup of lemon juice
- 1/4 cup of olive oil
- Salt and pepper as needed

Instructions:

1. Rice, parsley, dill, mint, lemon juice, olive oil, salt, and pepper Must all be combined in a bowl.
2. A grape leaf Must be placed glossy side down and stem end toward you on a flat surface.
3. Onto the center of the grape leaf, place a tiny portion of the rice Mixture (approximately 1 tbsp).
4. The leaf is folded over the filling on both sides before being tightly rolled up from the stem end to create a tidy cylinder.
5. With the remaining grape leaves and filling, repeat the procedure.
6. Seam side down, arrange the packed grape leaves in a single layer in a pot.
7. Fill the pot with water up to the grape leaves are submerged.
8. To keep the stuffed grape leaves from unraveling, place a heatproof plate on top of them.

9. Boil the Mixture while the pot is covered. When the rice is cooked and the grape leaves are soft, lower the heat and continue to simmer for around 45 mins.
10. Before serving, take the stuffed grape leaves out of the pot and let them to cool. They can be served chilled or at room temperature.

16. Molokhia

Time: 1 hr 30 mins
Servings: 4

Ingredients:

- 1 lb (450g) refrigerate molokhia leaves
- 4 cups of chicken or vegetable broth
- 4 cloves garlic, chop-up
- 1 onion, lightly chop-up
- 2 tbsp olive oil
- Salt and pepper as needed
- Lemon wedges, for serving
- Cooked rice or bread, for serving

Instructions:

1. Olive oil Must be heated in a sizable pot over medium heat. Add the chop-up onion and chop-up garlic, and cook up to they start to smell good and become a little golden.
2. After adding the broth to the pot, add the refrigerate molokhia leaves. The Mixture Must boil.
3. Stirring occasionally, lower the heat to a simmer, and cook the molokhia for about an hr. The leaves will deteriorate and become brittle.
4. As needed, add salt and pepper to the food. Add extra broth or water to thin down the Mixture if it is too thick.
5. Hot bread or cooked rice Must be served with the molokhia. For more sharpness, squeeze a lemon wedge over every dish.

NUTRITION INFO (per serving):
Cals: 180
Protein: 8g
Fat: 8g
Carbs: 20g
Fiber: 7g

17. Hawawshi

Time: 1 hr
Servings: 6

Ingredients:

- 1 lb (450g) ground beef or lamb
- 1 onion, lightly chop-up
- 2 cloves garlic, chop-up
- 1 green bell pepper, lightly chop-up
- 1 tomato, lightly chop-up
- 2 tbsp chop-up parsley
- 1 tsp ground cumin
- 1 tsp ground coriander
- Salt and pepper as needed
- 6 pita bread rounds

Instructions:

1. Set your oven's temperature to 375°F (190°C).
2. Combine the ground beef or lamb with the chop-up onion, chop-up garlic, bell pepper, tomato, parsley, cumin, coriander, salt, and pepper in a sizable combining bowl. Combine thoroughly up to all components are distributed equally.
3. Make a pocket out of every pita bread round by Cutting it open.
4. Put a fair amount of the ground meat Mixture into every pita pocket and gently press it down to cover the entire space.
5. The stuffed pitas Must be baked for 20 to 25 mins in a preheated oven, or up to the meat is thoroughly cooked and the pita bread is crunchy.
6. Hawawshi Must be served hot in a sandwich or with a side of salad.

NUTRITION INFO (per serving):
Cals: 350
Protein: 20g
Fat: 15g
Carbs: 30g
Fiber: 5g

18. Umm Ali

Time: 1 hr
Servings: 6

Ingredients:

- 4 cups of whole milk
- 1 cup of heavy cream
- 1 cup of sugar
- 1 tsp vanilla extract
- 6-8 stale croissants, torn into pieces
- 1/2 cup of slivered almonds
- 1/2 cup of raisins
- Ground cinnamon for sprinkling

Instructions:

1. Turn on the oven to 350 °F (175 °C).
2. The milk, heavy cream, sugar, and vanilla extract Must be heated in a saucepan over medium heat. Up to the sugar melts and the Mixture reveryes the desired temperature, stir occasionally. Don't let it to boil.
3. Place the shredded croissant pieces, slivered almonds, and raisins in a baking dish.
4. Making sure that every croissant piece is covered, pour the warm milk Mixture over the croissant combination.
5. Add some ground cinnamon on top.
6. Bake the baking dish for 30-35 mins, or up to the top is golden and crispy, in the preheated oven.
7. Before serving warm, take it out of the oven and let it cool for a while.

NUTRITION INFO (per serving):
Cals: 500
Protein: 10g
Fat: 25g
Carbs: 60g
Fiber: 2g

19. Egyptian Tomato Salad

Time: 15 mins
Servings: 4

Ingredients:

- 4 medium tomatoes, diced
- 1 mini cucumber, diced
- 1 mini red onion, thinly split
- 1/4 cup of fresh parsley, chop-up
- 2 tbsp fresh mint leaves, chop-up
- Juice of 1 lemon
- 2 tbsp olive oil
- Salt and pepper as needed

Instructions:

1. Diced tomatoes, cucumber, red onion, parsley, and mint leaves Must all be combined in a big bowl.
2. Combine the lemon juice, olive oil, salt, and pepper in a separate mini bowl.
3. After adding the dressing, gently toss the tomato Mixture to evenly coat all of the ingredients.
4. Leting time for the flavors to mingle together will help the salad taste better.
5. As a cool side dish, serve the Egyptian tomato salad chilled.

NUTRITION INFO (per serving):
Cals: 80
Protein: 2g
Fat: 6g
Carbs: 6g
Fiber: 2g

20. Mulukhiyah Soup

Time: 1 hr 30 mins
Servings: 6

Ingredients:

- 1 lb (450g) refrigerate mulukhiyah leaves
- 4 cups of chicken or vegetable broth
- 2 chicken breasts, cooked and shredded (non-compulsory)
- 4 cloves garlic, chop-up
- 1 onion, lightly chop-up
- 2 tbsp olive oil
- Salt and pepper as needed
- Lemon wedges, for serving
- Cooked rice, for serving

Instructions:

1. Olive oil Must be heated in a sizable pot over medium heat. Add the chop-up onion and chop-up garlic, and cook up to they start to smell good and become a little golden.
2. Add the broth to the pot, then the refrigerate mulukhiyah leaves. The Mixture Must boil.
3. Stirring occasionally, lower the heat to a simmer, and cook the mulukhiyah for about an hr. The leaves will deteriorate and become brittle.
4. Add cooked and shredded chicken breasts to the pot, if using. To blend, stir.
5. As needed, add salt and pepper to the food.
6. With cooked rice, serve the mulukhiyah soup hot. For more sharpness, squeeze a lemon wedge over every dish.

NUTRITION INFO (per serving):
Cals: 200
Protein: 18g
Fat: 8g
Carbs: 16g
Fiber: 7g

21. Bamya Bil Lahmeh

Time: 1 hr 30 mins

Servings: 4

Ingredients:

- 500 grams okra (bamya), trimmed and washed
- 500 grams beef or lamb, slice into cubes
- 1 onion, lightly chop-up
- 3 garlic cloves, chop-up
- 2 tomatoes, chop-up
- 2 tbsp tomato paste
- 2 tbsp olive oil
- 2 cups of water
- 1 tsp ground coriander
- 1 tsp ground cumin
- Salt and pepper as needed

Instructions:

1. Olive oil Must be heated in a sizable pot over medium heat. Add the chop-up garlic and onion, both chop-up. up to they are transparent, sauté.
2. Brown the beef cubes all over after adding them.
3. Add the tomato paste, diced tomatoes, ground cumin, ground coriander, salt, and pepper after stirring. Cook the tomatoes up to they begin to break down for a few mins.
4. Bring the water to a boil in the pot after adding it. Turn the heat down to low and simmer the Mixture for 30 mins.
5. When the meat is well cooked, add the okra to the saucepan and simmer for an additional 30 mins.
6. If necessary, adjust the seasoning. Hot rice or toast Must be served with the Bamya Bil Lahmeh.

NUTRITION INFO (per serving):

Cals: 350

Protein: 25g

Fat: 15g

Carbs: 30g

Fiber: 8g

22. Egyptian Fish Tagine

Time: 1 hr

Servings: 4

Ingredients:

- 500 grams white fish fillets
- 1 onion, lightly chop-up
- 3 garlic cloves, chop-up
- 2 tomatoes, chop-up
- 2 tbsp tomato paste
- 2 tbsp olive oil
- 2 tbsp lemon juice
- 1 tsp ground cumin
- 1 tsp ground coriander
- 1 tsp paprika
- Salt and pepper as needed
- Fresh cilantro for garnish

Instructions:

1. Set the oven's temperature to 180 C (350 F).
2. Heat the olive oil over medium heat in a sizable oven-safe dish or tagine. Add the chop-up garlic and onion, both chop-up. up to they are transparent, sauté.
3. Salt, pepper, paprika, tomato paste, ground cumin, ground coriander, and ground tomatoes Must all be added. Cook the tomatoes up to they begin to break down for a few mins.
4. Over the tomato Mixture in the plate, arrange the fish fillets. Over the fish, squeeze some lemon juice.
5. Place the dish or tagine in the preheated oven while it is covered. Bake the fish for 30 to 40 mins, or up to it is well cooked and flakes with a fork.
6. Before serving, garnish with fresh cilantro. Rice or bread Must be served with the Egyptian Fish Tagine.

NUTRITION INFO (per serving):

Cals: 220

Protein: 30g

Fat: 8g

Carbs: 10g

Fiber: 3g

23. Egyptian Fattoush Salad

Time: 20 mins

Servings: 4

Ingredients:

- 4 cups of combined salad greens
- 1 cucumber, diced
- 2 tomatoes, diced
- 1 green bell pepper, diced

- 1 red onion, thinly split
- 1 cup of fresh parsley leaves, chop-up
- 1 cup of fresh mint leaves, chop-up
- 2 tbsp olive oil
- 2 tbsp lemon juice
- 1 tsp sumac (non-compulsory)
- pepper and salt as desired
- Toasted and split up pita bread (for serving)

Instructions:

1. Combine salad greens, diced cucumber, diced tomatoes, diced green bell pepper, split red onion, chop-up parsley, and chop-up mint leaves in a sizable salad bowl.
2. To prepare the dressing, combine the sumac, olive oil, lemon juice, salt, and pepper in a mini bowl.
3. When the salad items are thoroughly coated, drizzle the dressing over them.
4. To keep their crispness, add the toasted pita bread pieces to the salad right before serving.
5. You can use the Egyptian Fattoush Salad as a light and energizing starter or side dish.

NUTRITION INFO (per serving):
Cals: 150
Protein: 3g
Fat: 8g
Carbs: 18g
Fiber: 5g

24. Egyptian Stuffed Eggplant

Time: 1 hr 30 mins
Servings: 4

Ingredients:

- 4 Big eggplants
- 500 grams ground beef or lamb
- 1 onion, lightly chop-up
- 3 garlic cloves, chop-up
- 2 tomatoes, chop-up
- 1/4 cup of chop-up fresh parsley
- 1/4 cup of chop-up fresh mint
- 1/4 cup of pine nuts
- 2 tbsp olive oil
- 2 tbsp tomato paste
- 1 tsp ground cumin
- 1 tsp ground coriander
- Salt and pepper as needed
- Lemon wedges for serving

Instructions:

1. Set the oven's temperature to 180 C (350 F).
2. The eggplants Must have their tops take outd before being slice in half lengthwise. Take out the flesh from every half, leaving a shell that is about 1/2 inch thick. Slice up and reserve the flesh that was scooped out.
3. Olive oil Must be heated in a sizable skillet over medium heat. Add the chop-up garlic and onion, both chop-up. up to they are transparent, sauté.
4. Cook the lamb or beef ground in a skillet till browned. Add the tomato paste, ground cumin, ground coriander, salt, and pepper after chopping the tomatoes and eggplant flesh into mini pieces. Cook the tomatoes up to they begin to break down for a few mins.
5. Add the pine nuts, chop-up mint, and chop-up parsley. Get rid of the heat.
6. Place the stuffed eggplant shells in a baking tray. Fill the eggplant shells with the meat Mixture.
7. Bake the eggplants in the preheated oven for 45–60 mins, or up to they are soft, with the foil covering the baking dish.
8. Egyptian Stuffed Eggplant Must be served hot with lemon wedges on the side.

NUTRITION INFO (per serving):
Cals: 300
Protein: 20g
Fat: 18g
Carbs: 15g
Fiber: 6g

25. Egyptian Chicken and Rice

Time: 1 hr 30 mins
Servings: 4

Ingredients:

- 4 chicken thighs, bone-in and skin-on
- 2 cups of basmati rice
- 1 onion, lightly chop-up
- 3 garlic cloves, chop-up
- 2 tomatoes, chop-up
- 2 tbsp olive oil
- 2 tbsp tomato paste
- 4 cups of chicken broth
- 1 tsp ground cumin
- 1 tsp ground coriander
- 1/2 tsp turmeric
- Salt and pepper as needed

- Fresh parsley for garnish

Instructions:

1. The olive oil Must be heated over medium heat in a big pot or Dutch oven. Add the chop-up garlic and onion, both chop-up. up to they are transparent, sauté.
2. Place the skin-side down chicken thighs in the pot and cook up to browned. Cook the chicken thighs for a short while longer on the other side. Chicken Must be taken out of the pot and placed aside.
3. Add the chop-up tomatoes, tomato paste, cumin, coriander, turmeric, salt, and pepper to the same pot. Cook the tomatoes up to they begin to break down for a few mins.
4. The rice Must be added to the pot and thoroughly combined with the tomato Mixture.
5. Over the rice in the pot, arrange the chicken thighs. Over the chicken and rice, pour the chicken broth.
6. Heat Must be turned down once the Mixture comes to a boil. For about 30 mins, or up to the rice is done and the chicken is tender, cover the saucepan and boil the food.
7. The chicken thighs Must be taken out of the pot and put aside. With a fork, fluff the rice.
8. Place a chicken thigh on top of a pile of rice while serving the Egyptian Chicken and Rice. Add fresh parsley as a garnish.

NUTRITION INFO (per serving):
Cals: 400
Protein: 25g
Fat: 12g
Carbs: 50g
Fiber: 2g

26. Baladi Bread

Time: 2 hrs
Servings: 6-8

Ingredients:

- 4 cups of all-purpose flour
- 2 tsp instant yeast
- 2 tsp sugar
- 2 tsp salt
- 2 cups of warm water

Instructions:

1. Combine the flour, yeast, sugar, and salt in a big bowl. Combine thoroughly.
2. Stirring with a wooden spoon, gradually add the heated water to the flour Mixture up to the dough comes together.
3. The dough Must be smooth and elastic after about 10 mins of kneading on a lightly dusted surface.
4. The dough Must be placed in a greased basin, covered with a kitchen towel, and leted to rise for about an hr, or up to it has doubled in size, in a warm location.
5. Set the oven's temperature to 475°F (245°C). Pre-heat the oven with a baking stone or baking sheet.
6. Punch down the dough, then divide it into 6 to 8 sections that are all equal. Make a ball out of every part.
7. The dough balls Must rest for about 10 mins after being placed on a baking sheet or hot baking stone.
8. In the preheated oven, bake the bread for 12 to 15 mins, or up to golden brown.
9. Before serving, take the bread out of the oven and let it cool on a wire rack.

27. Egyptian Lentil and Rice Pilaf

Time: 40 mins
Servings: 4

Ingredients:

- 1 cup of lentils, rinsed and drained
- 1 cup of basmati rice
- 1 onion, lightly chop-up
- 2 cloves garlic, chop-up
- 2 tbsp olive oil
- 2 cups of vegetable broth
- 1 tsp ground cumin
- 1/2 tsp ground coriander
- Salt and pepper as needed
- Fresh cilantro or parsley for garnish (non-compulsory)

Instructions:

1. In a sizable saucepan set over medium heat, warm the olive oil. Add the chop-up garlic and onion, both chop-up. Sauté the onion up to it turns translucent.

2. Rice, lentils, cumin, coriander, salt, and pepper Must all be added to the pan. The spices Must be thoroughly combined into the rice and lentils.
3. Bring the Mixture to a boil after adding the veggie broth. When the rice and lentils are cooked and soft, lower the heat to low, cover the pan, and simmer for 20 to 25 mins.
4. With the lid on, let the saucepan cool for about five mins after turning off the heat.
5. If desired, sprinkle the pilaf with fresh cilantro or parsley after fluffing it with a fork. Serve warm.

28. Konafa

Time: 1 hr
Servings: 8-10

Ingredients:

- 1 box/pkg (16 oz) konafa dough (shredded phyllo dough)
- 1 cup of unsalted butter, dilute
- 1 cup of granulated sugar
- 1 cup of water
- 1 tsp lemon juice
- 1 cup of lightly chop-up pistachios or walnuts

Instructions:

1. Set the oven's temperature to 350°F (175°C).
2. Using your fingers, separate the konafa dough strands into a sizable bowl, making sure they are fluffy and well-separated.
3. To uniformly cover the strands, drizzle the dilute butter over the konafa and give it a gentle spin.
4. A greased 9x13-inch baking dish Must have the bottom pressed with half of the konafa Mixture.
5. Combine the sugar, water, and lemon juice in a mini pot. Over medium heat, bring the Mixture to a boil while occasionally swirling to ensure that the sugar thoroughly dissolves. Take out the syrup from the heat and let it to cool slightly.
6. In the baking dish, evenly distribute the syrup over the konafa.
7. Over the konafa drenched in syrup, evenly distribute the chop-up nuts.
8. Gently press the remaining half of the konafa Mixture onto the nuts.
9. Bake the konafa in the preheated oven for 30 to 40 mins, or up to golden and crispy.
10. After taking it out of the oven, let it cool for a while before slicing. At room temperature or heated, serve.

29. Mahalabiya

Time: 30 mins (+ chilling time)
Servings: 4

Ingredients:

- 4 cups of milk
- 1/2 cup of sugar
- 1/4 cup of cornstarch
- 1 tsp rose water (non-compulsory)
- 1/4 cup of chop-up pistachios or almonds for garnish
- Ground cinnamon for garnish

Instructions:

1. Stir the milk, sugar, and cornstarch in a saucepan up to the sugar and cornstarch are completely dissolved.
2. Stirring continuously to avoid lumps, bring the Mixture to a simmer in the saucepan over medium heat.
3. As the Mixture thickens to a custard-like consistency, lower the heat to low and continue to simmer, stirring regularly.
4. If using rose water, turn off the heat source and stir it in.
5. Fill individual serving bowls or a big serving dish with the Mixture. Let it to cool to room temperature before chilling and setting in the fridge for at least two hrs.
6. Add ground cinnamon and chop-up almonds or pistachios as a garnish before serving.

30. Egyptian Stuffed Bell Peppers

Time: 1 hr
Servings: 6

Ingredients:

- 6 bell peppers (any color), tops take outd and seeds take outd
- 1 cup of cooked rice
- 1 cup of cooked ground beef or lamb
- 1 onion, lightly chop-up
- 2 cloves garlic, chop-up
- 1 tomato, lightly chop-up
- 2 tbsp tomato paste

- 1 tsp ground cumin
- 1 tsp ground coriander
- Salt and pepper as needed
- Olive oil for cooking

Instructions:

1. Set the oven's temperature to 375°F (190°C).
2. Melt some olive oil in a big skillet over medium heat. Add the chop-up garlic and onion, both chop-up. Sauté the onion up to it turns translucent.
3. Cook the lamb or beef ground in a skillet till browned. Take out any extra fat.
4. Add the chop-up tomato, tomato paste, cumin, coriander, salt, and pepper after stirring. The Mixture needs to be thoroughly blended and cooked through after a few mins of cooking.
5. Stir in the cooked rice after turning off the stove.
6. Place a little amount of water in a baking dish, then fill every bell pepper with the rice and meat Mixture.
7. When the bell peppers are soft, bake the baking dish in the preheated oven for 30 to 40 mins with the foil covering.
8. To slightly brown the peppers' tops, take out the foil and bake for an additional 5 to 10 mins.
9. Before serving, take them out of the oven and let them to cool for a while. Enjoy!

31. Mulukhiyah with Chicken:

Time: 1 hr
Servings: 4

Ingredients:

- 1 lb boneless, skinless chicken breasts, slice into cubes
- 2 cups of chop-up mulukhiyah leaves (also known as jute leaves or Jew's mlet)
- 4 cups of chicken broth
- 1 onion, lightly chop-up
- 4 cloves of garlic, chop-up
- 2 tbsp vegetable oil
- 1 tsp ground coriander
- 1 tsp ground cumin
- Salt and pepper as needed
- Juice of 1 lemon

Instructions:

1. Over medium heat, warm the vegetable oil in a big pot. Garlic and onions Must be added and sautéed up to transparent.
2. Cook the chicken cubes in the pot after adding them, stirring occasionally, up to evenly browned.
3. Add the salt, pepper, cumin, and ground coriander. one more min of cooking.
4. Bring to a boil after adding the chicken broth. For 30 mins, turn the heat down to low and simmer.
5. After adding the mulukhiyah leaves, boil the Mixture for a further ten mins.
6. Add the lemon juice and, if necessary, taste and adjust the seasoning.
7. Hot rice or toast Must be served with the mulukhiyah with chicken.

NUTRITION INFO (per serving):
Cals: 320
Protein: 30g
Fat: 12g
Carbs: 20g
Fiber: 5g

32. Egyptian Spiced Tea:

Time: 10 mins
Servings: 2

Ingredients:

- 2 cups of water
- 2 tsp black tea leaves
- 2 tsp sugar (adjust as needed)
- 2 whole cloves
- 2 cardamom pods, crushed
- 1 cinnamon stick
- 2 tsp dried mint leaves
- Juice of 1/2 lemon (non-compulsory)

Instructions:

1. Bring the water to a boil in a saucepan.
2. To the boiling water, add the black tea leaves, sugar, cinnamon stick, cloves, cardamom pods, and dried mint leaves.
3. For five mins, simmer over low heat.
4. After straining the tea into cups of, turn off the heat source.
5. If desired, add some lemon juice to the tea.
6. Egyptian spiced tea Must be served hot.

NUTRITION INFO (per serving):
Cals: 20
Protein: 0g
Fat: 0g
Carbs: 5g
Fiber: 0g

33. Egyptian Bean Salad:

Time: 20 mins
Servings: 4

Ingredients:

- 2 cups of cooked white beans (such as cannellini beans or navy beans)
- 1 cucumber, diced
- 1 tomato, diced
- 1 mini red onion, lightly chop-up
- 1/4 cup of chop-up fresh parsley
- 2 tbsp olive oil
- 2 tbsp lemon juice
- Salt and pepper as needed

Instructions:

1. White beans, cucumber, tomato, red onion, and parsley Must all be combined in a big bowl.
2. Combine the olive oil, lemon juice, salt, and pepper in a separate mini bowl.
3. The bean Mixture Must be poured the dressing over it, then gently combined.
4. If necessary, adjust the seasoning.
5. Serve the Egyptian bean salad at room temperature or cooled.

NUTRITION INFO (per serving):
Cals: 180
Protein: 9g
Fat: 6g
Carbs: 26g
Fiber: 8g

34. Egyptian Beef Kebabs:

Time: 30 mins (+ marinating time)
Servings: 4

Ingredients:

- 1 lb beef sirloin, slice into cubes
- 1 onion, lightly chop-up
- 2 cloves of garlic, chop-up
- 2 tbsp olive oil
- 1 tsp ground cumin
- 1 tsp ground coriander
- 1 tsp paprika
- Salt and pepper as needed
- Skewers (if using wooden skewers, soak them in water for 30 mins before using)

Instructions:

1. Combine the chop-up garlic, chop-up onion, olive oil, ground cumin, ground coriander, paprika, salt, and pepper in a bowl.
2. To evenly coat the beef cubes with the marinade, add them to the bowl and stir.
3. For better flavor, let the bowl covered in the refrigerator for at least an hr.
4. Get the grill or the broiler ready.
5. the skewers with the meat cubes that have been marinated.
6. The kebabs Must be grilled to the appropriate doneness on the grill or under the broiler for about 10 mins, flipping them once.
7. The kebabs Must be taken off the heat and given some time to rest.
8. Hot rice or bread Must be served with the Egyptian meat kebabs.

NUTRITION INFO (per serving):
Cals: 280
Protein: 26g
Fat: 18g
Carbs: 4g
Fiber: 1g

35. Rice-Stuffed Pigeon:

Time: 2 hrs
Servings: 4

Ingredients:

- 4 pigeons, cleaned and dressed
- 1 cup of long-grain rice
- 1 onion, lightly chop-up
- 4 cloves of garlic, chop-up
- 2 tbsp butter
- 1 tsp ground cinnamon
- 1 tsp ground allspice
- Salt and pepper as needed
- 4 cups of chicken broth

Instructions:

1. Set the oven's temperature to 350°F (175°C).
2. The pigeons Must be properly rinsed before being dried with paper towels.
3. Melt the butter in a pan over medium heat. Add the chop-up garlic and onion, and sauté up to they soften and turn golden.
4. Add the rice together with the salt, pepper, cinnamon and allspice powders. one more min of cooking.
5. Every pigeon Must be filled with the rice Mixture, and the openings Must be sealed with toothpicks or kitchen twine.
6. Put the stuffed pigeons in a baking dish, and then cover them with chicken broth.
7. For about 1.5 hrs, or up to the pigeons are cooked through and the rice is tender, cover the dish with foil and bake it in the preheated oven.
8. To enable the pigeons to softly brown during the final 15 mins of baking, take out the foil.
9. With a little of the boiling liquid spooned over them, serve the rice-stuffed pigeons hot.

NUTRITION INFO (per serving):
Cals: 410
Protein: 40g
Fat: 16g
Carbs: 22g
Fiber: 2g

36. Egyptian Beetroot Salad:

Time: 15 mins
Servings: 4

Ingredients:

- 4 medium beetroots, cooked and diced
- 1 mini red onion, thinly split
- 2 tbsp fresh lemon juice
- 2 tbsp olive oil
- Salt and pepper as needed
- Fresh parsley, chop-up (for garnish)

Instructions:

1. Red onion slices and diced beets Must be combined in a big basin.
2. Combine the lemon juice, olive oil, salt, and pepper in a separate mini bowl.
3. Then, add the dressing and well toss to coat the beetroot Mixture.
4. Serve chilled with fresh parsley as a garnish.

NUTRITION INFO (per serving):
Cals: 120
Fat: 7g
Carbs: 12g
Protein: 2g
Fiber: 3g

37. Basboosa Bil Nisrina:

Time: 50 mins
Servings: 8

Ingredients:

- 2 cups of semolina
- 1 cup of desiccated coconut
- 1 cup of sugar
- 1 cup of milk
- 1/2 cup of unsalted butter, dilute
- 1 tsp baking powder
- 1/4 cup of blanched almonds, halved
- 1 tbsp rosewater

Instructions:

1. Grease a baking dish and set the oven to 180°C (350°F) before baking.
2. Semolina, desiccated coconut, sugar, dilute butter, milk, and baking powder Must all be combined in a sizable basin.
3. Smooth the top after pouring the batter into the oiled baking dish.
4. On top of the Mixture, arrange the halves of the almonds.
5. Bake for about 40 mins, or up to golden brown, in the preheated oven.
6. After removing from the oven, top with rosewater.
7. Before slicing it into diamond- or square-shaped pieces, let it cool.

NUTRITION INFO (per serving):
Cals: 350
Fat: 20g
Carbs: 37g
Protein: 5g
Fiber: 3g

38. Egyptian Grilled Fish:

Time: 30 mins
Servings: 4

Ingredients:

- 4 fish fillets (such as tilapia or sea bass)
- 4 cloves garlic, chop-up
- 2 tbsp lemon juice
- 2 tbsp olive oil
- 1 tsp ground cumin
- 1 tsp ground coriander
- Salt and pepper as needed
- Fresh parsley, chop-up (for garnish)

Instructions:

1. Combine chop-up garlic, lemon juice, olive oil, cumin, coriander, salt, and pepper in a mini bowl to make a marinade.
2. In a shlet dish, arrange the fish fillets and pour the marinade over them. Assure even coating of the fish.
3. Give the fish around 15 mins to marinade.
4. A grill or grill pan Must be preheated to high heat.
5. The fish fillets Must be cooked through and attractively browned after grilling them for around 5-7 mins on every side.
6. Before serving, take out from the grill and top with more parsley.

NUTRITION INFO (per serving):
Cals: 220
Fat: 12g
Carbs: 1g
Protein: 26g
Fiber: 0g

39. Kushari Pizza:

Time: 1 hr 30 mins
Servings: 6

Ingredients:

- 1 pre-made pizza dough
- 1 cup of cooked rice
- 1 cup of cooked macaroni
- 1 cup of cooked brown lentils
- 1 cup of tomato sauce
- 1/2 cup of chickpeas, cooked
- 1/2 cup of caramelized onions
- 1/4 cup of vinegar
- 2 tbsp olive oil
- 1 tsp cumin
- Salt and pepper as needed
- Fresh parsley, chop-up (for garnish)

Instructions:

1. As directed on the pizza dough, preheat the oven.
2. The pizza dough Must be rolled out to the desired thickness and shape.
3. Rice, macaroni, lentils, tomato sauce, chickpeas, caramelized onions, vinegar, olive oil, cumin, salt, and pepper Must all be combined in a bowl.
4. Over the pizza crust, distribute the rice and lentil Mixture evenly.
5. Pizza dough Must be baked in the preheated oven for the specified amount of time or up to the crust is golden brown.
6. Serve hot after removing from the oven and garnishing with fresh parsley.

NUTRITION INFO (per serving):
Cals: 380
Fat: 10g
Carbs: 62g
Protein: 12g
Fiber: 5g

40. Egyptian Carrot Salad:

Time: 20 mins
Servings: 4

Ingredients:

- 4 medium carrots, finely grated
- 1/4 cup of raisins
- 1/4 cup of fresh orange juice
- 2 tbsp lemon juice
- 2 tbsp olive oil
- 1 tbsp honey
- 1/4 tsp ground cinnamon
- Salt and pepper as needed
- Chop-up fresh mint (for garnish)

Instructions:

1. Raspberries and finely grated carrots Must be combined in a big bowl.
2. Combine the orange juice, lemon juice, olive oil, honey, cinnamon, salt, and pepper in a separate mini bowl.
3. Then, after adding the dressing, stir the carrot Mixture thoroughly.
4. Serve chilled with chop-up fresh mint as a garnish.

NUTRITION INFO (per serving):
Cals: 150
Fat: 7g
Carbs: 23g
Protein: 1g
Fiber: 3g

41. Egyptian Spinach and Cheese Pastry

Time: 45 mins
Servings: 4

Ingredients:

- 1 box/pkg refrigerate spinach, thawed and drained
- 1 cup of feta cheese, cut up
- 1/2 cup of finely grated Parmesan cheese
- 1/4 cup of chop-up fresh parsley
- 2 cloves garlic, chop-up
- 1/4 tsp ground nutmeg
- Salt and pepper as needed
- 12 sheets phyllo dough
- 1/2 cup of dilute butter

Instructions:

1. Set your oven's temperature to 375°F (190°C).
2. Spinach, feta cheese, Parmesan cheese, parsley, garlic, nutmeg, salt, and pepper Must all be combined in a combining bowl. Combine thoroughly.
3. One phyllo dough sheet Must be placed on a spotless board and lightly buttered. Five more sheets Must be used in similar manner, stacked on top of one another.
4. Over the top sheet of phyllo dough, evenly distribute half of the spinach and cheese Mixture.
5. On top of the spinach and cheese Mixture, arrange six more sheets of phyllo dough, coating every one with dilute butter.
6. Over the top phyllo dough layer, evenly distribute the remaining spinach and cheese Mixture.
7. Then, arrange the remaining six phyllo dough pieces on top, coating every one with dilute butter.
8. Slice the phyllo dough layers into squares or triangles using a sharp knife.
9. The pastries Must be baked for 25 to 30 mins, or up to golden and crispy, on a baking sheet.
10. Before serving, take them out of the oven and let them to cool for a while.

Nutrition (per serving):
Cals: 320
Protein: 12g
Carbs: 28g
Fat: 18g
Fiber: 3g

42. Egyptian Fish Soup

Time: 1 hr
Servings: 6

Ingredients:

- 1 lb (450g) white fish fillets, slice into bite-sized pieces
- 2 tbsp vegetable oil
- 1 onion, lightly chop-up
- 2 cloves garlic, chop-up
- 1 carrot, diced
- 1 celery stalk, diced
- 1 can (14 oz/400g) diced tomatoes
- 4 cups of fish or vegetable broth
- 1 tsp ground cumin
- 1 tsp ground coriander
- 1/2 tsp ground turmeric
- 1/4 tsp cayenne pepper (non-compulsory)
- Salt and pepper as needed
- Juice of 1 lemon
- Fresh cilantro, chop-up (for garnish)

Instructions:

1. Over medium heat, warm the vegetable oil in a big pot.
2. The onion and garlic Must be added to the pot and sautéed up to transparent and tender.
3. The carrot and celery Must soften after being added to the pot and cooked for a few mins.
4. Add the fish or vegetable broth, diced tomatoes, cumin, coriander, turmeric, cayenne (if using), salt, and pepper. The soup Must boil.
5. To let the flavors to mingle, turn the heat down to low and let the soup simmer for about 30 mins.
6. When the fish is cooked through and flakes easily with a fork, add the fish pieces to the pot and simmer for an additional 5-7 mins.
7. Add the lemon juice and, if necessary, taste and adjust the seasoning.
8. Serve the heated soup in dishes with fresh cilantro as a garnish.

Nutrition (per serving):
Cals: 190
Protein: 18g
Carbs: 10g
Fat: 8g
Fiber: 2g

43. Egyptian Lemonade

Time: 10 mins

Servings: 4

Ingredients:

- 4 lemons, juiced
- 4 cups of cold water
- 1/2 cup of granulated sugar (adjust according as needed)
- Ice cubes
- Fresh mint leaves (for garnish)

Instructions:

1. Lemon juice, cold water, and sugar Must all be combined in a pitcher. Stir the sugar up to it dissolves.
2. If necessary, add extra sugar to the lemonade after tasting it to regulate the sweetness.
3. Ice cubes Must be placed in glasses before adding the lemonade.
4. Add a fresh mint sprig to the rim of every glass.
5. Before serving, thoroughly stir.

Nutrition (per serving):
Cals: 85
Protein: 0g
Carbs: 22g
Fat: 0g
Fiber: 0g

44. Egyptian Sweet Rice with Nuts

Time: 40 mins

Servings: 6

Ingredients:

- 1 cup of basmati rice
- 2 cups of water
- 1/4 cup of unsalted butter
- 1/2 cup of chop-up combined nuts (such as almonds, pistachios, and cashews)
- 1/4 cup of raisins
- 1/4 cup of granulated sugar
- 1/2 tsp ground cinnamon
- 1/4 tsp ground cardamom
- Pinch of salt

Instructions:

1. Basmati rice Must be well rinsed in cold water up to the water is clear. Flow freely.
2. Bring the water to a boil in a medium-sized saucepan. Add a dash of salt and the washed rice. Stir, put a lid on, and turn down the heat. Cook the rice for 15 to 20 mins, or up to the water has been absorbed and the rice is soft.
3. Melt the butter over medium heat in a separate pan. The chop-up nuts Must be added now and sautéed for a few mins up to gently toasted.
4. To the pan containing the nuts, add the raisins, sugar, cinnamon, and cardamom. To blend, thoroughly stir.
5. Gently stir the cooked rice into the nut and sugar Mixture in the pan after adding it.
6. To let the flavors to mingle, cover the pan and let the rice sit for 5 mins.
7. With a fork, fluff the rice before transferring it to a serving bowl.
8. As a dessert or side dish, serve the heated sweet rice.

Nutrition (per serving):
Cals: 290
Protein: 4g
Carbs: 41g
Fat: 13g
Fiber: 2g

45. Egyptian Meat Stew

Time: 2 hrs 30 mins

Servings: 6

Ingredients:

- 2 lbs (900g) beef stew meat, slice into bite-sized pieces
- 2 tbsp vegetable oil
- 2 onions, lightly chop-up
- 4 cloves garlic, chop-up
- 2 carrots, peel off and diced
- 2 celery stalks, diced
- 2 potatoes, peel off and cubed
- 1 can (14 oz/400g) diced tomatoes
- 4 cups of beef broth
- 2 tbsp tomato paste
- 2 tsp ground cumin

- 2 tsp ground coriander
- 1 tsp ground cinnamon
- 1/2 tsp ground turmeric
- Salt and pepper as needed
- Fresh parsley, chop-up (for garnish)

Instructions:

1. Over medium heat, warm the vegetable oil in a big pot.
2. Brown the beef stew meat completely in the pot before adding it. The meat Must be taken out of the pot and set aside.
3. Add the chop-up garlic and onion in the same pot. Sauté up to they are transparent and supple.
4. To the pot, add the diced potatoes, celery, and carrots. Cook for a short while up to they start to soften.
5. Add the diced tomatoes, beef broth, tomato paste, cumin, coriander, cinnamon, turmeric, salt, and pepper to the saucepan along with the browned beef stew meat.
6. After bringing the stew to a boil, turn down the heat. For about two hrs, or up to the meat is soft and the flavors are well-balanced, simmer the Mixture in a covered pot.
7. If necessary, taste the stew to determine the seasoning.
8. Serve the stew hot with rice or toast and sprinkle with freshly chop-up parsley.

Nutrition (per serving):
Cals: 380
Protein: 32g
Carbs: 15g
Fat: 20g
Fiber: 3g

46. Egyptian Pumpkin Soup

Time: 1 hr
Servings: 4

Ingredients:

- 1 mini pumpkin (about 2 lbs/900g), peel off, seeded, and cubed
- 1 onion, chop-up
- 2 cloves garlic, chop-up
- 2 tbsp olive oil
- 4 cups of vegetable broth
- 1/2 tsp ground cumin
- 1/2 tsp ground coriander
- 1/4 tsp ground nutmeg
- Salt and pepper as needed
- 1/2 cup of heavy cream (non-compulsory)
- Pumpkin seeds (for garnish)

Instructions:

1. Olive oil Must be heated in a sizable pot over medium heat.
2. Add the chop-up garlic and onion to the saucepan. Sauté up to they are aromatic and tender.
3. The pumpkin Must be added to the pot and cooked for a few mins while being stirred occasionally.
4. Add the salt, pepper, nutmeg, cumin, coriander, and vegetable broth. The Mixture Must boil.
5. The soup Must simmer for about 30 to 40 mins, or up to the pumpkin is soft and can be easily mashed with a fork, on low heat with the lid on.
6. Pour the soup into a blender or use an immersion blender to purée it up to it's smooth and creamy.
7. Add the heavy cream (if using) and bring the soup back to a simmer in the pot. Warm the soup completely over a low heat.
8. Serve the hot pumpkin soup in dishes with pumpkin seeds as a garnish.

Nutrition (per serving):
Cals: 220
Protein: 3g
Carbs: 18g
Fat: 16g
Fiber: 3g

47. Egyptian Chicken Molokhia

Time: 1 hr
Servings: 4

Ingredients:

- 4 chicken breasts
- 2 tbsp vegetable oil
- 1 onion, lightly chop-up
- 4 garlic cloves, chop-up
- 1 bunch fresh molokhia leaves, washed and chop-up
- 4 cups of chicken broth
- Salt and pepper as needed
- Lemon wedges for serving

Instructions:

1. Over medium heat, warm the vegetable oil in a big pot. Add the chop-up garlic and onion, both chop-up. Sauté the onion up to it turns translucent.
2. The chicken breasts Must be added to the pot and cooked up to both sides are browned.
3. Bring to a boil after adding the chicken broth. When the chicken is thoroughly cooked, lower the heat and let the dish simmer for about 30 mins.
4. Shred the cooked chicken into mini pieces after removing it from the pot.
5. Add the chop-up molokhia leaves and the shredded chicken back to the pot. another 10 mins of cooking.
6. As needed, add salt and pepper to the food.
7. With rice or toast, serve the Egyptian Chicken Molokhia hot. Lemon wedges are used as a garnish.

NUTRITION INFO: (per serving)
Cals: 320
Fat: 12g
Carbs: 10g
Protein: 40g

48. Egyptian Cheese Pie

Time: 1 hr
Servings: 6

Ingredients:

- 2 sheets of puff pastry
- 2 cups of finely grated Egyptian cheese (such as feta or akkawi)
- 1 cup of shredded mozzarella cheese
- 2 eggs, beaten
- 1/4 cup of chop-up fresh parsley
- Salt and pepper as needed

Instructions:

1. Set the oven's temperature to 350°F (175°C).
2. One sheet of puff pastry is rolled out and placed in a pie dish that has been buttered.
3. Finely grated Egyptian cheese, shredded mozzarella cheese, beaten eggs, parsley, salt, and pepper Must all be combined in a combining dish. Combine thoroughly.
4. On top of the puff pastry in the pie dish, pour the cheese Mixture.
5. The second sheet of puff pastry Must be rolled out and positioned on top of the cheese Mixture. The sides Must be sealed with the bottom pastry.
6. For a golden crust, brush the pie with beaten egg.
7. The pie Must be golden brown after 40 mins in the preheated oven.
8. Before slicing and serving, let the pie cool for a few mins.

NUTRITION INFO: (per serving)
Cals: 380
Fat: 26g
Carbs: 22g
Protein: 15g

49. Egyptian Shrimp and Rice

Time: 40 mins
Servings: 4

Ingredients:

- 1 lb shrimp, peel off and deveined
- 2 tbsp vegetable oil
- 1 onion, lightly chop-up
- 2 garlic cloves, chop-up
- 1 cup of long-grain rice
- 2 cups of chicken broth
- 1 tsp ground cumin
- 1 tsp ground coriander
- 1/2 tsp turmeric
- Salt and pepper as needed
- Fresh parsley for garnish

Instructions:

1. Over medium heat, warm the vegetable oil in a big skillet. Add the chop-up garlic and onion, both chop-up. Sauté the onion up to it turns translucent.
2. Cook the shrimp in the skillet up to they are opaque and pink. The shrimp Must be taken out of the skillet and put aside.
3. Add the rice, cumin, coriander, turmeric, salt, and pepper to the same skillet. The spices Must be thoroughly combined into the rice.
4. Bring to a boil after adding the chicken broth. Once the rice is done and has absorbed the liquid, turn the heat down, cover the skillet, and simmer for about 20 mins.

5. Reintroduce the cooked shrimp to the skillet and combine.
6. Egyptian Shrimp and Rice Must be served hot and with fresh parsley on top.

NUTRITION INFO: (per serving)

Cals: 320

Fat: 8g

Carbs: 37g

Protein: 24g

50. Egyptian Cucumber Yogurt Salad

Time: 15 mins

Servings: 4

Ingredients:

- 2 cucumbers, peel off and diced
- 1 cup of plain yogurt
- 1 garlic clove, chop-up
- 2 tbsp chop-up fresh mint
- 1 tbsp fresh lemon juice
- Salt and pepper as needed

Instructions:

1. Cucumber dice, plain yogurt, chop-up garlic, chop-up mint, lemon juice, salt, and pepper Must all be combined in a combining dish. Combine thoroughly.
2. If necessary, taste and adjust the seasoning.
3. Before serving, the Egyptian Cucumber Yogurt Salad Must be chilled in the fridge for at least 30 mins.
4. As a cooling side dish, serve chilled.

NUTRITION INFO: (per serving)

Cals: 70

Fat: 3g

Carbs: 8g

Protein: 4g

51. Egyptian Meatballs

Time: 45 mins

Servings: 4

Ingredients:

- 1 lb ground beef
- 1 onion, lightly chop-up
- 2 garlic cloves, chop-up
- 1/4 cup of breadcrumbs
- 1/4 cup of chop-up fresh parsley
- 1 tsp ground cumin
- 1 tsp ground coriander
- 1/2 tsp ground cinnamon
- Salt and pepper as needed
- Vegetable oil for frying

Instructions:

1. Ground beef, chop-up onion, breadcrumbs, chop-up parsley, ground cumin, ground coriander, ground cinnamon, salt, and pepper Must all be combined in a combining bowl. Combine thoroughly.
2. Create little meatballs using the ingredients that are about one inch in diameter.
3. Over medium heat, warm vegetable oil in a big skillet. The meatballs Must be cooked through and evenly browned as you fry them in batches.
4. The meatballs Must be taken out of the skillet and put on a plate covered with paper towels to absorb any extra oil.
5. As an appetizer or as a main meal with rice and salad, serve the Egyptian meatballs hot.

NUTRITION INFO: (per serving)

Cals: 280

Fat: 18g

Carbs: 7g

Protein: 22g

52. Egyptian Bread Pudding

Time: 1 hr 30 mins

Servings: 6

Ingredients:

- 6 cups of stale bread, slice into cubes
- 4 cups of milk
- 1 cup of sugar
- 4 eggs
- 1 tsp vanilla extract
- 1/2 tsp ground cinnamon
- 1/4 cup of raisins (non-compulsory)
- Butter for greasing the baking dish
- Powdered sugar for dusting

Instructions:

1. Set the oven's temperature to 350°F (175°C). A baking dish Must be butter-greased.
2. Combine the milk, sugar, eggs, vanilla extract, and ground cinnamon in a sizable combining basin. Up up to a smooth combine, whisk.
3. The milk Mixture Must now contain the stale bread cubes. Let them soak for approximately 10 mins. Occasionally stir the bread to make sure it's all saturated.
4. Drain any raisins you plan to use before adding them to the bread Mixture. Combine thoroughly.
5. Spread the bread Mixture evenly throughout the oiled baking dish.
6. The top Must be golden brown and the pudding Must be set, which takes about an hr in a preheated oven.
7. Take it out of the oven, then let it to cool.
8. Sprinkle some powdered sugar over the top of the bread pudding.
9. Warm or room temperature servings of Egyptian Bread Pudding are acceptable.

53. Egyptian Roasted Chicken:

Time: 1 hr 30 mins
Servings: 4-6

Ingredients:

- 1 whole chicken
- 4 tbsp olive oil
- 2 tsp ground cumin
- 2 tsp ground coriander
- 2 tsp paprika
- 1 tsp ground cinnamon
- 1 tsp salt
- 1/2 tsp black pepper
- 4 cloves garlic, chop-up
- Juice of 1 lemon

Instructions:

1. Set the oven's temperature to 400°F (200°C).
2. Olive oil, cumin, coriander, paprika, cinnamon, salt, pepper, chop-up garlic, and lemon juice Must all be combined in a mini bowl.
3. Place the chicken in a roasting pan and coat it completely and evenly with the spice Mixture.
4. When the chicken's internal temperature reveryes 165°F (74°C), roast it in the preheated oven for about an hr and fifteen mins.
5. Before Cutting, let the chicken rest for a few mins. Serve warm.

Nutrition (per serving):
Cals: 350
Protein: 28g
Fat: 24g
Carbs: 2g
Fiber: 1g

54. Egyptian Chickpea Salad:

Time: 15 mins
Servings: 4

Ingredients:

- 2 cups of cooked chickpeas
- 1 cucumber, diced
- 1 tomato, diced
- 1/2 red onion, thinly split
- 1/4 cup of chop-up fresh parsley
- 1/4 cup of chop-up fresh mint
- Juice of 1 lemon
- 2 tbsp olive oil
- Salt and pepper as needed

Instructions:

1. Chickpeas, cucumber, tomato, red onion, parsley, and mint Must all be combined in a big bowl.
2. Combine the lemon juice, olive oil, salt, and pepper in a mini bowl.
3. After adding the dressing, blend the chickpea Mixture thoroughly.
4. If necessary, adjust the seasoning. Offer cold.

Nutrition (per serving):
Cals: 220
Protein: 8g
Fat: 8g
Carbs: 29g
Fiber: 8g

55. Egyptian Lamb Kofta:

Time: 30 mins

Servings: 4

Ingredients:

- 1 lb ground lamb
- 1/2 cup of lightly chop-up onion
- 2 cloves garlic, chop-up
- 1/4 cup of chop-up fresh parsley
- 1/4 cup of chop-up fresh mint
- 1 tsp ground cumin
- 1 tsp ground coriander
- 1/2 tsp ground cinnamon
- 1/2 tsp ground paprika
- Salt and pepper as needed
- Olive oil for cooking

Instructions:

1. Combine the ground lamb with the onion, garlic, parsley, mint, cumin, coriander, cinnamon, paprika, salt, and pepper in a sizable bowl.
2. Create little oval-shaped patties out of the ingredients.
3. In a skillet over medium heat, warm the olive oil. The kofta patties Must be fried for 4 to 5 mins on every side, or up to they are well heated through.
4. Tzatziki sauce and pita bread Must be served hot.

Nutrition (per serving):

Cals: 360
Protein: 23g
Fat: 28g
Carbs: 6g
Fiber: 1g

56. Egyptian Phyllo Meat Pie:

Time: 1 hr
Servings: 8

Ingredients:

- 1 lb ground beef or lamb
- 1/2 cup of lightly chop-up onion
- 2 cloves garlic, chop-up
- 2 tbsp olive oil
- 1 tsp ground cumin
- 1 tsp ground coriander
- 1/2 tsp ground cinnamon
- Salt and pepper as needed
- 10 sheets phyllo dough
- 1/4 cup of dilute butter

Instructions:

1. Set the oven's temperature to 350°F (175°C).
2. Olive oil Must be heated in a sizable skillet over medium heat. Cook the onion and garlic after being added up to tender.
3. Cook the lamb or beef ground in a skillet till browned. Take out any extra fat.
4. Add the salt, pepper, cinnamon, cumin, and coriander. another 2 mins of cooking. Take it off the fire and give it a min to cool.
5. Dilute butter Must be used to brush a 9x13-inch baking dish.
6. In the baking dish, arrange 5 sheets of phyllo dough, coating every one with dilute butter.
7. Over the phyllo dough, evenly distribute the meat Mixture.
8. Repeatedly smearing every sheet of phyllo dough with dilute butter, layer the remaining 5 sheets of dough on top.
9. Trim any extra phyllo dough that is protruding over the baking dish's sides.
10. The phyllo dough's top layer Must be scored into squares or triangles.
11. The phyllo dough Must be baked in the preheated oven for 30 to 40 mins, or up to golden brown.
12. Prior to serving, let it cool for a while.

Nutrition (per serving):

Cals: 330
Protein: 15g
Fat: 20g
Carbs: 24g
Fiber: 2g

57. Egyptian Coconut Cookies:

Time: 45 mins
Servings: 24

Ingredients:

- 2 cups of shredded coconut
- 1 cup of granulated sugar
- 3 egg whites
- 1/2 tsp vanilla extract

Instructions:

1. Set the oven's temperature to 325°F (160°C). Use parchment paper to cover a baking sheet.
2. The sugar and coconut shreds Must be combined in a combining dish.

3. The egg whites Must be beaten up to firm peaks form in a different bowl.
4. Gently fold the egg whites into the coconut Mixture after beating them.
5. Combine thoroughly after adding the vanilla extract.
6. Spoonfuls of the Mixture Must be dropped onto the prepared baking sheet, about 2 inches apart.
7. Bake the cookies for 20 to 25 mins, or up to golden brown.
8. Before serving, take the cookies out of the oven and let them cool fully.

Nutrition (per serving - 1 cookie):
Cals: 70
Protein: 1g
Fat: 3g -Carbs: 10g
Fiber: 1g

58. Egyptian Spiced Rice:

Time: 40 mins
Servings: 4

Ingredients:

- 1 cup of basmati rice
- 1 tbsp olive oil
- 1 mini onion, lightly chop-up
- 2 cloves garlic, chop-up
- 1 tsp ground cumin
- 1 tsp ground coriander
- 1/2 tsp ground cinnamon
- 1/4 tsp ground turmeric
- 2 cups of vegetable or chicken broth
- Salt and pepper as needed
- Chop-up fresh cilantro for garnish

Instructions:

1. Rice Must be thoroughly rinsed in cold water up to the water is clear. Drain, then set apart.
2. In a sizable saucepan set over medium heat, warm the olive oil. Cook the onion and garlic after being added up to tender.
3. To the pot, add the cumin, coriander, cinnamon, and turmeric. The spices Must be thoroughly combined with the onion and garlic.
4. Stir the spices into the rice after adding it to the pan.
5. Add the chicken or vegetable broth and season with salt and pepper.
6. Once the Mixture has reveryed a rolling boil, turn the heat down to low, cover the pan, and let the Mixture simmer for 15 to 20 mins, or up to the rice is done and the liquid has been absorbed.
7. Before serving, fluff the rice with a fork and top with lightly chop-up fresh cilantro.

Nutrition (per serving):
Cals: 180
Protein: 3g
Fat: 4g
Carbs: 33g
Fiber: 2g

59. Egyptian Egg Salad:

Time: 15 mins
Servings: 4

Ingredients:

- 6 hard-boiled eggs, peel off and chop-up
- 1/4 cup of chop-up fresh parsley
- 1/4 cup of chop-up fresh dill
- 1/4 cup of chop-up green onions
- 1/4 cup of chop-up cucumber
- 1/4 cup of chop-up tomato
- 2 tbsp olive oil
- 2 tbsp lemon juice
- Salt and pepper as needed

Instructions:

1. The chop-up eggs, parsley, dill, green onions, cucumber, and tomato Must all be combined in a big bowl.
2. Combine the olive oil, lemon juice, salt, and pepper in a mini bowl.
3. After adding the dressing, gently toss the egg Mixture to coat.
4. If necessary, adjust the seasoning.
5. Enjoy while serving chilled!

60. Egyptian Beef and Potato Stew:

Time: 1 hr and 30 mins
Servings: 6

Ingredients:

- 1 kg beef stew meat, slice into cubes
- 2 tbsp vegetable oil
- 1 onion, chop-up

- 2 garlic cloves, chop-up
- 2 tsp ground cumin
- 2 tsp ground coriander
- 1/2 tsp ground cinnamon
- Salt and pepper as needed
- 4 cups of beef broth
- 4 potatoes, peel off and diced
- 1/4 cup of chop-up fresh cilantro (coriander)

Instructions:

1. Vegetable oil Must be heated in a sizable pot over medium heat.
2. Brown the beef cubes all over after adding them.
3. To the pot, add the chop-up garlic and onion, and cook up to aromatic.
4. Add the salt, pepper, cinnamon, cumin, and coriander.
5. Bring to a boil after adding the beef broth.
6. Simmer for a full hr on low heat with the lid on.
7. When the potatoes are ready, add the diced potatoes and simmer for a further 30 mins.
8. Before serving, garnish with chop-up cilantro.

61. Egyptian Lentil Salad:

Time: 30 mins

Servings: 4

Ingredients:

- 1 cup of dried lentils
- 1/2 cup of chop-up cucumber
- 1/2 cup of chop-up tomato
- 1/4 cup of chop-up red onion
- 1/4 cup of chop-up fresh parsley
- 2 tbsp olive oil
- 2 tbsp lemon juice
- 1 tsp ground cumin
- Salt and pepper as needed

Instructions:

1. The lentils Must be thoroughly rinsed before cooking them as directed on the packet.
2. After cooking, drain the lentils and let them cool.
3. Combine the lentils, lightly diced cucumber, tomato, red onion, and parsley in a Big bowl.
4. Combine the olive oil, lemon juice, cumin, salt, and pepper in a mini bowl.
5. The lentil Mixture Must be drizzled with the dressing, then gently combined.
6. If necessary, adjust the seasoning.
7. At least an hr Must pass before serving.

62. Egyptian Stuffed Zucchini:

Time: 1 hr and 15 mins

Servings: 6

Ingredients:

- 6 medium zucchini
- 500g ground beef
- 1/2 cup of cooked rice
- 1 onion, lightly chop-up
- 2 garlic cloves, chop-up
- 2 tbsp chop-up fresh dill
- 2 tbsp chop-up fresh parsley
- 1 tbsp tomato paste
- 1 tsp ground cumin
- 1/2 tsp ground cinnamon
- Salt and pepper as needed
- 2 cups of tomato sauce

Instructions:

1. Set the oven's temperature to 180 C (350 F).
2. Slice off the zucchini's tops and take out the pulp, leaving a shell.
3. Ground beef, cooked rice, diced onion, chop-up garlic, dill, parsley, tomato paste, cumin, cinnamon, salt, and pepper Must all be combined in a bowl.
4. Place the meat Mixture within the zucchini shells.
5. In a baking dish, spread the tomato sauce over the stuffed zucchini.
6. Bake the dish for 45 mins while it is covered with aluminum foil.
7. When the beef is fully cooked and the zucchini are tender, take out the foil and bake for an additional 15 mins.
8. Serve warm.

63. Egyptian Shish Kebabs:

Time: 40 mins

Servings: 4

Ingredients:

- 500g beef or lamb cubes
- 1/4 cup of olive oil

- 2 tbsp lemon juice
- 2 garlic cloves, chop-up
- 1 tsp ground cumin
- 1 tsp ground coriander
- 1/2 tsp ground paprika
- Salt and pepper as needed
- Skewers (if using wooden skewers, soak them in water for 30 mins before using)

Instructions:

1. Make the marinade in a bowl by combining the olive oil, lemon juice, chop-up garlic, cumin, coriander, paprika, salt, and pepper.
2. Cubes of lamb or beef Must be added to the marinade and combined to coat thoroughly.
3. For at least 30 mins, marinate the beef in the refrigerator with the bowl covered.
4. Get the grill or the broiler ready.
5. Onto skewers, thread the marinated meat.
6. The kebabs Must be grilled or broiled for 10 to 12 mins, rotating once or twice, or up to the meat is cooked to your preference.
7. Serve hot with pita bread or rice.

64. Egyptian Date Cookies:

Time: 1 hr and 30 mins
Servings: 24 cookies

Ingredients:

- 2 cups of all-purpose flour
- 1 cup of unsalted butter, melted
- 1/2 cup of powdered sugar
- 1/2 tsp vanilla extract
- 1/4 tsp salt
- 1 cup of dates, pitted and chop-up
- 1/4 cup of chop-up walnuts (non-compulsory)

Instructions:

1. Set the oven's temperature to 180 C (350 F).
2. The melted butter and powdered sugar Must be combined in a combining dish and creamed up to light and fluffy.
3. Add salt and vanilla extract after that.
4. Combine in the flour gradually up to a dough forms.
5. Make little balls out of the dough, every about 1 tbsp in size.
6. With your palms flattened, drop a few chop-up dates and some chop-up walnuts (if using) in the center of every ball.
7. To create a cookie shape, fold the dough over the filling and bind the edges.
8. On a baking sheet covered with parchment paper, spread out the cookies.
9. Bake for 12 to 15 mins, or up to the edges are golden brown, in a preheated oven.
10. Before serving, take the cookies out of the oven and let them cool on a wire rack.

65. Egyptian Okra and Lamb Stew

Time: 2 hrs
Servings: 4-6 servings

Ingredients:

- 1 lb lamb, slice into cubes
- 1 lb okra, trimmed and halved
- 1 onion, lightly chop-up
- 3 cloves garlic, chop-up
- 2 tbsp vegetable oil
- 2 tbsp tomato paste
- 4 cups of chicken or vegetable broth
- 1 tsp ground cumin
- 1 tsp ground coriander
- Salt and pepper as needed
- Fresh cilantro, chop-up (for garnish)

Instructions:

1. Over medium heat, warm the vegetable oil in a big pot. Add the lamb cubes and sauté them up to evenly browned. Lamb Must be taken out of the saucepan and placed aside.
2. Add the chop-up garlic and onion to the same pot. Sauté the onion up to it turns translucent.
3. Salt, pepper, tomato paste, cumin, and coriander Must be added to the pot. The spices Must be thoroughly combined with the onions and garlic.
4. Add the chicken or vegetable broth to the pot with the lamb cubes once more. Once it begins to boil, turn the heat down, cover, and simmer for about an hr, or up to the lamb is cooked.
5. When the okra is fully cooked, add it to the stew and boil it for an additional 30 mins.
6. If necessary, adjust the seasoning. Serve the stew hot with fresh cilantro on top. Enjoy!

NUTRITION INFO (per serving):
Cals: 320
Protein: 22g
Carbs: 14g
Fat: 20g

Fiber: 5g

55. Egyptian Yogurt with Honey

Time: 5 mins
Servings: 2 servings

Ingredients:

- 1 cup of plain Greek yogurt
- 2 tbsp honey
- 1/4 tsp vanilla extract (non-compulsory)
- Fresh berries or split fruits (non-compulsory, for topping)

Instructions:

1. Greek yogurt, honey, and vanilla extract (if used) Must all be combined in a bowl. Combine thoroughly up to the Mixture is smooth and the honey is distributed evenly.
2. If necessary, add additional honey after tasting to regulate the sweetness.
3. To serve, divide the yogurt Mixture among dishes.
4. If desired, garnish with split fruit or fresh berries.
5. Enjoy this cooling yogurt from Egypt with honey right away!

NUTRITION INFO (per serving):
Cals: 180
Protein: 18g
Carbs: 25g
Fat: 0.5g
Fiber: 0g

56. Egyptian Lamb and Rice

Time: 1 hr
Servings: 4 servings

Ingredients:

- 1 lb lamb, slice into cubes
- 1 onion, lightly chop-up
- 2 cloves garlic, chop-up
- 2 tbsp vegetable oil
- 1 cup of basmati rice
- 2 cups of chicken or vegetable broth
- 1 tsp ground cinnamon
- 1/2 tsp ground cumin
- Salt and pepper as needed
- Fresh parsley, chop-up (for garnish)

Instructions:

1. Over medium heat, warm the vegetable oil in a big pot. Add the lamb cubes and sauté them up to evenly browned. Lamb Must be taken out of the saucepan and placed aside.
2. Add the chop-up garlic and onion to the same pot. Sauté the onion up to it turns translucent.
3. The rice Must be added to the pot and thoroughly combined with the onion and garlic.
4. Add the chicken or vegetable broth to the pot with the lamb cubes once more. Add the salt, pepper, cumin, and cinnamon powders.
5. Heat Must be turned down once the Mixture comes to a boil. For about 30 to 40 mins, or up to the rice is cooked and the liquid has been absorbed, simmer the pot covered.
6. Before serving, fluff the rice with a fork. Add fresh parsley as a garnish. Enjoy this delicious lamb and rice dish from Egypt!

NUTRITION INFO (per serving):
Cals: 450
Protein: 25g
Carbs: 40g
Fat: 20g
Fiber: 2g

57. Egyptian Cabbage Salad

Time: 20 mins
Servings: 4 servings

Ingredients:

- 1 mini cabbage, thinly split
- 1 mini red onion, thinly split
- 1 cucumber, peel off and thinly split
- 1 bell pepper, thinly split
- 2 tomatoes, diced
- 1/4 cup of fresh lemon juice
- 2 tbsp olive oil
- 1 tsp ground cumin
- Salt and pepper as needed
- Fresh mint leaves, chop-up (for garnish)

Instructions:

1. Split cabbage, red onion, cucumber, bell pepper, and chop-up tomatoes Must all be combined in a big bowl.
2. Combine the lemon juice, olive oil, ground cumin, salt, and pepper in a separate mini bowl.

3. To ensure that everything is equally coated, pour the dressing over the salad items and toss thoroughly.
4. Before serving, let the salad sit in the marinade for about 10 mins to let the flavors blend.
5. Serve this cooling Egyptian cabbage salad as a side dish or light supper, garnished with fresh mint leaves. Enjoy!

NUTRITION INFO (per serving):
Cals: 120
Protein: 2g
Carbs: 15g
Fat: 7g
Fiber: 4g

58. Egyptian Lamb Chops

Time: 30 mins
Servings: 4 servings

Ingredients:

- 8 lamb chops
- 2 cloves garlic, chop-up
- 2 tbsp olive oil
- 1 tsp ground cumin
- 1 tsp ground coriander
- 1/2 tsp ground paprika
- Salt and pepper as needed
- Lemon wedges (for serving)

Instructions:

1. Heat your grill or grill pan on the stovetop to medium-high.
2. Combine the chop-up garlic, olive oil, cumin, coriander, paprika, salt, and pepper in a mini bowl. For a paste, thoroughly combine.
3. Make sure to evenly coat the lamb chops with the spice paste as you rub.
4. To cook the lamb chops to your preferred doneness, place them on the prepared grill and cook for about 4-5 mins per side for medium-rare.
5. The lamb chops Must be taken off the grill and given some time to rest before serving.
6. Lemon wedges Must be placed on the side of the lamb chops. Enjoy these succulent lamb chops from Egypt!

NUTRITION INFO (per serving):
Cals: 350
Protein: 22g
Carbs: 1g
Fat: 28g
Fiber: 0g

59. Egyptian Spinach Stew

Time: 40 mins
Servings: 4 servings

Ingredients:

- 1 lb fresh spinach, washed and chop-up
- 1 onion, lightly chop-up
- 2 cloves garlic, chop-up
- 2 tbsp vegetable oil
- 1 cup of vegetable broth
- 1 cup of canned chickpeas, rinsed and drained
- 1 tbsp tomato paste
- 1 tsp ground ccumin
- 1/2 tsp ground coriander
- Salt and pepper as needed
- Juice of 1 lemon
- Fresh parsley, chop-up (for garnish)

Instructions:

1. Over medium heat, warm the vegetable oil in a big pot. Add the chop-up garlic and onion, both chop-up. Sauté the onion up to it turns translucent.
2. Add salt, pepper, tomato paste, ground cumin, and ground coriander to the pot. The spices Must be thoroughly combined with the onions and garlic.
3. Stir the saucepan while adding the chop-up spinach up to it wilts.
4. Add the veggie broth, then boil the Mixture. Cook the spinach for 15 to 20 mins, or up to it is soft.
5. To fully reheat the chickpeas, stir them in and simmer for an additional 5 mins.
6. Add the lemon juice after turning off the stove. If necessary, taste and adjust the seasoning.
7. Serve the hot spinach stew with fresh parsley on top. Enjoy this filling stew of Egyptian spinach!

NUTRITION INFO (per serving):
Cals: 150
Protein: 8g
Carbs: 20g
Fat: 6g
Fiber: 7g

60. Egyptian Chicken Shawarma

Time: 1 hr

Servings: 4

Ingredients:

- 4 boneless, skinless chicken breasts
- 2 tbsp olive oil
- 2 tbsp lemon juice
- 2 cloves garlic, chop-up
- 1 tsp ground cumin
- 1 tsp ground coriander
- 1 tsp paprika
- 1/2 tsp ground turmeric
- 1/2 tsp ground cinnamon
- Salt and pepper, as needed
- 4 pita bread rounds
- Toppings: diced tomatoes, split cucumbers, tahini sauce

Instructions:

1. Olive oil, lemon juice, chop-up garlic, cumin, coriander, paprika, turmeric, cinnamon, salt, and pepper are all combined in a bowl. Combine thoroughly.
2. Spread the marinade evenly over the chicken breasts before adding them. Give the chicken at least 30 mins to marinate.
3. Over medium-high heat, preheat the grill or grill pan on the stove.
4. The marinated chicken breasts Must be grilled for 6 to 8 mins on every side, or up to done and slightly browned.
5. After taking the chicken off the grill, give it some time to rest. Then slice the chicken very thin.
6. In the oven or a skillet, reheat the pita bread rounds.
7. Place the split chicken atop the warmed pita bread rounds to assemble the shawarma. Add diced tomatoes and cucumber slices on top, then drizzle with tahini sauce.
8. If necessary, fasten the pita bread roll with a toothpick.
9. Enjoy the warm Egyptian Chicken Shawarma!

NUTRITION INFO: (per serving)
Cals: 320
Fat: 10g
Carbs: 30g
Protein: 28g

61. Egyptian Breaded Fish

Time: 40 mins

Servings: 4

Ingredients:

- 4 fish fillets (such as tilapia or cod)
- 1 cup of breadcrumbs
- 1/4 cup of all-purpose flour
- 1 tsp ground cumin
- 1 tsp ground coriander
- 1/2 tsp paprika
- Salt and pepper, as needed
- 2 eggs, beaten
- Vegetable oil, for frying
- Lemon wedges, for serving

Instructions:

1. Combine breadcrumbs, flour, cumin, coriander, paprika, salt, and pepper in a shlet dish.
2. Make sure every fish fillet is completely coated by dipping it into the beaten eggs.
3. Apply the breadcrumb Mixture to the fish fillets, gently pressing to adhere.
4. In a frying pan, heat vegetable oil to a medium-high temperature.
5. The breaded fish fillets Must be fried for three to four mins on every side, or up to golden and crispy.
6. Fish Must be taken out of the pan and put on a dish covered with paper towels to absorb any extra oil.
7. Enjoy the Egyptian Breaded Fish together with wedges of lemon!

NUTRITION INFO: (per serving)
Cals: 290
Fat: 9g
Carbs: 20g
Protein: 30g

62. Egyptian Sesame Cookies

Time: 1 hr

Servings: 24 cookies

Ingredients:

- 1 cup of unsalted butter, melted
- 1 cup of granulated sugar
- 2 eggs
- 1 tsp vanilla extract
- 3 cups of all-purpose flour

- 1 tsp baking powder
- 1/2 tsp baking soda
- 1/4 tsp salt
- 1/2 cup of sesame seeds

Instructions:

1. A baking sheet Must be lined with parchment paper and the oven Must be preheated to 350°F (175°C).
2. The melted butter and sugar Must be creamed up to light and fluffy in a combining dish.
3. One at a time, beat in every egg, then add the vanilla essence.
4. Combine the flour, baking soda, baking powder, and salt in a another basin.
5. As you gradually include the dry ingredients, blend them thoroughly with the butter Mixture.
6. Make little, 1 inch-diameter balls out of the dough.
7. Sesame seeds Must be put in a shlet dish. As you uniformly coat every dough ball in sesame seeds, continue.
8. Place the covered dough balls on the baking sheet that has been prepared, leting space between every cookie.
9. Bake the cookies in the preheated oven for 12 to 15 mins, or up to golden brown.
10. The cookies Must be taken out of the oven and leted to cool on a wire rack.
11. When the Egyptian Sesame Cookies have cooled, place them in an airtight container.

NUTRITION INFO: (per cookie)
Cals: 150
Fat: 8g
Carbs: 17g
Protein: 2g

63. Egyptian Tomato and Cucumber Salad

Time: 15 mins
Servings: 4

Ingredients:

- 2 Big tomatoes, diced
- 1 English cucumber, diced
- 1 mini red onion, thinly split
- 1/4 cup of fresh parsley, chop-up
- 1/4 cup of fresh mint leaves, chop-up
- 2 tbsp lemon juice
- 2 tbsp extra-virgin olive oil
- Salt and pepper, as needed

Instructions:

1. Diced tomatoes, cucumber, red onion, parsley, and mint leaves Must all be combined in a big bowl.
2. Combine the lemon juice, olive oil, salt, and pepper in a mini bowl.
3. Over the tomato and cucumber Mixture, drizzle the dressing. Combine thoroughly by tossing.
4. If necessary, taste and adjust the seasoning.
5. Before serving, let the salad sit in the marinade for at least 10 mins to let the flavors blend.
6. As a cooling side dish, serve the Egyptian Tomato and Cucumber Salad cold.

NUTRITION INFO: (per serving)
Cals: 80
Fat: 6g
Carbs: 7g
Protein: 1g

64. Egyptian Lamb and Potato Stew

Time: 2 hrs 30 mins
Servings: 6

Ingredients:

- 2 lbs lamb Muster, slice into cubes
- 2 tbsp vegetable oil
- 1 Big onion, chop-up
- 3 cloves garlic, chop-up
- 2 tsp ground cumin
- 2 tsp ground coriander
- 1 tsp ground turmeric
- 1 tsp paprika
- 1/2 tsp cinnamon
- Salt and pepper, as needed
- 4 cups of beef or vegetable broth
- 4 medium potatoes, peel off and cubed
- 1 cup of canned chickpeas, drained and rinsed
- 1/4 cup of chop-up fresh cilantro
- Lemon wedges, for serving

Instructions:

1. Over medium heat, warm vegetable oil in a big pot or Dutch oven.
2. Add the lamb cubes and sauté them up to evenly browned. Lamb Must be taken out of the saucepan and placed aside.
3. Add the chop-up garlic and onion to the same pot. Sauté the onion up to it turns translucent.
4. Return the lamb to the saucepan and season with salt, pepper, ground cumin, ground coriander, ground turmeric, ground paprika, and ground cinnamon. Stir the spices into the meat and onions thoroughly.
5. Bring the Mixture to a boil before adding the beef or veggie broth. For an hr, simmer the Mixture on low heat with the lid on.
6. Add the drained chickpeas and cubed potatoes to the stew an hr later. To blend, stir.
7. Once more covering the pot, simmer for another hr, or up to the lamb is soft and the potatoes are fully cooked.
8. If necessary, taste the stew to determine the seasoning.
9. Before serving, top the stew with fresh cilantro that has been chop-up.
10. Serve hot lemon wedges alongside the Egyptian Lamb and Potato Stew.

NUTRITION INFO: (per serving)
Cals: 420
Fat: 20g
Carbs: 26g
Protein: 34g

65. Egyptian Lentil and Vegetable Stew

Time: 1 hr 30 mins
Servings: 6

Ingredients:

- 1 cup of dried red lentils, rinsed
- 2 tbsp vegetable oil
- 1 Big onion, chop-up
- 3 cloves garlic, chop-up
- 2 carrots, diced
- 2 celery stalks, diced
- 1 red bell pepper, diced
- 1 tsp ground cumin
- 1 tsp ground coriander
- 1 tsp ground turmeric
- 1/2 tsp paprika
- 1/4 tsp cinnamon
- Salt and pepper, as needed
- 4 cups of vegetable broth
- 1 can (14 ozs) diced tomatoes
- 1 tbsp tomato paste
- Juice of 1 lemon
- Chop-up fresh cilantro, for garnish

Instructions:

1. Vegetable oil Must be heated over medium heat in a big pot or Dutch oven.
2. Add the chop-up garlic and onion, both chop-up. Sauté the onion up to it turns translucent.
3. To the pot, add diced carrots, celery, and red bell pepper. Vegetables Must be sautéed for a few mins up to they begin to soften.
4. Add the ground cumin, coriander, turmeric, paprika, cinnamon, salt, and pepper after stirring in the ground spices. The spices Must be thoroughly combined into the vegetables.
5. Pour the vegetable broth into the pot with the rinsed red lentils.
6. Add the tomato paste and diced tomatoes after that.
7. As soon as the Mixture comes to a boil, turn the heat down to low and cover the pan. For approximately an hr, or up to the lentils are cooked through and the flavors are well-balanced, let the stew simmer.
8. Add the lemon juice and, if necessary, taste and adjust the seasoning.
9. Egyptian Lentil and Vegetable Stew Must be poured into dishes and topped with lightly chop-up fresh cilantro.
10. Enjoy the stew right away!

NUTRITION INFO: (per serving)
Cals: 230
Fat: 6g
Carbs: 36g
Protein: 11g

66. Egyptian Stuffed Artichokes:

Time: 1 hr 30 mins
Servings: 4

Ingredients:

- 4 Big artichokes
- 1 cup of breadcrumbs
- 1/2 cup of finely grated Parmesan cheese

- 1/4 cup of chop-up fresh parsley
- 2 cloves garlic, chop-up
- 1/4 cup of olive oil
- 1/2 cup of water
- Salt and pepper as needed

Instructions:

1. Set the oven's temperature to 375°F (190°C).
2. Take out any tough outer leaves and trim the artichokes' stems.
3. Breadcrumbs, Parmesan cheese, parsley, garlic, salt, and pepper Must all be combined in a basin.
4. Every artichoke's leaves Must be fanned out carefully before the breadcrumb Mixture is stuffed in between the leaves.
5. In a baking dish, place the stuffed artichokes. Pour water into the dish and drizzle olive oil on top.
6. Bake the dish for an hr while it is covered with aluminum foil.
7. Once the artichokes are soft and the breadcrumbs are golden brown, take out the cover and bake for an additional 15 mins.
8. Serve warm.

67. Egyptian Beef Shawarma:

Time: 2 hrs 30 mins
Servings: 6

Ingredients:

- 2 lbs beef sirloin, thinly split
- 1/4 cup of olive oil
- 4 cloves garlic, chop-up
- 2 tbsp ground cumin
- 2 tbsp ground coriander
- 2 tbsp paprika
- 1 tbsp ground turmeric
- 1 tbsp ground cinnamon
- Juice of 2 lemons
- Salt and pepper as needed
- Pita bread and tahini sauce for serving

Instructions:

1. Olive oil, chop-up garlic, cumin, coriander, paprika, turmeric, cinnamon, lemon juice, salt, and pepper are all combined in a bowl.
2. Slices of beef Must be added to the bowl and combined around to evenly distribute the marinade. For at least two hrs, let the meat marinade in the refrigerator.
3. Heat a skillet or grill to a medium-high temperature.
4. Slices of marinated beef Must be cooked on the grill or in a skillet for 3–4 mins on every side, or up to they revery the appropriate D of doneness.
5. After the beef has finished cooking, turn off the heat and give it some time to rest.
6. The beef Must be thinly split.
7. Serve the meat shawarma with tahini sauce on pita bread.

68. Egyptian Semolina Cake:

Time: 1 hr
Servings: 8

Ingredients:

- 1 cup of semolina
- 1 cup of sugar
- 1 cup of plain yogurt
- 1/2 cup of vegetable oil
- 1/2 tsp vanilla extract
- 1/2 tsp baking powder
- 1/4 tsp baking soda
- Zest of 1 lemon
- Syrup:
- 1 cup of sugar
- 1 cup of water
- Juice of 1 lemon

Instructions:

1. Prepare a round cake pan with greasing and preheat the oven to 350°F (175°C).
2. Semolina, sugar, yogurt, vegetable oil, vanilla extract, baking soda, baking powder, and lemon zest Must all be combined in a combining dish. Well combine up to smooth.
3. After smoothing the top, pour the batter into the prepared cake pan.
4. A toothpick inserted in the center Must come out clean after baking for about 30-35 mins, or up to the top is golden brown.
5. Make the syrup by combining the sugar, water, and lemon juice in a saucepan while the cake is baking. Boil for a few mins before simmering.
6. When the cake is finished baking, take it from the oven and drizzle the hot syrup over the warm cake right away.
7. Before serving, let the cake cool in the pan.

69. Egyptian Roasted Vegetables:

Time: 45 mins

Servings: 4

Ingredients:

- 2 Big eggplants, cubed
- 2 Big zucchinis, split
- 2 bell peppers, split
- 1 red onion, split
- 4 tomatoes, chop-up
- 4 cloves garlic, chop-up
- 3 tbsp olive oil
- 1 tbsp ground cumin
- 1 tbsp ground coriander
- Salt and pepper as needed

Instructions:

1. Set the oven's temperature to 400°F (200°C).
2. Combine the cubed eggplant, split zucchini, bell peppers, split red onion, and chop-up tomatoes in a sizable baking dish.
3. Combine the chop-up garlic, olive oil, cumin, coriander, salt, and pepper in a mini bowl.
4. Sprinkle the vegetables in the baking dish with the garlic and spice Mixture. Toss thoroughly to evenly coat the vegetables.
5. 30-35 mins, or up to the veggies are soft and gently browned, Must be spent roasting in the preheated oven.
6. Serve as a side dish or a vegetarian main course after removing from the oven.

70. Egyptian Lamb and Eggplant Stew:

Time: 2 hrs

Servings: 6

Ingredients:

- 2 lbs lamb stew meat, cubed
- 2 eggplants, cubed
- 2 onions, chop-up
- 4 cloves garlic, chop-up
- 2 tbsp tomato paste
- 2 cups of beef or vegetable broth
- 1 tsp ground cumin
- 1 tsp ground coriander
- 1 tsp ground cinnamon
- 1/2 tsp ground turmeric
- Salt and pepper as needed
- Chop-up fresh parsley for garnish

Instructions:

1. Over medium-high heat, preheat a Big saucepan or Dutch oven. Stir in the lamb stew meat and heat it up to it is evenly browned.
2. To the pot, add the chop-up garlic and lightly chop-up onions. The onions Must be sautéed up to transparent and tender.
3. Add the tomato paste along with the spices (cumin, coriander, cinnamon, turmeric, salt, pepper). To enable the flavors to mingle, cook for a few mins.
4. Add the beef or vegetable broth to the pot along with the cubed eggplants. To blend, thoroughly stir.
5. After bringing the stew to a boil, turn down the heat. Once the lamb is cooked and the flavors are well-balanced, simmer the dish with the lid on for about 1 1/2 to 2 hrs.
6. Before serving, taste the food and add more seasoning if necessary.
7. Serve the stew hot with rice or toast and top with freshly chop-up parsley.

71. Egyptian Bulgur Salad:

Time: 30 mins

Servings: 4

Ingredients:

- 1 cup of bulgur wheat
- 2 cups of boiling water
- 1 cucumber, diced
- 2 tomatoes, diced
- 1 red bell pepper, diced
- 1/2 cup of chop-up fresh parsley
- 1/4 cup of chop-up fresh mint
- 1/4 cup of olive oil
- Juice of 2 lemons
- Salt and pepper as needed

Instructions:

1. Pour the boiling water over the bulgur wheat that has been placed in a big bowl. For about 15 to 20 mins, or up to the bulgur is tender and has absorbed the water, cover the bowl and let it to settle.
2. The cooked bulgur Must be fluffed with a fork and let to cool to room temperature.

3. Add the diced cucumber, tomatoes, red bell pepper, chop-up parsley, and chop-up mint to the bowl when the bulgur has cooled. Blend thoroughly.
4. Combine the olive oil, lemon juice, salt, and pepper in a separate mini bowl.
5. When all the ingredients are coated, drizzle the dressing over the bulgur salad and toss to combine.
6. If necessary, adjust the seasoning.
7. The bulgur salad can be served cold or at room temperature.

72. Egyptian Lamb Kebabs:

Time: 1 hr 30 mins
Servings: 4

Ingredients:

- 1 lb (450g) lamb, slice into cubes
- 1 onion, lightly chop-up
- 2 cloves garlic, chop-up
- 2 tbsp olive oil
- 1 tbsp lemon juice
- 1 tsp ground cumin
- 1 tsp ground coriander
- 1/2 tsp ground cinnamon
- Salt and pepper as needed

Instructions:

1. Combine the chop-up garlic, chop-up onion, olive oil, lemon juice, cumin, coriander, cinnamon, salt, and pepper in a bowl.
2. To evenly coat them, add the lamb cubes to the marinade and toss. Refrigerate the lamb for at least an hr to let it marinate.
3. Activate the broiler or grill and heat it to medium-high.
4. To cook the lamb to the desired doneness, thread it onto skewers and grill or broil for about 10 mins, flipping it once or twice.
5. Warm pita bread and tzatziki sauce Must be served alongside the Egyptian lamb kebabs.

73. Egyptian Green Bean Stew:

Time: 1 hr 15 mins
Servings: 6

Ingredients:

- 1 lb (450g) green beans, trimmed and slice into bite-sized pieces
- 2 tbsp olive oil
- 1 onion, lightly chop-up
- 2 cloves garlic, chop-up
- 1 can (14 oz/400g) diced tomatoes
- 1 tsp ground cumin
- 1 tsp ground coriander
- 1/2 tsp ground turmeric
- Salt and pepper as needed
- Fresh cilantro or parsley for garnish (non-compulsory)

Instructions:

1. In a big pot, warm up the olive oil over medium heat. When the onion is transparent, add the chop-up garlic and the diced onion.
2. To the pot, add the chop-up tomatoes, salt, pepper, ground cumin, ground coriander, and ground turmeric. To blend, thoroughly stir.
3. Stir the green beans into the tomato sauce after adding them to the pot. Up to the green beans are cooked, simmer the pot with the lid on for about 45 mins.
4. If necessary, adjust the seasoning. If preferred, garnish with fresh cilantro or parsley.
5. Hot rice or toast Must be served with the Egyptian green bean stew.

74. Egyptian Chicken and Vegetable Tagine:

Time: 1 hr 30 mins
Servings: 4

Ingredients:

- 4 chicken thighs, bone-in and skin-on
- 1 onion, lightly chop-up
- 2 cloves garlic, chop-up
- 2 carrots, peel off and split
- 1 zucchini, split
- 1 eggplant, diced
- 1 can (14 oz/400g) diced tomatoes
- 1 tsp ground cumin
- 1 tsp ground coriander
- 1/2 tsp ground cinnamon
- Salt and pepper as needed
- Fresh parsley for garnish (non-compulsory)

Instructions:

1. Heat some olive oil in a sizable saucepan or tagine over medium heat. The chicken thighs are browned on all sides, then they are take outd.
2. Sauté the chop-up onion and chop-up garlic in the same pot up to the onion is transparent.
3. Cook the carrots, zucchini, and eggplant in the saucepan for a few mins, or up to they are just beginning to soften.
4. Add the diced tomatoes, ground cumin, ground coriander, ground cinnamon, salt, and pepper to the pot with the chicken thighs. To blend, thoroughly stir.
5. Once the chicken is cooked through and the vegetables are soft, take out the lid and let the Mixture simmer for about an hr.
6. If desired, garnish with fresh parsley.
7. With couscous or toast, serve the delicious Egyptian chicken and vegetable tagine.

75. Egyptian Rice and Lentil Soup:

Time: 45 mins

Servings: 6

Ingredients:

- 1 cup of brown lentils
- 1 onion, lightly chop-up
- 2 cloves garlic, chop-up
- 1 carrot, diced
- 1 celery stalk, diced
- 1 cup of rice
- 6 cups of vegetable or chicken broth
- 1 tsp ground cumin
- 1 tsp ground coriander
- Salt and pepper as needed
- Fresh lemon wedges for serving

Instructions:

1. Put the lentils aside after giving them a cold water rinse.
2. The chop-up onion and chop-up garlic Must be cooked in a big pot up to the onion is transparent.
3. Cook for a few mins after adding the diced carrot and celery to the saucepan.
4. Add the rice, lentils, ground cumin, ground coriander, salt, pepper, and vegetable or chicken broth to the pot. To blend, thoroughly stir.
5. When the rice and lentils are fully cooked, turn down the heat, cover the pot, and simmer for about 30 mins.
6. If necessary, adjust the seasoning.
7. Egyptian rice and lentil soup Must be served hot and with a squeeze of lemon juice.

76. Egyptian Stuffed Onions:

Time: 1 hr 30 mins

Servings: 4

Ingredients:

- 4 Big onions
- 1 lb (450g) ground beef or lamb
- 1/2 cup of cooked rice
- 2 tbsp olive oil
- 1 tsp ground cumin
- 1 tsp ground coriander
- 1/2 tsp ground cinnamon
- Salt and pepper as needed
- Tomato sauce for serving

Instructions:

1. Set the oven's temperature to 350°F (175°C).
2. Slice off the tops and peel the onions. Take out the centers, leaving a 1/4-inch-thick shell in their place.
3. Ground beef or lamb, cooked rice, olive oil, ground cumin, ground coriander, ground cinnamon, salt, and pepper Must all be combined in a bowl.
4. Put the meat and rice Mixture within the onion shells, packing it down firmly.
5. In a baking dish, cover the stuffed onions with foil.
6. Bake for approximately an hr, or up to the meat is thoroughly cooked and the onions are soft.
7. With tomato sauce, serve the Egyptian-style stuffed onions hot.

77. Egyptian Lamb Curry:

Time: 2 hrs

Servings: 6

Ingredients:

- 2 lbs (900g) lamb Muster, slice into chunks
- 2 onions, lightly chop-up
- 3 cloves garlic, chop-up
- 2 tbsp olive oil
- 2 tbsp Egyptian curry powder

- 1 tsp ground cumin
- 1 tsp ground coriander
- 1/2 tsp ground turmeric
- 1/2 tsp ground cinnamon
- 1/4 tsp ground cloves
- 1 can (14 oz/400g) diced tomatoes
- 1 cup of coconut milk
- Salt and pepper as needed
- Fresh cilantro for garnish (non-compulsory)

Instructions:

1. Over medium heat, warm the olive oil in a big pot or Dutch oven. When the onions are transparent, add the chop-up garlic and the chop-up onions.
2. Cook the lamb chunks in the pot up to they are evenly browned.
3. Add the ground cumin, ground coriander, ground turmeric, ground cinnamon, and powdered cloves to the saucepan along with the Egyptian curry powder. The spices Must be thoroughly combined in to coat the lamb.
4. Add the coconut milk and diced tomatoes. Add salt and pepper as needed.
5. When the lamb is soft and the flavors are well-balanced, simmer the dish with the lid on for around 1.5 to 2 hrs.
6. If necessary, adjust the seasoning.
7. If desired, garnish with fresh cilantro.
8. Warm rice or naan bread Must be served with the Egyptian lamb curry.

78. Egyptian Rice and Chicken Soup

Time: 1 hr
Servings: 4

Ingredients:

- 1 cup of Egyptian rice
- 2 chicken breasts, boneless and skinless, diced
- 1 onion, lightly chop-up
- 2 cloves of garlic, chop-up
- 2 carrots, peel off and split
- 2 celery stalks, chop-up
- 4 cups of chicken broth
- 1 tsp ground cumin
- 1 tsp ground coriander
- Salt and pepper as needed
- Fresh parsley, chop-up (for garnish)

Instructions:

1. Heat some oil in a big saucepan on a medium heat. Garlic and onion Must be added and sautéed up to transparent.
2. Cook the chicken breasts, diced, in the pot up to no longer pink.
3. Add the salt, pepper, cumin, coriander, carrots, and celery after stirring. Cook the vegetables for a few mins, or up to they start to soften.
4. Add the chicken stock and Egyptian rice to the pot. Once the Mixture has to a boil, turn down the heat, cover it, and simmer for 30 mins, or up to the rice is done and the flavors have combined.
5. If necessary, adjust the seasoning. Hot soup Must be served with fresh parsley on top.

NUTRITION INFO (per serving):

Cals: 320
Protein: 28g
Fat: 5g
Carbs: 40g
Fiber: 3g

79. Egyptian Stuffed Mushrooms

Time: 45 mins
Servings: 6

Ingredients:

- 18 Big mushrooms, stems take outd
- 1 cup of cooked Egyptian rice
- 1 mini onion, lightly chop-up
- 2 cloves of garlic, chop-up
- 1/4 cup of chop-up fresh parsley
- 1/4 cup of chop-up fresh dill
- 1/4 cup of finely grated Parmesan cheese
- Salt and pepper as needed
- Olive oil for drizzling

Instructions:

1. Turn on the oven to 350 °F (175 °C). Place the gill side up of the mushroom caps on a baking sheet.
2. Egyptian rice that has been cooked with chop-up onion, chop-up garlic, parsley, dill, Parmesan cheese, salt, and pepper Must all be combined in a bowl. Combine thoroughly.
3. Gently push the rice Mixture into every mushroom cap after spooning it in. Olive oil Must be drizzled on the stuffed mushrooms.

4. Bake in the preheated oven for about 25 to 30 mins, or up to the filling is golden brown and the mushrooms are soft.
5. Before serving, take them out of the oven and let them to cool for a while.

NUTRITION INFO (per serving):
Cals: 120
Protein: 5g
Fat: 3g
Carbs: 20g
Fiber: 2g

80. Egyptian Lamb and Potato Curry

Time: 2 hrs
Servings: 6

Ingredients:

- 2 lbs lamb stew meat, cubed
- 2 onions, lightly chop-up
- 4 cloves of garlic, chop-up
- 2 tbsp vegetable oil
- 2 tbsp Egyptian curry powder
- 1 tsp ground turmeric
- 1 tsp ground cumin
- 1 tsp ground coriander
- 1 tsp ground cinnamon
- 4 potatoes, peel off and cubed
- 2 cups of beef or vegetable broth
- Salt and pepper as needed
- Fresh cilantro, chop-up (for garnish)

Instructions:

1. Over medium heat, warm the vegetable oil in a big pot. Sauté the onions and garlic after being added up to they are fragrant and tender.
2. Brown the lamb stew meat completely in the pot before adding it.
3. Add the cinnamon, turmeric, cumin, coriander, and Egyptian curry powder. The spices Must cook for one min to toast.
4. Cubed potatoes and broth Must be added to the pot. The dish Must be brought to a boil, then simmered for 1.5 to 2 hrs, covered, up to the lamb is fork-tender and the flavors are well-balanced.
5. Depending on your taste, add salt and pepper to the dish. Warm lamb and potato curry Must be served with fresh cilantro on top.

NUTRITION INFO (per serving):
Cals: 430
Protein: 28g
Fat: 20g
Carbs: 35g
Fiber: 5g

81. Egyptian Spinach and Lentil Soup

Time: 45 mins
Servings: 4

Ingredients:

- 1 cup of red lentils, rinsed
- 1 onion, lightly chop-up
- 2 cloves of garlic, chop-up
- 2 tbsp olive oil
- 4 cups of vegetable broth
- 1 lb fresh spinach, washed and chop-up
- 1 tsp ground cumin
- 1 tsp ground coriander
- Salt and pepper as needed
- Lemon wedges (for serving)

Instructions:

1. Olive oil Must be heated in a sizable pot over medium heat. Garlic and onion Must be added and sautéed up to transparent.
2. In the pot, combine the red lentils, vegetable broth, cumin and coriander powders, salt, and pepper. When the lentils are cooked, about 30 mins after bringing the stew to a boil, turn the heat down and let it simmer.
3. The spinach Must be wilted after an additional 5–10 mins of cooking after being stirred in.
4. If necessary, adjust the seasoning. A squeeze of lemon juice Must be added to the hot spinach and lentil soup before serving.

NUTRITION INFO (per serving):
Cals: 250
Protein: 15g
Fat: 7g
Carbs: 35g
Fiber: 10g

82. Egyptian Chicken and Potato Tagine

Time: 1 hr 30 mins
Servings: 4

Ingredients:

- 4 chicken thighs, bone-in and skin-on
- 4 potatoes, peel off and quartered
- 1 onion, thinly split
- 3 cloves of garlic, chop-up
- 1 tsp ground cumin
- 1 tsp ground coriander
- 1 tsp ground turmeric
- 1 tsp ground cinnamon
- 1 cup of chicken broth
- 1/4 cup of chop-up fresh cilantro
- Salt and pepper as needed

Instructions:

1. Set your oven's temperature to 375°F (190°C).
2. Salt, pepper, cumin, coriander, turmeric, and cinnamon are used to season the chicken thighs.
3. Heat up some oil in a sizable oven-safe saucepan or tagine. The chicken thighs Must be browned on both sides before being taken out of the pot and placed aside.
4. Split onion and chop-up garlic Must be cooked in the same pot up to tender and aromatic.
5. Add the quartered potatoes, chicken broth, and the chicken thighs back to the pot. Place the saucepan in the preheated oven while it is covered.
6. Bake the potatoes and chicken for about an hr, or up to the chicken is cooked through.
7. Add freshly slice cilantro as a garnish before serving.

NUTRITION INFO (perserving):
Cals: 380
Protein: 25g
Fat: 12g
Carbs: 40g
Fiber: 6g

83. Egyptian Rice and Vermicelli Pilaf

Time: 30 mins
Servings: 4

Ingredients:

- 1 cup of Egyptian rice
- 1/2 cup of vermicelli noodles, broken into mini pieces
- 2 tbsp butter
- 2 cups of chicken or vegetable broth
- Salt as needed

Instructions:

1. Melt the butter in a medium-sized pot over medium heat. Vermicelli noodles Must be added and cooked up to golden brown, stirring constantly to avoid scorching.
2. Egyptian rice Must be added to the pot and cooked for an additional min while stirring to evenly distribute the butter throughout the rice and vermicelli.
3. Add salt as needed and then pour in the chicken or veggie broth. The Mixture Must boil.
4. Once the rice is soft and the liquid has been absorbed, turn the heat down to low, cover the pot, and simmer for 15 to 20 mins.
5. Before serving, fluff the rice and vermicelli pilaf with a fork.

NUTRITION INFO (per serving):
Cals: 220
Protein: 4g
Fat: 7g
Carbs: 36g
Fiber: 2g

84. Egyptian Okra and Tomato Stew:

Time: 1 hr 30 mins
Servings: 4-6

Ingredients:

- 2 tbsp vegetable oil
- 1 onion, lightly chop-up
- 2 cloves garlic, chop-up
- 1 lb (450g) okra, stems take outd
- 2 cups of diced tomatoes
- 1 tsp ground cumin
- 1 tsp ground coriander
- 1/2 tsp ground turmeric
- Salt and pepper as needed
- Juice of 1 lemon

Instructions:

1. Over medium heat, warm the vegetable oil in a big pot. Add the chop-up garlic and onion, and cook up to the onion is transparent.
2. While stirring occasionally, add the okra to the stew and cook for about 5 mins.
3. Add the diced tomatoes along with the salt, pepper, turmeric, cumin, and coriander. When the okra is ready, turn the heat down to low, cover the pan, and simmer for about an hr.

4. Pour lemon juice over the stew right before serving, and stir well. If needed, adjust the seasoning.
5. Egyptian Okra and Tomato Stew is best served hot with rice or bread.

85. Egyptian Chicken Fatta:

Time: 2 hrs
Servings: 6-8

Ingredients:

- 2 lbs (900g) boneless, skinless chicken breasts
- 1 tsp ground cumin
- 1 tsp ground coriander
- 1 tsp ground cinnamon
- Salt and pepper as needed
- 2 tbsp vegetable oil
- 2 cups of long-grain rice
- 4 cups of chicken broth
- 4 pita bread rounds, toasted and slice into mini pieces
- 4 cups of garlic yogurt sauce (yogurt combined with chop-up garlic and salt)
- Chop-up fresh parsley for garnish

Instructions:

1. Salt, pepper, cinnamon, coriander, and cumin are used to season the chicken breasts.
2. Over medium heat, warm the vegetable oil in a big pot. Cook the chicken breasts with the seasoning up to they are browned on both sides.
3. Chicken Must be taken out of the pot and placed aside. The rice Must be added to the pot and heated through for a few mins.
4. Bring it to a boil after adding the chicken broth. Once the rice is done and the liquid has been absorbed, turn the heat down to low, cover the pot, and simmer for about 20 mins.
5. Shred the cooked chicken into mini pieces while the rice is cooking.
6. Place the cooked rice, shredded chicken, toasted pita bread, and garlic yogurt sauce in a serving dish.
7. Serve the Egyptian Chicken Fatta warm and garnish with lightly chop-up fresh parsley.

86. Egyptian Fava Bean Salad:

Time: 30 mins
Servings: 4-6

Ingredients:

- 2 cans (15 oz every) fava beans, drained and rinsed
- 1/2 cup of chop-up fresh parsley
- 1/4 cup of chop-up fresh dill
- 2 cloves garlic, chop-up
- 2 tbsp lemon juice
- 2 tbsp olive oil
- Salt and pepper as needed

Instructions:

1. The fava beans, chop-up garlic, chop-up dill, parsley, lemon juice, and olive oil Must all be combined in a big basin.
2. Combine thoroughly after adding salt and pepper as needed.
3. Before serving, give the flavors about 15 mins to meld.
4. Egyptian Fava Bean Salad is best served cold or at room temperature.

87. Egyptian Lamb and Spinach Tagine

Time: 2 hrs
Servings: 4

Ingredients:

- 1 kg lamb, slice into cubes
- 2 tbsp vegetable oil
- 1 onion, lightly chop-up
- 3 garlic cloves, chop-up
- 2 tsp ground cumin
- 1 tsp ground coriander
- 1 tsp ground turmeric
- 1 tsp ground cinnamon
- 1 tsp salt
- 1/2 tsp black pepper
- 400 grams fresh spinach, washed and chop-up
- 2 tomatoes, diced
- 1 cup of vegetable broth
- Fresh cilantro, for garnish

Instructions:

1. Over medium heat, warm the vegetable oil in a big pot. Add the lamb cubes and sauté them up to evenly browned. Lamb Must be taken out of the saucepan and placed aside.

2. Add the chop-up garlic and onion to the same pot. Sauté the onion up to it turns translucent.
3. To the pot, add the ground cumin, coriander, cinnamon, turmeric, salt, and black pepper. The spices Must be thoroughly combined with the onions and garlic.
4. Add the diced tomatoes and add the lamb back to the saucepan. Combine all of the ingredients.
5. Bring the Mixture to a boil after adding the veggie broth. Turn down the heat to low, cover the pan, and simmer the lamb for one and a half hrs, or up to it is cooked.
6. Stir in the chop-up spinach after adding it to the pot. Once more covering the pot, simmer it for another 15 mins, letting the spinach wilt.
7. Serve the tagine hot with fresh cilantro as a garnish. It goes great with bread or rice.

NUTRITION INFO per serving:
Cals: 450
Protein: 35g
Carbs: 12g
Fat: 30g
Fiber: 5g

88. Egyptian Rice Pudding with Rosewater

Time: 1 hr
Servings: 6

Ingredients:

- 1 cup of medium-grain rice
- 4 cups of whole milk
- 1/2 cup of granulated sugar
- 1 tsp rosewater
- 1/4 cup of raisins
- Ground cinnamon, for garnish

Instructions:

1. Rice Must be thoroughly rinsed in cold water up to the water is clear. Rice Must be drained and left aside.
2. Rice, milk, and sugar are combined in a big pot. Over medium heat, bring the Mixture to a boil while stirring often to keep the rice from sticking to the bottom.
3. Stirring occasionally, lower the heat to a simmer, and let the Mixture simmer for about 40 mins, or up to the rice is cooked and the pudding thickens.
4. Rosewater and raisins have been added. Cook for a further five mins.
5. Rice pudding Must cool to room temperature after the saucepan has been taken off the heat.
6. After the pudding has cooled, place it in serving bowls and top with ground cinnamon.
7. Before serving, place the rice pudding in the fridge for at least two hrs. Both cold and room temperature versions are acceptable.

NUTRITION INFO per serving:
Cals: 280
Protein: 6g
Carbs: 56g
Fat: 5g
Fiber: 1g

89. Egyptian Stuffed Squash

Time: 1 hr 30 mins
Servings: 4

Ingredients:

- 4 medium-sized squash
- 300 grams ground beef
- 1/2 cup of short-grain rice
- 1 onion, lightly chop-up
- 2 garlic cloves, chop-up
- 2 tbsp vegetable oil
- 1 tsp ground cumin
- 1 tsp ground coriander
- 1/2 tsp ground cinnamon
- Salt and pepper, as needed
- 2 cups of tomato sauce
- Fresh parsley, for garnish

Instructions:

1. Set the oven's temperature to 180 C (350 F).
2. Squash tops are take outd, and the meat and seeds are scooped out to leave hollow shells. Set aside the shells.
3. Ground beef, rice, chop-up onion, chop-up garlic, vegetable oil, cumin, coriander, cinnamon, salt, and pepper are all combined in a bowl. Combine thoroughly up to all components are distributed equally.
4. Stuff the steak and rice Mixture into the hollow

squash shells. Put the squash in a roasting dish after stuffing it.
5. Make sure the stuffed squash is well covered with tomato sauce before adding more.
6. The baking dish Must be covered with aluminum foil and baked for an hr in a preheated oven.
7. When the squash is soft and the tops are golden, take out the foil and bake for a further 30 mins.
8. Warm stuffed squash Must be served with fresh parsley on top.

NUTRITION INFO per serving:
Cals: 350
Protein: 15g
Carbs: 35g
Fat: 15g
Fiber: 6g

90. Egyptian Lamb and Egg Tagine

Time: 2 hrs 30 mins
Servings: 6

Ingredients:
- 1 kg lamb, slice into cubes
- 2 tbsp vegetable oil
- 2 onions, lightly chop-up
- 4 garlic cloves, chop-up
- 2 tsp ground cumin
- 1 tsp ground coriander
- 1 tsp ground cinnamon
- 1 tsp ground paprika
- 1 tsp salt
- 1/2 tsp black pepper
- 2 tomatoes, diced
- 1/2 cup of tomato sauce
- 1 cup of water
- 6 eggs
- Fresh cilantro, for garnish

Instructions:
1. Over medium heat, warm the vegetable oil in a big pot. Add the lamb cubes and sauté them up to evenly browned. Lamb Must be taken out of the saucepan and placed aside.
2. Add the chop-up garlic and onion in the same pot. The onions Must be sautéed up to transparent.
3. Add salt, black pepper, paprika, cinnamon, coriander, and ground cumin to the pot. The spices Must be thoroughly combined with the onions and garlic.
4. Add the diced tomatoes, tomato sauce, and water to the pot with the lamb once more. Combine all of the ingredients.
5. The Mixture Must be brought to a boil, then simmer for two hrs, covered, with the heat reduced to low.
6. The eggs Must be cracked into the tagine evenly spaced. Once more covering the saucepan, boil the eggs for a further 10 mins, or up to they are done to your preference.
7. Serve the hot lamb and egg tagine with fresh cilantro on top. It is frequently eaten with rice or toast.

NUTRITION INFO per serving:
Cals: 420
Protein: 30g
Carbs: 12g
Fat: 28g
Fiber: 3g

91. Egyptian Lentil and Chickpea Salad

Time: 30 mins
Servings: 4

Ingredients:
- 1 cup of green lentils
- 1 cup of cooked chickpeas
- 1 cucumber, diced
- 2 tomatoes, diced
- 1 red onion, lightly chop-up
- 1/2 cup of fresh parsley, chop-up
- 1/4 cup of fresh mint, chop-up
- 3 tbsp lemon juice
- 2 tbsp extra virgin olive oil
- 1 tsp ground cumin
- Salt and pepper, as needed

Instructions:
1. The green lentils Must be cooked as directed on the box/pkg up to they are soft but firm. Drain, then leave to cool.
2. The cooked lentils, chickpeas, diced cucumber, diced tomatoes, chop-up red onion, fresh parsley, and fresh mint Must all be combined in a big bowl.
3. Combine the lemon juice, extra virgin olive oil, ground cumin, salt, and pepper in a mini bowl.

4. Over the Mixture of lentils and chickpeas, drizzle the dressing. Combine everything thoroughly and drizzle the dressing over everything.
5. To let the flavors to mingle, let the salad sit for about 15 mins.
6. The lentil and chickpea salad can be served cold or warm. It can be eaten as a light main course or as a side dish.

NUTRITION INFO per serving:
Cals: 320
Protein: 15g
Carbs: 50g
Fat: 8g
Fiber: 14g

92. Egyptian Lamb and Green Bean Stew

Time: 1 hr 30 mins
Servings: 4

Ingredients:

- 500 grams lamb, slice into cubes
- 2 tbsp vegetable oil
- 1 onion, lightly chop-up
- 3 garlic cloves, chop-up
- 2 tsp ground cumin
- 1 tsp ground coriander
- 1 tsp ground turmeric
- 1 tsp ground cinnamon
- 1 tsp salt
- 1/2 tsp black pepper
- 400 grams green beans, trimmed and slice into bite-sized pieces
- 2 tomatoes, diced
- 2 cups of vegetable broth
- Fresh parsley, for garnish

Instructions:

1. Over medium heat, warm the vegetable oil in a big pot. Add the lamb cubes and sauté them up to evenly browned. Lamb Must be taken out of the saucepan and placed aside.
2. Add the chop-up garlic and onion to the same pot. Sauté the onion up to it turns translucent.
3. To the pot, add the ground cumin, coriander, cinnamon, turmeric, salt, and black pepper. The spices Must be thoroughly combined with the onions and garlic.
4. Add the diced tomatoes and add the lamb back to the saucepan. Combine all of the ingredients.
5. Bring the Mixture to a boil after adding the veggie broth. Turn the heat down to low, cover the pan, and simmer the lamb for one hr, or up to it is cooked.
6. Stir in the green beans after adding them to the pot. Once more covering the pot, simmer it for a further 15 mins, or up to the beans are done to your preference.
7. Warm lamb and green bean stew Must be served with fresh parsley on top. It goes great with bread or rice.

NUTRITION INFO per serving:
Cals: 380
Protein: 25g
Carbs: 14g
Fat: 25g
Fiber: 5g

93. Egyptian Lamb and Chickpea Stew

Time: 2 hrs
Servings: 4

Ingredients:

- 1 lb (450g) lamb, cubed
- 1 onion, chop-up
- 3 cloves garlic, chop-up
- 2 tbsp olive oil
- 1 can (14 oz/400g) chickpeas, drained and rinsed
- 2 carrots, peel off and split
- 2 potatoes, peel off and cubed
- 1 can (14 oz/400g) diced tomatoes
- 2 cups of (480ml) vegetable broth
- 1 tsp ground cumin
- 1 tsp ground coriander
- 1/2 tsp ground turmeric
- Salt and pepper as needed
- Fresh cilantro or parsley for garnish

Instructions:

1. Over medium heat, warm the olive oil in a big pot. Add the lamb and cook it up to it is well-browned all over.
2. In the pot, combine the chop-up garlic and chop-up onion, and cook up to the onion is transparent.
3. Salt, pepper, turmeric, cumin, and coriander Must all be stirred in. For the flavors to come out, cook for one min.

4. Diced tomatoes, potatoes, carrots, chickpeas, and vegetable broth Must be added to the saucepan. When the lamb is tender and the flavors are well-balanced, bring to a boil, then lower the heat and simmer for 1.5 to 2 hrs.
5. If necessary, taste and adjust the seasonings. Serve the stew hot with fresh cilantro or parsley as a garnish.

NUTRITION INFO (per serving):
Cals: 380
Protein: 29g
Carbs: 30g
Fat: 16g
Fiber: 8g

94. Egyptian Stuffed Cabbage Rolls

Time: 1 hr 30 mins
Servings: 6

Ingredients:
- 12 Big cabbage leaves
- 1 lb (450g) ground lamb or beef
- 1 cup of cooked rice
- 1 onion, lightly chop-up
- 2 cloves garlic, chop-up
- 1 tsp ground cumin
- 1 tsp ground coriander
- 1/2 tsp ground cinnamon
- Salt and pepper as needed
- 1 can (14 oz/400g) diced tomatoes
- 1 cup of (240ml) vegetable broth
- Fresh parsley for garnish

Instructions:
1. Bring water in a big pot to a boil. When the cabbage leaves are soft, add them and simmer for another 5 mins. Take out of the water, then place aside.
2. Ground lamb or beef, cooked rice, chop-up onion, cumin, coriander, cinnamon, salt, and pepper are all combined in a bowl. To thoroughly combine all the ingredients, stir well.
3. Place a dollop of the meat and rice Mixture in the middle of a cabbage leaf. As you roll the leaf tightly, tuck the sides in. Repeat with the rest of the filling and leaves.
4. Place the stuffed cabbage rolls side by side in a big saucepan. Over the rolls, pour the vegetable broth and diced tomatoes.
5. When the cabbage rolls are fully cooked and the flavors have combined, simmer the dish covered for about an hr over low heat.
6. Hot cabbage rolls with filling Must be served with fresh parsley on top.

NUTRITION INFO (per serving):
Cals: 330
Protein: 18g
Carbs: 21g
Fat: 20g
Fiber: 5g

95. Egyptian Lamb Tagine with Prunes

Time: 2 hrs
Servings: 4

Ingredients:
- 1.5 lbs (680g) lamb Muster, cubed
- 1 onion, chop-up
- 3 cloves garlic, chop-up
- 2 tbsp olive oil
- 1 tsp ground cumin
- 1 tsp ground coriander
- 1/2 tsp ground cinnamon
- 1/2 tsp ground ginger
- Salt and pepper as needed
- 1 cup of pitted prunes
- 1/4 cup of slivered almonds
- Fresh cilantro for garnish

Instructions:
1. In a tagine or big pot, warm the olive oil over medium heat. Add the lamb and cook it up to it is well-browned all over.
2. In the pot, combine the chop-up garlic and chop-up onion, and cook up to the onion is transparent.
3. Add the salt, pepper, cinnamon, ginger, cumin, and coriander. For the flavors to come out, cook for one min.
4. Just cover the meat with water in the pot. Bring to a boil, then lower the heat to a simmer, cover the pot, and cook the lamb for 1.5 to 2 hrs, or up to it is tender.
5. For an additional 10 mins of cooking, stir in the pitted prunes.
6. The slivered almonds Must be lightly toasted till golden brown in a separate pan.

7. Serve the hot lamb tagine with fresh cilantro and roasted almonds as garnishes.

NUTRITION INFO (per serving):
Cals: 480
Protein: 33g
Carbs: 26g
Fat: 28g
Fiber: 4g

96. Egyptian Stuffed Tomatoes

Time: 1 hr
Servings: 4

Ingredients:

- 4 Big tomatoes
- 1 cup of cooked rice
- 1 onion, lightly chop-up
- 2 cloves garlic, chop-up
- 1/4 cup of chop-up fresh parsley
- 1/4 cup of chop-up fresh mint
- 2 tbsp olive oil
- 1 tsp ground cumin
- 1 tsp ground coriander
- Salt and pepper as needed

Instructions:

1. Set the oven's temperature to 375°F (190°C).
2. To create a hollow shell, carefully scrape out the pulp and seeds from the tops of the tomatoes. Put the pulp aside.
3. Cooked rice, chop-up onion, chop-up garlic, parsley, mint, olive oil, cumin, coriander, salt, and pepper Must all be combined in a bowl. To thoroughly combine all the ingredients, stir well.
4. Chop the tomato pulp that was set aside and stir it into the rice Mixture. To blend, stir.
5. Place a substantial amount of the rice Mixture inside every tomato shell.
6. Bake the stuffed tomatoes for 30 to 40 mins, or up to the tomatoes are soft and the Mixture is thoroughly cooked.
7. The stuffed tomatoes are best served hot as a side dish or a quick supper.

NUTRITION INFO (per serving):
Cals: 180
Protein: 3g
Carbs: 25g
Fat: 7g
Fiber: 3g

97. Egyptian Lamb and Okra Stew

Time: 1 hr 30 mins
Servings: 4

Ingredients:

- 1 lb (450g) lamb, cubed
- 1 onion, chop-up
- 3 cloves garlic, chop-up
- 2 tbsp olive oil
- 1 lb (450g) okra, ends trimmed
- 1 can (14 oz/400g) diced tomatoes
- 2 cups of (480ml) vegetable broth
- 1 tsp ground cumin
- 1 tsp ground coriander
- 1/2 tsp ground turmeric
- Salt and pepper as needed
- Fresh cilantro for garnish

Instructions:

1. Over medium heat, warm the olive oil in a big pot. Add the lamb and cook it up to it is well-browned all over.
2. In the pot, combine the chop-up garlic and chop-up onion, and cook up to the onion is transparent.
3. Salt, pepper, turmeric, cumin, and coriander Must all be stirred in. For the flavors to come out, cook for one min.
4. To the pot, add the diced tomatoes and vegetable broth. Bring to a boil, then turn down the heat and simmer the lamb for approximately an hr, or up to it is tender.
5. Okra Must be blanched in boiling water for 5 mins while you wait. Drain, then set apart.
6. When the okra is cooked and the flavors are blended, add the blanched okra to the saucepan and simmer for an additional 20 to 30 mins.
7. If necessary, taste and adjust the seasonings. Serve the hot stew of lamb and okra with fresh cilantro on top.

NUTRITION INFO (per serving):
Cals: 320
Protein: 23g
Carbs: 20g
Fat: 18g
Fiber: 6g

98. Egyptian Quinoa Salad

Time: 30 mins

Servings: 4

Ingredients:

- 1 cup of quinoa
- 2 cups of water
- 1 cucumber, diced
- 1 tomato, diced
- 1 bell pepper, diced
- 1/4 cup of chop-up fresh parsley
- 1/4 cup of chop-up fresh mint
- 1/4 cup of chop-up fresh cilantro
- 2 tbsp lemon juice
- 2 tbsp olive oil
- Salt and pepper as needed

Instructions:

1. In order to get rid of any bitterness, rinse the quinoa in cold water. Quinoa and water are combined in a pan. Bring to a boil, then lower the heat to a simmer, cover the pan, and cook the quinoa for 15 to 20 mins, or up to the water is absorbed.
2. After cooking, take the quinoa off the fire and let it cool.
3. Cucumber, tomato, bell pepper, parsley, mint, and cilantro dices, cooked quinoa, and other ingredients are combined in a sizable bowl.
4. Combine the lemon juice, olive oil, salt, and pepper in a separate mini bowl. Toss the quinoa salad with the dressing after pouring it over it.
5. If necessary, adjust the seasoning. The Egyptian quinoa salad can be served cold or warm.

NUTRITION INFO (per serving):

Cals: 250

Protein: 6g

Carbs: 32g

Fat: 11g

Fiber: 5g

99. Egyptian Chicken and Okra Tagine:

Time: 1 hr 30 mins

Servings: 4

Ingredients:

- 1 lb (450g) chicken pieces
- 1 onion, lightly chop-up
- 2 garlic cloves, chop-up
- 1 tsp ground cumin
- 1 tsp ground coriander
- 1 tsp ground turmeric
- 1/2 tsp ground cinnamon
- Salt and pepper as needed
- 2 cups of (500ml) chicken broth
- 1 lb (450g) okra, trimmed
- 1 lemon, juiced
- Fresh cilantro, chop-up (for garnish)

Instructions:

1. Over medium heat, warm some oil in a big pot. Brown the chicken pieces all over after adding them. Take out of the pot and reserve.
2. Add the chop-up garlic and onion to the same pot. up to melted, sauté.
3. Stir in the ground cumin, coriander, cinnamon, turmeric, and salt. The spices Must be thoroughly combined with the onions and garlic.
4. Add the chicken stock to the pot with the chicken chunks still inside. After bringing to a boil, lower the heat, and let the Mixture simmer for 30 mins.
5. When the okra is soft, return the clipped pieces to the saucepan and simmer for an additional 20 mins.
6. Add the lemon juice and, if necessary, taste and adjust the seasoning.
7. Serve the tagine hot with fresh cilantro as a garnish. Enjoy!

100. Egyptian Rice and Beef Soup:

Time: 1 hr 15 mins

Servings: 6

Ingredients:

- 1 lb (450g) beef stew meat, cubed
- 1 onion, chop-up
- 2 carrots, diced
- 2 celery stalks, diced
- 3 garlic cloves, chop-up
- 1 cup of (200g) rice
- 6 cups of (1.5L) beef broth
- 1 tsp ground cumin
- 1 tsp ground coriander

- Salt and pepper as needed
- Fresh parsley, chop-up (for garnish)

Instructions:

1. Over medium heat, warm some oil in a big pot. Brown the beef cubes all over after adding them. Take out of the pot and reserve.
2. Add the diced carrots, diced celery, diced onion, and chop-up garlic to the same saucepan. Sauté the vegetables just up to they start to soften.
3. Rice, beef broth, ground coriander, cumin, and salt Must all be added. Stir thoroughly.
4. Back in the pot, add the beef cubes. Cook for 45 mins, or up to the beef is cooked, after bringing to a boil.
5. If necessary, adjust the seasoning.
6. Hot soup Must be served with fresh parsley on top. Enjoy!

101. Egyptian Stuffed Peppers with Rice:

Time: 1 hr
Servings: 4

Ingredients:

- 4 bell peppers
- 1 cup of (200g) rice
- 1 onion, chop-up
- 2 tomatoes, diced
- 2 garlic cloves, chop-up
- 1/4 cup of (60ml) tomato sauce
- 1 tsp ground cumin
- 1 tsp ground coriander
- Salt and pepper as needed
- Fresh mint, chop-up (for garnish)

Instructions:

1. Set the oven's temperature to 350°F (180°C).
2. The bell peppers' tops Must be slice off, and the seeds and membranes Must be take outd.
3. Rice, chop-up onion, diced tomatoes, chop-up garlic, tomato sauce, cumin, ground coriander, salt, and pepper Must all be combined in a bowl.
4. Place the bell peppers in a baking dish after stuffing them with the rice Mixture.
5. The dish Must be covered with foil and baked for 45 mins, or up to the rice is done and the peppers are soft.
6. After taking them out of the oven, give them some time to cool.
7. Serve the stuffed peppers hot with fresh mint as a garnish. Enjoy!

102. Egyptian Lamb and Cauliflower Curry:

Time: 1 hr 30 mins
Servings: 4

Ingredients:

- 1 lb (450g) lamb, cubed
- 1 onion, lightly chop-up
- 2 garlic cloves, chop-up
- 1 tsp ground cumin
- 1 tsp ground coriander
- 1 tsp ground turmeric
- 1/2 tsp ground cinnamon
- Salt and pepper as needed
- 1 cauliflower, slice into florets
- 1 cup of (240ml) coconut milk
- 2 tbsp tomato paste
- Fresh cilantro, chop-up (for garnish)

Instructions:

1. Over medium heat, warm some oil in a big pot. Brown the lamb cubes all over after adding them. Take out of the pot and reserve.
2. Add the chop-up garlic and onion to the same pot. up to melted, sauté.
3. Stir in the ground cumin, coriander, cinnamon, turmeric, and salt. The spices Must be thoroughly combined with the onions and garlic.
4. Add the cauliflower florets, tomato paste, coconut milk, and meat cubes back to the pot. To blend, stir.
5. When the lamb is soft and the cauliflower is cooked, bring to a boil, then lower the heat and simmer for one hr.
6. If necessary, adjust the seasoning.
7. With fresh cilantro as a garnish, serve the curry hot. Enjoy!

103. Egyptian Spinach and Chickpea Soup:

Time: 45 mins

Servings: 6

Ingredients:

- 2 tbsp olive oil
- 1 onion, chop-up
- 3 garlic cloves, chop-up
- 1 lb (450g) spinach, chop-up
- 1 can (15 oz/425g) chickpeas, drained and rinsed
- 6 cups of (1.5L) vegetable broth
- 1 tsp ground cumin
- 1 tsp ground coriander
- Salt and pepper as needed
- Lemon wedges (for serving)

Instructions:

1. Over medium heat, warm the olive oil in a big pot. Add the chop-up garlic and onion, both chop-up. up to melted, sauté.
2. Cook the spinach up to it wilts after being added.
3. Add the ground cumin, ground coriander, salt, and pepper along with the chickpeas and vegetable broth. Stir thoroughly.
4. After bringing to a boil, lower the heat, and let the Mixture simmer for 30 mins.
5. If necessary, adjust the seasoning.
6. With a squeeze of lemon juice on top, serve the soup hot. Enjoy!

104. Egyptian Chicken and Eggplant Tagine:

Time: 1 hr 30 mins

Servings: 4

Ingredients:

- 1 lb (450g) chicken pieces
- 1 onion, lightly chop-up
- 2 garlic cloves, chop-up
- 1 tsp ground cumin
- 1 tsp ground coriander
- 1 tsp ground paprika
- 1/2 tsp ground cinnamon
- Salt and pepper as needed
- 1 eggplant, cubed
- 2 tomatoes, diced
- 1/2 cup of (120ml) chicken broth
- Fresh parsley, chop-up (for garnish)

Instructions:

1. Over medium heat, warm some oil in a big pot. Brown the chicken pieces all over after adding them. Take out of the pot and reserve.
2. Add the chop-up garlic and onion to the same pot. up to melted, sauté.
3. Add the ground cinnamon, salt, pepper, paprika, coriander, and cumin. The spices Must be thoroughly combined with the onions and garlic.
4. Add the cubed eggplant, diced tomatoes, and chicken stock to the saucepan along with the chicken pieces once more. To blend, stir.
5. Bring to a boil, then lower the heat and simmer for an hr, or up to the eggplant is soft.
6. If necessary, adjust the seasoning.
7. Serve the tagine hot with fresh parsley as a garnish. Enjoy!

105. Egyptian Rice and Lentil Pilaf with Caramelized Onions:

Time: 1 hr

Servings: 4

Ingredients:

- 1 cup of basmati rice
- 1/2 cup of brown lentils
- 2 onions, thinly split
- 4 tbsp vegetable oil
- 1 tsp ground cumin
- 1/2 tsp ground coriander
- Salt, as needed
- Water, as needed

Instructions:

1. Separately, rinse the rice and lentils in cool water.
2. 2 tbsp of vegetable oil Must be heated on medium heat in a big pot. Split onions Must be added and cooked up to they are golden brown and caramelized. Half of the onions are take outd, and they are left aside for garnish.
3. Add salt, cumin, coriander, and the 2 tbsp of leftover oil to the same saucepan. Stir up to fragrant after a min.
4. Stir thoroughly after adding the rice and lentils to the saucepan so that they are well-coated.
5. Add water up to the rice and lentils are covered by approximately 1 inch. Bring to a boil, then lower the heat to a simmer, cover the pan, and

cook the rice and lentils for about 30 mins, or up to they are cooked and soft.
6. With a fork, fluff the pilaf and transfer it to a serving bowl. Add the saved caramelized onions on top. Serve warm.

NUTRITION INFO: (per serving)
Cals: 360
Fat: 14g
Carbs: 50g
Protein: 8g

106. Egyptian Stuffed Cabbage Leaves with Rice and Beef:

Time: 1 hr 30 mins
Servings: 6

Ingredients:

- 12 Big cabbage leaves
- 1 lb ground beef
- 1/2 cup of rice, uncooked
- 1 onion, lightly chop-up
- 2 cloves garlic, chop-up
- 1/4 cup of chop-up fresh parsley
- 1/4 cup of chop-up fresh mint
- 2 tbsp tomato paste
- 2 tbsp lemon juice
- 1 tsp ground cumin
- 1/2 tsp ground cinnamon
- Salt and pepper, as needed
- 2 cups of vegetable broth
- 1 cup of crushed tomatoes

Instructions:

1. Big saucepan of salted water Must be brought to a boil. The cabbage leaves Must be blanched in the boiling water for 5 mins or up to they are tender. Drain, then set apart.
2. Ground beef, rice, onion, garlic, parsley, mint, tomato paste, lemon juice, cumin, cinnamon, salt, and pepper Must all be combined in a combining dish. All the components Must be thoroughly combined.
3. Place roughly 2 tsp of the meat Mixture in the middle of every cabbage leaf. Wrap the filling tightly in the leaf by folding the leaf's sides over it.
4. In a big pot, put the stuffed cabbage rolls. Add the tomato juice and veggie broth. The liquid ought to saturate the rolls.
5. When the rice is tender and the cabbage rolls are cooked, turn the heat down to low, cover the pot, and simmer for about an hr.
6. Hot, with some of the cooking liquid spooned over, serve the packed cabbage leaves.

NUTRITION INFO: (per serving)
Cals: 320
Fat: 12g
Carbs: 29g
Protein: 23g

107. Egyptian Lamb Tagine with Artichokes and Olives:

Time: 2 hrs
Servings: 4

Ingredients:

- 2 lbs lamb Muster, slice into chunks
- 2 tbsp vegetable oil
- 1 onion, chop-up
- 3 cloves garlic, chop-up
- 2 tsp ground cumin
- 1 tsp ground coriander
- 1 tsp ground turmeric
- 1 tsp ground cinnamon
- 1/2 tsp ground ginger
- Salt and pepper, as needed
- 1 cup of chop-up tomatoes
- 1 cup of chicken broth
- 1 cup of canned artichoke hearts, drained and quartered
- 1/2 cup of green olives
- 2 tbsp chop-up fresh cilantro

Instructions:

1. In a sizable saucepan or tagine, heat the vegetable oil over medium-low heat. Add the lamb chunks and sauté them up to they are evenly browned. Lamb Must be taken out of the saucepan and placed aside.
2. Add the chop-up garlic and onion to the same pot. Sauté the onion up to it turns translucent.
3. Add the cumin, coriander, turmeric, cinnamon, ginger, salt, and pepper to the saucepan with the lamb once more. The spices Must be thoroughly combined in to coat the lamb.

4. Add the chicken broth and diced tomatoes. When the lamb is tender, simmer the dish for around 1 hr and 30 mins after turning down the heat and covering it.
5. Cook for a further 15 mins after adding the artichoke hearts and green olives.
6. Prior to serving, top the tagine with the chop-up cilantro. Serve warm with toast or rice.

NUTRITION INFO: (per serving)
Cals: 480
Fat: 32g
Carbs: 11g
Protein: 38g

108. Egyptian Rice and Chicken Stuffed Grape Leaves:

Time: 1 hr
Servings: 4

Ingredients:

- 1 cup of long-grain rice
- 1 lb boneless chicken breasts, cooked and shredded
- 1/4 cup of chop-up fresh dill
- 1/4 cup of chop-up fresh parsley
- 2 tbsp lemon juice
- 1 tsp ground cumin
- Salt and pepper, as needed
- 20-30 grape leaves, blanched and drained
- 2 cups of chicken broth
- 2 tbsp olive oil

Instructions:

1. Rice, chicken that has been shredden, dill, parsley, lemon juice, cumin, salt, and pepper Must all be combined in a combining dish. To thoroughly incorporate all ingredients, stir well.
2. Place about 1 spoonful of the rice and chicken Mixture in the center of every grape leaf as you go. Wrap the filling tightly in the leaf by folding the leaf's sides over it.
3. In a big pot, arrange the packed grape leaves. Olive oil and chicken broth Must be added. The grape leaves Must be submerged in the liquid.
4. To retain the stuffed grape leaves in the liquid, place a heatproof plate or cover on top of them. They won't unravel when cooking if this is done.
5. When the rice is cooked and soft, turn off the heat, cover the pot, and let it simmer for 30 to 40 mins.
6. Place the packed grape leaves on a serving dish after carefully removing them from the pot. Whether hot or cool, serve.

NUTRITION INFO: (per serving)
Cals: 380
Fat: 10g
Carbs: 45g
Protein: 26g

109. Egyptian Stuffed Bell Peppers with Rice and Lamb:

Time: 1 hr 30 mins
Servings: 4

Ingredients:

- 4 Big bell peppers (any color)
- 1/2 cup of long-grain rice
- 1/2 lb ground lamb
- 1 onion, lightly chop-up
- 2 cloves garlic, chop-up
- 1 tsp ground cumin
- 1 tsp ground coriander
- 1/2 tsp ground cinnamon
- 1/4 tsp cayenne pepper (non-compulsory)
- Salt and pepper as needed
- 2 tbsp tomato paste
- 2 cups of vegetable or chicken broth
- Fresh parsley, chop-up (for garnish)

Instructions:

1. Set your oven's temperature to 375°F (190°C).
2. The bell peppers' tops Must be slice off, and the seeds and membranes Must be take outd.
3. Rice, ground lamb, onion, garlic, cumin, coriander, cinnamon, cayenne pepper, salt, and pepper Must all be combined in a big bowl. Combine thoroughly.
4. Place the rice and lamb Mixture inside the bell peppers.
5. Whisk the tomato paste and broth in a baking dish. Fill the dish with the stuffed bell peppers.
6. Bake the dish for 45 mins with the foil covering.
7. When the peppers are cooked through and the filling is soft, take out the foil and bake for an additional 15 mins.

8. Serve the filled bell peppers hot with fresh parsley added as a garnish.

110. Egyptian Egg and Tomato Tagine:

Time: 30 mins
Servings: 4

Ingredients:

- 2 tbsp olive oil
- 1 onion, lightly chop-up
- 2 cloves garlic, chop-up
- 4 tomatoes, diced
- 1 tsp ground cumin
- 1 tsp ground paprika
- 1/2 tsp ground turmeric
- Salt and pepper as needed
- 4 eggs
- Fresh parsley, chop-up (for garnish)

Instructions:

1. Over medium heat, warm the olive oil in a Big skillet.
2. To the skillet, add the onion and garlic, and cook up to tender.
3. Tomatoes, cumin, paprika, turmeric, salt, and pepper Must also be added. While intermittently stirring, cook for 5 mins.
4. Crack the eggs into the tomato Mixture wells that you have created.
5. Cook the eggs under cover for about 5 mins, or up to they are done to your preference.
6. Serve hot and top with fresh parsley.

111. Egyptian Rice and Vermicelli Soup:

Time: 40 mins
Servings: 6

Ingredients:

- 1 cup of vermicelli noodles, broken into mini pieces
- 1 tbsp butter
- 1 onion, lightly chop-up
- 2 cloves garlic, chop-up
- 1 cup of long-grain rice
- 6 cups of vegetable or chicken broth
- Salt and pepper as needed
- Fresh parsley, chop-up (for garnish)

Instructions:

1. Melt the butter in a Big pot over medium heat.
2. As you stir regularly to prevent burning, add the vermicelli noodles and cook up to they are golden brown.
3. Sauté the onion and garlic in the pot up to they are tender.
4. Add the rice and stir before cooking for a few mins.
5. Add the broth and salt and pepper as needed.
6. Once the soup has reveryed a rolling boil, turn down the heat, cover it, and simmer it for about 20 mins, or up to the rice is cooked through.
7. Hot soup Must be served with fresh parsley on top.

112. Egyptian Stuffed Eggplant with Rice and Ground Beef:

Time: 1 hr 30 mins
Servings: 4

Ingredients:

- 2 Big eggplants
- Salt
- 1/2 cup of long-grain rice
- 1/2 lb ground beef
- 1 onion, lightly chop-up
- 2 cloves garlic, chop-up
- 1 tsp ground cumin
- 1 tsp ground coriander
- 1/2 tsp ground cinnamon
- Salt and pepper as needed
- 2 tbsp tomato paste
- 2 cups of vegetable or beef broth
- Fresh parsley, chop-up (for garnish)

Instructions:

1. Set your oven's temperature to 375°F (190°C).
2. Scoop out the meat after Cutting the eggplants in half lengthwise, leaving roughly a 1/4-inch shell behind.
3. The eggplant shells Must be salted and left to stand for 15 mins. Towel dry after rinsing.
4. Rice, ground beef, onion, garlic, cumin, coriander, cinnamon, salt, and pepper Must all be combined in a big bowl. Combine thoroughly.

5. Put the rice and meat Mixture inside the eggplant shells.
6. Whisk the tomato paste and broth in a baking dish. In the dish, put the stuffed eggplants.
7. Bake the dish for 45 mins with the foil covering.
8. When the eggplants are cooked through and soft, take out the foil and bake for an additional 15 mins.
9. Hot filled eggplants Must be served with fresh parsley on top.

113. Egyptian Lamb and Okra Tagine with Tomatoes:

Time: 1 hr 30 mins
Servings: 4

Ingredients:

- 1 lb lamb, slice into cubes
- 2 tbsp olive oil
- 1 onion, lightly chop-up
- 2 cloves garlic, chop-up
- 1 tsp ground cumin
- 1 tsp ground coriander
- 1 tsp paprika
- 1/2 tsp ground cinnamon
- Salt and pepper as needed
- 1 can (14 ozs) diced tomatoes
- 1 cup of water
- 1 lb okra, ends trimmed
- Fresh cilantro, chop-up (for garnish)

Instructions:

1. Heat the olive oil in a sizable saucepan or tagine over medium heat.
2. Add the lamb and cook it up to it is well-browned all over. Lamb Must be taken out of the saucepan and placed aside.
3. Sauté the onion and garlic in the same saucepan up to they are tender.
4. Add the cumin, coriander, paprika, cinnamon, salt, and pepper to the saucepan with the lamb once more. Stir thoroughly.
5. Add water and the diced tomatoes. After bringing to a boil, turn down the heat, cover the pan, and simmer for one hr.
6. When the okra is tender, add it to the saucepan and boil for an additional 15 mins.
7. The lamb and okra tagine Must be served hot with fresh cilantro as a garnish.

114. Egyptian Lentil and Bulgur Salad:

Time: 30 mins
Servings: 4

Ingredients:

- 1 cup of green lentils
- 1/2 cup of fine bulgur
- 2 tomatoes, diced
- 1 cucumber, diced
- 1 green bell pepper, diced
- 1/2 red onion, lightly chop-up
- 1/4 cup of fresh parsley, chop-up
- 1/4 cup of fresh mint, chop-up
- 1/4 cup of olive oil
- 2 tbsp lemon juice
- 1 clove garlic, chop-up
- Salt and pepper as needed

Instructions:

1. As directed on the packaging, cook the lentils. Drain, then leave to cool.
2. Bulgur Must be soaked in boiling water for 15 mins, or up to it becomes soft, in a separate basin. Empty any extra water.
3. The cooked lentils, bulgur, tomatoes, cucumber, bell pepper, red onion, parsley, and mint Must all be combined in a sizable combining basin.
4. Combine the olive oil, lemon juice, garlic, salt, and pepper in a mini bowl.
5. Over the Mixture of lentils and bulgur, drizzle the dressing. Combine thoroughly by tossing.
6. If necessary, adjust the seasoning.
7. The lentil and bulgur salad can be served cold or warm.

115. Egyptian Chicken and Spinach Tagine with Chickpeas

Time: 1 hr
Servings: 4

Ingredients:

- 4 chicken thighs, bone-in and skin-on
- 1 onion, chop-up

- 3 cloves of garlic, chop-up
- 1 tsp ground cumin
- 1 tsp ground coriander
- 1/2 tsp ground turmeric
- 1/2 tsp ground cinnamon
- Salt and pepper as needed
- 1 can (14 oz) diced tomatoes
- 1 can (14 oz) chickpeas, drained and rinsed
- 4 cups of fresh spinach leaves
- Fresh cilantro, chop-up (for garnish)

Instructions:

1. Heat some oil in a big tagine or a deep pan over medium heat. Add the chicken thighs and sauté them up to both sides are browned. Chicken Must be taken out and put aside.
2. Add the chop-up garlic and onion to the same pan. Sauté the onion up to it turns translucent.
3. Stir in the ground cumin, coriander, cinnamon, turmeric, and salt. The spices Must be thoroughly combined with the onion and garlic.
4. Add the diced tomatoes and their liquids to the pan along with the chicken back in it. Simmer the Mixture for a short while.
5. For about 30 mins, or up to the chicken is fully cooked, cover the pan and let it cook.
6. Add the spinach and chickpeas to the pan. The spinach Must wilt after another five mins of cooking after a good stir.
7. Before serving, take out from heat and garnish with fresh cilantro. Serve alongside rice or couscous.

NUTRITION INFO: (Per serving)
Cals: 420
Fat: 15g
Carbs: 33g
Protein: 40g
Fiber: 9g

116. Egyptian Rice and Milk Pudding with Cinnamon

Time: 1 hr (+ chilling time)
Servings: 6

Ingredients:

- 1 cup of long-grain rice
- 4 cups of whole milk
- 1/2 cup of granulated sugar
- 1 tsp vanilla extract
- Ground cinnamon, for garnish

Instructions:

1. Rice Must be thoroughly rinsed in cold water up to the water is clear. Rinse the rice.
2. Rice, milk, and sugar are combined in a big pot. Stir thoroughly.
3. Bring the Mixture to a boil in the saucepan over medium heat. Stirring regularly, lower the heat to a simmer for about 45 mins, or up to the rice is cooked through and the stew thickens.
4. Add the vanilla extract after turning off the heat in the saucepan. Room temperature Must be reveryed by the pudding.
5. Transfer the pudding to a big serving bowl or individual serving dishes once it has cooled. On top, sprinkle cinnamon powder.
6. Before serving, cover and chill for at least two hrs in the refrigerator.

NUTRITION INFO: (Per serving)
Cals: 260
Fat: 5g
Carbs: 47g
Protein: 7g
Fiber: 0g

117. Egyptian Stuffed Zucchini with Rice and Lamb

Time: 1 hr 30 mins
Servings: 4

Ingredients:

- 4 Big zucchini
- 1/2 lb ground lamb
- 1/2 cup of long-grain rice
- 1 onion, lightly chop-up
- 2 cloves of garlic, chop-up
- 1 tbsp tomato paste
- 1 tsp ground cumin
- 1 tsp ground coriander
- 1/2 tsp ground cinnamon
- Salt and pepper as needed
- 2 cups of chicken or vegetable broth
- Fresh parsley, chop-up (for garnish)

Instructions:

1. Take out the zucchini's tops and use a spoon to hollow them out, leaving a 1/4-inch-thick shell

behind. Save the pulp from the zucchini for later use.
2. Cook the ground lamb in a Big skillet over medium heat. The lamb Must be taken out of the skillet and placed aside.
3. Add the chop-up garlic and onion to the same skillet. Sauté the onion up to it turns translucent.
4. Rice, tomato paste, cumin, coriander, cinnamon, salt, and pepper Must all be included. The spices Must be thoroughly combined into the rice and onion.
5. Add the saved zucchini pulp to the skillet with the browned lamb. To blend, thoroughly stir.
6. Fill the zucchini hollows with the rice and lamb Mixture.
7. Pour the chicken or vegetable stock over the filled zucchini in the big pot. The zucchini must be submerged in the liquid.
8. After bringing the pot to a boil, lower the heat. Rice and zucchini Must be fully cooked after around 45 mins of simmering with the cover on.
9. Place the stuffed zucchini on a serving platter after removing them from the pot. Before serving, garnish with fresh parsley.

NUTRITION INFO: (Per serving)
Cals: 320
Fat: 14g
Carbs: 24g
Protein: 22g
Fiber: 4g

118. Egyptian Lamb and Potato Tagine with Green Peas

Time: 1 hr 30 mins
Servings: 4

Ingredients:

- 1 lb lamb Muster, cubed
- 2 tbsp vegetable oil
- 1 onion, chop-up
- 3 cloves of garlic, chop-up
- 1 tsp ground cumin
- 1 tsp ground coriander
- 1 tsp ground paprika
- Salt and pepper as needed
- 2 Big potatoes, peel off and cubed
- 1 cup of green peas
- 1 cup of water
- Fresh cilantro, chop-up (for garnish)

Instructions:

1. Heat the vegetable oil over medium heat in a big tagine or a deep skillet. Brown the lamb cubes all over after adding them. The lamb Must be take outd and put aside.
2. Add the chop-up garlic and onion to the same pan. Sauté the onion up to it turns translucent.
3. Go back to the pan with the browned lamb. Add the salt, pepper, paprika, and ground cumin and coriander. Stir vigorously to evenly distribute the spices over the meat and onion.
4. To the pan, add the diced potatoes, green peas, and water. To blend, stir.
5. For approximately an hr, or up to the lamb is soft and the potatoes are cooked through, simmer the dish covered over low heat. When stirring, add a little water at a time. 6.At the point of serving, take out from the heat and top with fresh cilantro. Serve alongside rice or toast.

NUTRITION INFO: (Per serving)
Cals: 450
Fat: 22g
Carbs: 30g
Protein: 34g
Fiber: 6g

119. Egyptian Spinach and Lentil Salad

Time: 30 mins
Servings: 4

Ingredients:

- 4 cups of fresh spinach leaves
- 1 cup of cooked lentils
- 1/2 cup of cherry tomatoes, halved
- 1/4 cup of red onion, thinly split
- 1/4 cup of fresh parsley, chop-up
- 1/4 cup of fresh mint leaves, chop-up
- Juice of 1 lemon
- 2 tbsp olive oil
- Salt and pepper as needed

Instructions:

1. The spinach leaves, cooked lentils, cherry tomatoes, red onion, parsley, and mint Must all be combined in a sizable combining basin.
2. Combine the lemon juice, olive oil, salt, and pepper in a mini bowl.
3. Over the salad, drizzle the dressing and toss to blend.

4. Salad can be served cold or at room temperature.

NUTRITION INFO: (Per serving)
Cals: 180
Fat: 7g
Carbs: 23g
Protein: 9g
Fiber: 6g

120. Egyptian Chicken and Okra Stew with Tomatoes

Time: 1 hr 30 mins
Servings: 4

Ingredients:

- 4 chicken thighs, bone-in and skin-on
- 1 onion, chop-up
- 3 cloves of garlic, chop-up
- 1 tsp ground cumin
- 1 tsp ground coriander
- 1/2 tsp ground turmeric
- 1/2 tsp ground cinnamon
- Salt and pepper as needed
- 2 cups of okra, trimmed and halved
- 1 can (14 oz) diced tomatoes
- 1 cup of chicken broth
- Fresh cilantro, chop-up (for garnish)

Instructions:

1. Heat some oil over medium heat in a big pot or Dutch oven. Add the chicken thighs and sauté them up to both sides are browned. Chicken Must be taken out and put aside.
2. Add the chop-up garlic and onion to the same pot. Sauté the onion up to it turns translucent.
3. Stir in the ground cumin, coriander, cinnamon, turmeric, and salt. The spices Must be thoroughly combined with the onion and garlic.
4. Put the chicken back in the pot. Add the chicken broth, diced tomatoes, and okra. To blend, stir.
5. Heat Must be turned down once the Mixture comes to a boil. Once the chicken is cooked through and the okra is soft, cover and simmer for approximately an hr.
6. Before serving, take out from heat and garnish with fresh cilantro. Serve alongside toast or rice.

NUTRITION INFO: (Per serving)
Cals: 380
Fat: 18g
Carbs: 24g
Protein: 32g
Fiber: 6g

121. Egyptian Spinach and Chickpea Salad:

Time: 20 mins
Servings: 4

Ingredients:

- 4 cups of fresh spinach leaves
- 1 can chickpeas, drained and rinsed
- 1 mini red onion, thinly split
- 1 cup of cherry tomatoes, halved
- 1/2 cup of cut up feta cheese
- 1/4 cup of chop-up fresh parsley
- 2 tbsp lemon juice
- 2 tbsp olive oil
- Salt and pepper as needed

Instructions:

1. Spinach, chickpeas, red onion, cherry tomatoes, feta cheese, and parsley Must all be combined in a sizable salad bowl.
2. Combine the lemon juice, olive oil, salt, and pepper in a mini bowl.
3. Over the salad, drizzle the dressing, and toss just enough to combine.
4. Serve right away.

122. Egyptian Chicken and Egg Tagine with Potatoes:

Time: 1 hr 30 mins
Servings: 6

Ingredients:

- 6 chicken thighs
- 4 eggs
- 4 potatoes, peel off and slice into chunks
- 1 onion, lightly chop-up
- 4 garlic cloves, chop-up
- 2 tsp ground cumin
- 2 tsp ground coriander
- 1 tsp ground turmeric
- 1 tsp paprika
- 1/2 tsp ground cinnamon

- 1/4 tsp cayenne pepper (non-compulsory)
- 1 cup of chicken broth
- 2 tbsp olive oil
- Salt and pepper as needed

Instructions:

1. Over medium heat, warm the olive oil in a big tagine or deep skillet.
2. Add the chicken thighs and sauté them up to they are evenly browned. Chicken Must be taken out of the pan and put aside.
3. Add the onions and garlic to the same pan and sauté for a few mins up to tender.
4. Add the salt, pepper, cayenne pepper (if used), cumin, coriander, turmeric, paprika, cinnamon, and so on. The spices Must be thoroughly combined with the onions and garlic.
5. Add the potatoes, chicken broth, and chicken back to the pan. For one hr, simmer covered.
6. Add the eggs gently to the tagine, cover once more, and cook for a further 10 mins, or up to the eggs are cooked to your preference.
7. Serve the heated tagine with rice or couscous.

123. Egyptian Rice and Vermicelli Pilaf with Chickpeas:

Time: 40 mins

Servings: 4

Ingredients:

- 1 cup of basmati rice
- 1/2 cup of vermicelli noodles, broken into mini pieces
- 1 can chickpeas, drained and rinsed
- 1 onion, lightly chop-up
- 2 cloves garlic, chop-up
- 2 tbsp vegetable oil
- 2 cups of vegetable broth
- 1 tsp ground cumin
- 1 tsp ground coriander
- Salt and pepper as needed

Instructions:

1. Vegetable oil Must be heated in a sizable pan over medium heat.
2. As you stir regularly to prevent burning, add the vermicelli noodles and cook up to they are golden brown.
3. Cook up to the onion is transparent after adding the chop-up garlic and onion.
4. Rice, chickpeas, cumin, coriander, salt, and pepper Must all be combined. To toast the rice, cook for a little time.
5. The veggie broth Must be added and brought to a boil. Once the rice is done and the liquid has been absorbed, turn the heat down to low, cover the pot, and simmer for 15 to 20 mins.
6. Before serving, fluff the rice pilaf with a fork.

124. Egyptian Stuffed Bell Peppers with Rice and Vegetables:

Time: 1 hr 15 mins

Servings: 6

Ingredients:

- 6 bell peppers (any color), tops take outd and seeded
- 1 cup of cooked rice
- 1 cup of combined vegetables (carrots, peas, corn, etc.), cooked
- 1 onion, lightly chop-up
- 2 cloves garlic, chop-up
- 1 can diced tomatoes
- 1/2 cup of tomato sauce
- 1/4 cup of chop-up fresh parsley
- 2 tbsp olive oil
- 1 tsp ground cumin
- 1/2 tsp ground coriander
- Salt and pepper as needed

Instructions:

1. Set the oven's temperature to 375°F (190°C).
2. Olive oil Must be heated in a sizable skillet over medium heat. Cook the onion and garlic after being added up to tender.
3. Add the cooked rice, combined veggies, tomato sauce, diced tomatoes, coriander, cumin, parsley, salt, and pepper. To blend, thoroughly stir.
4. Place the bell peppers upright in a baking dish after stuffing them with the rice and veggie Mixture.
5. Bake the dish for 45 mins with the foil covering.
6. When the peppers are soft and slightly browned, take out the foil and bake for an additional 15 mins.
7. The filled bell peppers Must be served hot.

125. Egyptian Lamb Tagine with Olives and Lemon:

Time: 2 hrs

Servings: 4

Ingredients:

- 2 lbs lamb Muster, slice into cubes
- 1 onion, lightly chop-up
- 4 cloves garlic, chop-up
- 1 preserved lemon, pulp take outd, rind thinly split
- 1 cup of green olives
- 1/4 cup of chop-up fresh cilantro
- 2 tbsp olive oil
- 1 tsp ground cumin
- 1 tsp ground coriander
- 1/2 tsp ground ginger
- 1/4 tsp ground cinnamon
- 1/4 tsp saffron threads (non-compulsory)
- Salt and pepper as needed

Instructions:

1. Heat the olive oil in a big Dutch oven or tagine over medium heat.
2. Brown the lamb cubes all over after adding them. Lamb Must be taken out of the pan and placed aside.
3. Add the chop-up garlic and onion to the same pan. Cook the onion up to it turns translucent.
4. Add the cumin, coriander, ginger, cinnamon, saffron (if using), salt, and pepper to the pan with the lamb once more. The spices Must be thoroughly combined in to coat the lamb.
5. Fill the pan with water so that it covers the meat. Bring to a boil, lower the heat to a simmer, cover the pot, and cook for one hr and thirty mins, or up to the lamb is cooked.
6. After adding the olives and preserved lemon slices, simmer the tagine for a further 15 mins.
7. Before serving, garnish with chop-up cilantro.

126. Egyptian Rice and Chicken Stuffed Grape Leaves with Mint:

Time: 1 hr 30 mins

Servings: 6

Ingredients:

- 1 jar grape leaves in brine (about 50 leaves)
- 1 cup of cooked rice
- 1 cup of cooked chicken, shredded
- 1 onion, lightly chop-up
- 2 cloves garlic, chop-up
- 1/4 cup of chop-up fresh mint leaves
- 1/4 cup of lemon juice
- 2 tbsp olive oil
- Salt and pepper as needed

Instructions:

1. Take the grape leaves out of the container and give them a thorough cold water rinse. Drain, then set apart.
2. Olive oil Must be heated in a sizable skillet over medium heat. Cook up to melted after adding the chop-up garlic and diced onion.
3. Add the cooked rice, diced chicken, mint leaves, salt, pepper, and lemon juice. To blend, thoroughly stir.
4. A grape leaf Must be placed glossy side down on a level surface. If required, take out the stem.
5. Place a mini quantity of the chicken and rice Mixture in the leaf's middle. The leaf is rolled up firmly by crossing the bottom over the filling and then folding the sides inside.
6. With the remaining grape leaves and filling, repeat the procedure.
7. Make sure the stuffed grape leaves are securely packed and set them seam side down in a sizable pot.
8. Fill the pot with water up to the grape leaves are submerged. The packed grape leaves Must be placed on top of a heatproof plate to keep them in position.
9. After the water comes to a boil, turn down the heat, cover the pan, and simmer it for 45 mins.
10.

127. Egyptian Rice and Chicken Stuffed Bell Peppers:

Time: 1 hr 30 mins

Servings: 4

Ingredients:

- 4 bell peppers
- 1 cup of cooked rice
- 1 cup of cooked chicken, shredded
- 1 mini onion, lightly chop-up
- 2 cloves garlic, chop-up
- 1 tsp cumin
- 1 tsp paprika
- Salt and pepper as needed
- 1 cup of tomato sauce
- Fresh parsley for garnish

Instructions:

1. Set the oven's temperature to 375°F (190°C).
2. The bell peppers' tops Must be slice off, and the seeds and membranes Must be take outd.
3. Cooked rice, chicken that has been shredded, onion, garlic, cumin, paprika, salt, and pepper Must all be combined in a combining dish. Combine thoroughly.
4. Place the rice and chicken Mixture inside the bell peppers.
5. In a baking dish, put the filled bell peppers and cover them with tomato sauce.
6. Bake for an hr with the foil covering the baking dish.
7. When the bell peppers are cooked, take out the cover and bake for another 15 mins.
8. Serve hot and garnish with fresh parsley.

128. Egyptian Stuffed Grape Leaves with Rice and Vegetables:

Time: 1 hr 30 mins
Servings: 4

Ingredients:

- 1 cup of grape leaves (fresh or preserved)
- 1 cup of cooked rice
- 1 mini onion, lightly chop-up
- 2 cloves garlic, chop-up
- 1 tomato, diced
- 1/4 cup of fresh parsley, chop-up
- 1/4 cup of fresh mint, chop-up
- 2 tbsp olive oil
- 1 lemon, juiced
- Salt and pepper as needed

Instructions:

1. When using fresh grape leaves, blanch them briefly in boiling water before rinsing under cold water. When using preserved grape leaves, thoroughly rinse them to get rid of the extra salt.
2. Cooked rice, chop-up onion, chop-up garlic, diced tomato, parsley, mint, olive oil, lemon juice, salt, and pepper Must all be combined in a combining dish. Combine thoroughly.
3. A grape leaf Must be laid flat and shiny side down on a work area. Place a spoonful or more of the rice Mixture in the leaf's middle.
4. The leaf is formed into a compact cylinder by folding the sides over the filling and then tightly rolling the leaf from bottom to top. Repeat with the remaining rice and grape leaves.
5. Seam side down, arrange the packed grape leaves in a single layer in a pot.
6. The grape leaves Must be covered with water, and a heavy plate or lid Must be placed on top to keep them submerged throughout cooking.
7. After bringing the water to a boil, turn the heat down low and let it simmer for a full hr.
8. Before serving, take out the packed grape leaves from the heat and let them to cool. Serve refrigerated or at room temperature.

129. Egyptian Lamb Tagine with Prunes and Almonds:

Time: 2 hrs
Servings: 4

Ingredients:

- 2 lbs lamb Muster, cubed
- 1 onion, lightly chop-up
- 2 cloves garlic, chop-up
- 1 tsp ground cumin
- 1 tsp ground coriander
- 1/2 tsp ground cinnamon
- Salt and pepper as needed
- 1 cup of pitted prunes
- 1/2 cup of slivered almonds
- 2 tbsp olive oil
- 1 cup of chicken broth
- Fresh cilantro for garnish

Instructions:

1. Over medium heat, warm the olive oil in a Big saucepan or tagine.
2. Add the lamb cubes and sauté them up to evenly browned. Lamb Must be taken out of the saucepan and placed aside.
3. Add the chop-up garlic and onion to the same pot. The onion Must be cooked up to tender and transparent.
4. Add the ground cumin, coriander, cinnamon, salt, and pepper to the saucepan with the lamb once more. The spices Must be thoroughly combined in to coat the lamb.
5. To the pot, add the pitted prunes, almond slivers, and chicken broth. To blend, stir.
6. For one and a half hrs, or up to the lamb is cooked, simmer the Mixture with the lid on over low heat.

7. Serve hot with rice or couscous and garnish with fresh cilantro.

130. Egyptian Rice and Beef Stuffed Cabbage Leaves:

Time: 1 hr 30 mins

Servings: 4

Ingredients:

- 8 Big cabbage leaves
- 1 cup of cooked rice
- 1/2 lb ground beef
- 1 mini onion, lightly chop-up
- 2 cloves garlic, chop-up
- 1/2 tsp ground cinnamon
- 1/4 tsp ground allspice
- Salt and pepper as needed
- 1 cup of tomato sauce
- 1 cup of beef broth
- Fresh dill for garnish

Instructions:

1. Big saucepan of salted water Must be brought to a boil. Add the cabbage leaves and cook them in the boiling water for 2 mins or up to they are soft. The leaves Must be taken out and put aside to cool.
2. Cooked rice, ground beef, chop-up garlic, chop-up onion, ground cinnamon, ground allspice, salt, and pepper Must all be combined in a combining dish. Combine thoroughly.
3. A cabbage leaf Must be placed flat on a work surface, and the middle of the leaf Must be covered with about a spoonful of the rice and meat Mixture.
4. The leaf is formed into a compact cylinder by folding the sides over the filling and then tightly rolling the leaf from bottom to top. Repeat with the remaining rice and cabbage leaves.
5. Tomato sauce and beef broth Must be combined in a big pot. Seam side down, arrange the stuffed cabbage leaves in a single layer in the saucepan.
6. Once the liquid has reveryed a rolling boil, turn down the heat, cover the pot, and simmer the Mixture for one hr.
7. Before serving, take the stuffed cabbage leaves off the stove and let them to cool somewhat. Serve hot and garnish with fresh dill.

131. Egyptian Stuffed Eggplant with Rice and Chickpeas:

Time: 1 hr 30 mins

Servings: 4

Ingredients:

- 2 Big eggplants
- 1 cup of cooked rice
- 1 cup of cooked chickpeas
- 1 mini onion, lightly chop-up
- 2 cloves garlic, chop-up
- 1 tomato, diced
- 1/4 cup of fresh parsley, chop-up
- 1/4 cup of fresh cilantro, chop-up
- 2 tbsp olive oil
- 1 lemon, juiced
- Salt and pepper totaste

Instructions:

1. Set the oven's temperature to 375°F (190°C).
2. The eggplants Must be split lengthwise. Take out the flesh, leaving a shell that is about 1/4 inch thick. Slice the eggplant flesh into pieces and reserve it.
3. Olive oil Must be heated in a skillet over medium heat. Add the chop-up onion, garlic, and eggplant flesh. Sauté the vegetables up to they are soft.
4. Add the diced tomato, parsley, cilantro, lemon juice, salt, and pepper to the skillet along with the cooked rice and chickpeas. To blend, thoroughly stir.
5. Place the rice and chickpea Mixture inside the eggplant shells.
6. In a baking dish, place the packed eggplants, and cover with foil.
7. Take out the foil after 45 mins of baking and continue baking for a further 15 mins to let the tops to brown.
8. Before serving, take the stuffed eggplants out of the oven and let them to cool somewhat. Serve hot.

132. Egyptian Lamb and Cauliflower Tagine with Chickpeas:

Time: 2 hrs

Servings: 4

Ingredients:

- 2 lbs lamb Muster, cubed

- 1 onion, lightly chop-up
- 2 cloves garlic, chop-up
- 1 tsp ground cumin
- 1 tsp ground coriander
- 1/2 tsp ground turmeric
- 1/4 tsp ground cinnamon
- Salt and pepper as needed
- 1 cauliflower, slice into florets
- 1 can (15 ozs) chickpeas, drained and rinsed
- 2 tbsp olive oil
- 1 cup of vegetable broth
- Fresh parsley for garnish

Instructions:

1. Over medium heat, warm the olive oil in a Big saucepan or tagine.
2. Add the lamb cubes and sauté them up to evenly browned. Lamb Must be taken out of the saucepan and placed aside.
3. Add the chop-up garlic and onion to the same pot. The onion Must be cooked up to tender and transparent.
4. Add the ground cumin, coriander, turmeric, cinnamon, salt, and pepper to the saucepan with the lamb once more. The spices Must be thoroughly combined in to coat the lamb.
5. Add the chickpeas and cauliflower florets to the pot. To blend, stir.
6. Add the veggie broth, and then boil the Mixture.
7. When the lamb is soft and the cauliflower is cooked through, simmer the Mixture with the lid on for 1 hr and 30 mins over low heat.
8. Serve hot with rice or couscous and garnish with fresh parsley.

133. Egyptian Stuffed Zucchini with Rice and Chickpeas

Time: 1 hr 30 mins
Servings: 4

Ingredients:

- 8 mini zucchini
- 1 cup of cooked rice
- 1 cup of cooked chickpeas
- 1 onion, lightly chop-up
- 2 cloves garlic, chop-up
- 2 tbsp olive oil
- 1 tsp cumin
- 1 tsp coriander
- 1/2 tsp paprika
- Salt and pepper as needed
- 2 tbsp tomato paste
- 1 cup of vegetable broth
- Fresh parsley, chop-up (for garnish)

Instructions:

1. Set the oven's temperature to 375°F (190°C).
2. Take out the zucchini's tops, scoop out the meat, and then discard the shells. Put the flesh aside for later use.
3. Olive oil is heated in a skillet at a medium temperature. Sauté up to melted after adding the chop-up garlic and diced onion.
4. The reserved zucchini flesh Must be chop-up and added to the skillet. Till tender, cook for a few mins.
5. To the skillet, add the cooked rice, chickpeas, cumin, coriander, paprika, salt, and pepper. To thoroughly incorporate all ingredients, stir well.
6. Fill every zucchini hollow with a Mixture of rice and chickpeas.
7. Spread the tomato paste equally on the bottom of a baking dish. The filled zucchini Must be placed on top of the tomato paste.
8. Around the zucchini in the baking dish, pour the vegetable broth.
9. Bake for 45 mins while the baking dish is covered with aluminum foil.
10. When the zucchini is soft, take out the cover and bake for a further 10-15 mins.
11. Serve the heated stuffed zucchini with freshly chop-up parsley on top.

NUTRITION INFO (per serving):
Cals: 250
Protein: 8g
Carbs: 40g
Fat: 7g
Fiber: 8g

134. Egyptian Lamb and Potato Tagine with Green Beans

Time: 2 hrs
Servings: 6

Ingredients:

- 1 kg lamb, slice into chunks
- 4 potatoes, peel off and cubed
- 1 onion, lightly chop-up
- 4 cloves garlic, chop-up

- 2 tbsp olive oil
- 2 tsp ground cumin
- 2 tsp ground coriander
- 1 tsp ground turmeric
- 1 tsp paprika
- Salt and pepper as needed
- 1 cup of chicken or vegetable broth
- 1 cup of green beans, trimmed
- Fresh cilantro, chop-up (for garnish)

Instructions:

1. Over medium heat, warm the olive oil in a Big saucepan or tagine. Sauté up to melted after adding the chop-up garlic and diced onion.
2. Cook the lamb chunks in the pot up to they are evenly browned.
3. Add the ground paprika, turmeric, cumin, coriander, salt, and pepper. The spices Must be thoroughly combined in to coat the lamb.
4. Add the chicken or vegetable broth, then boil the Mixture. The lamb Must be tender after an hr of cooking under cover.
5. Green beans and potatoes, chop-up, Must be added to the saucepan. Stir the spices into the lamb to combine.
6. Once more covering the pot, simmer it for 30 more mins, or up to the potatoes are tender and the flavors are well-balanced.
7. Serve the hot lamb and potato tagine with freshly chop-up cilantro on the side.

NUTRITION INFO (per serving):

Cals: 380

Protein: 25g

Carbs: 25g

Fat: 20g

Fiber: 4g

135. Egyptian Spinach and Lentil Soup with Lemon

Time: 1 hr

Servings: 6

Ingredients:

- 1 cup of dried lentils
- 1 onion, lightly chop-up
- 3 cloves garlic, chop-up
- 2 tbsp olive oil
- 1 bunch spinach, washed and chop-up
- 4 cups of vegetable broth
- 2 cups of water
- Juice of 1 lemon
- Salt and pepper as needed
- Ground cumin for garnish

Instructions:

1. The dried lentils Must be rinsed before storing.
2. Olive oil is heated over medium heat in a big pot. Sauté up to melted after adding the chop-up garlic and diced onion.
3. Stir the onion and garlic in the pot before adding the washed lentils.
4. Add the water and veggie broth. The lentils Must be soft after about 40 mins of simmering over a low heat after bringing to a boil.
5. Cook the spinach for an additional 10 mins, or up to it wilts, after adding the chop-up spinach to the pot.
6. Smoothen the soup using a standard blender or an immersion blender.
7. Reheat the soup in the same container over low heat.
8. Add the salt, pepper, and lemon juice. To fully combine the flavors, stir thoroughly.
9. Serve the hot spinach and lentil soup with a dash of ground cumin as a garnish.

NUTRITION INFO (per serving):

Cals: 180

Protein: 9g

Carbs: 27g

Fat: 5g

Fiber: 8g

136. Egyptian Chicken and Okra Stew with Potatoes

Time: 1 hr 30 mins

Servings: 4

Ingredients:

- 4 chicken thighs, bone-in and skin-on
- 1 onion, lightly chop-up
- 3 cloves garlic, chop-up
- 2 tbsp olive oil
- 2 tsp ground cumin
- 2 tsp ground coriander
- 1 tsp ground turmeric

- 1/2 tsp paprika
- Salt and pepper as needed
- 2 potatoes, peel off and cubed
- 2 cups of okra, trimmed
- 2 cups of chicken broth
- Fresh cilantro, chop-up (for garnish)

Instructions:

1. Olive oil Must be heated over medium heat in a big pot or Dutch oven. Sauté up to melted after adding the chop-up garlic and diced onion.
2. Place the chicken thighs skin-side down in the pot. Cook the food up to the skin is crispy and browned. The other side of the chicken thighs Must also be browned. Chicken Must be taken out of the pot and placed aside.
3. Add the ground cumin, ground coriander, ground turmeric, ground paprika, salt, and pepper to the same pot. The spices Must be thoroughly combined with the onions and garlic.
4. To the pot, add the diced potatoes and the trimmed okra. Stir the spices into the Mixture.
5. Put the chicken thighs back in the saucepan on top of the veggies.
6. Add the chicken broth, then boil the Mixture. For 45 mins, or up to the chicken is thoroughly cooked and the vegetables are tender, cover the saucepan and let it cook.
7. Serve the hot chicken and okra stew with freshly chop-up cilantro on the side.

NUTRITION INFO (per serving):
Cals: 380
Protein: 25g
Carbs: 25g
Fat: 15g
Fiber: 6g

138. Egyptian Rice and Milk Pudding with Pistachios

Time: 1 hr 30 mins
Servings: 6

Ingredients:

- 1 cup of short-grain rice
- 4 cups of milk
- 1/2 cup of sugar
- 1 tsp vanilla extract
- 1/4 cup of pistachios, chop-up (+ extra for garnish)
- Ground cinnamon for garnish

Instructions:

1. Rice Must be thoroughly rinsed in cold water up to the water is clear. Drain, then set apart.
2. Combine the washed rice, milk, and sugar in a big pot. Over medium heat, bring to a boil while stirring occasionally.
3. Stirring regularly to avoid sticking, reduce the heat to low and simmer the rice and milk combination for approximately an hr, or up to the rice is tender and the sauce thickens.
4. Add the chop-up pistachios and vanilla extract after that. Cook for a further five mins.
5. Once the rice pudding has reveryed room temperature, turn off the heat and let it cool. Further thickening will occur as it cools.
6. Divide the rice pudding into serving bowls once it has cooled. Add more chop-up pistachios and a dash of ground cinnamon as garnish.
7. Rice and milk pudding can be served cold or at room temperature.

NUTRITION INFO (per serving):
Cals: 280
Protein: 7g
Carbs: 50g
Fat: 6g
Fiber: 1g

139. Egyptian Stuffed Eggplant with Rice and Lentils

Time: 1 hr 30 mins
Servings: 4

Ingredients:

- 4 Big eggplants
- 1 cup of cooked rice
- 1 cup of cooked lentils
- 1 onion, lightly chop-up
- 3 cloves garlic, chop-up
- 2 tbsp olive oil
- 1 tsp ground cumin
- 1 tsp ground coriander
- 1/2 tsp paprika
- Salt and pepper as needed
- 2 tbsp tomato paste
- 1 cup of vegetable broth
- Fresh parsley, chop-up (for garnish)

Instructions:

1. Set the oven's temperature to 375°F (190°C).
2. Take out the eggplants' tops, then slice them in half lengthwise. Take out the flesh, leaving a shell that is hollow. Put the flesh aside for later use.
3. Olive oil is heated in a skillet at a medium temperature. Sauté up to melted after adding the chop-up garlic and diced onion.
4. The reserved eggplant flesh Must be chop-up and added to the skillet. Till tender, cook for a few mins.
5. To the skillet, add the cooked rice, lentils, cumin, coriander, paprika, salt, and pepper. To thoroughly incorporate all ingredients, stir well.
6. Fill every hollowed-out eggplant half with a Mixture of rice and lentils.
7. Spread the tomato paste equally on the bottom of a baking dish. On top of the tomato paste, arrange the stuffed eggplants.
8. Around the eggplants in the baking dish, pour the vegetable broth.
9. Bake for 45 mins while the baking dish is covered with aluminum foil.
10. When the eggplants are cooked, take out the cover and bake for an additional 10-15 mins.
11. With freshly chop-up parsley as a garnish, serve the stuffed eggplants hot.

NUTRITION INFO (per serving):
Cals: 260
Protein: 10g
Carbs: 45g
Fat: 6g
Fiber: 12g

140. Egyptian Lamb and Cauliflower Tagine with Tomatoes

Time: 1 hr 30 mins
Servings: 4

Ingredients:

- 1 lb (450g) lamb, cubed
- 1 cauliflower, slice into florets
- 1 onion, chop-up
- 3 cloves of garlic, chop-up
- 2 tomatoes, diced
- 2 tbsp olive oil
- 1 tsp ground cumin
- 1 tsp ground coriander
- 1/2 tsp ground turmeric
- 1/2 tsp ground cinnamon
- Salt and pepper as needed
- Fresh cilantro, chop-up (for garnish)

Instructions:

1. Over medium heat, warm the olive oil in a sizable saucepan or tagine. Add the lamb, then sear it thoroughly.
2. Sauté the onion and garlic in the pot up to they are tender.
3. Add the salt, pepper, cinnamon, turmeric, cumin, and coriander.
4. Stir thoroughly after adding the tomatoes and cauliflower to the pot.
5. When the lamb is soft and the cauliflower is fully cooked, boil the Mixture with the lid on for about an hr.
6. Serve the tagine hot with fresh cilantro as a garnish.

NUTRITION INFO (per serving):
Cals: 340
Protein: 25g
Fat: 18g
Carbs: 21g
Fiber: 6g

141. Egyptian Spinach and Chickpea Soup with Cumin

Time: 40 mins
Servings: 6

Ingredients:

- 1 onion, chop-up
- 3 cloves of garlic, chop-up
- 1 lb (450g) fresh spinach, washed and chop-up
- 1 can (15 oz) chickpeas, drained and rinsed
- 4 cups of vegetable broth
- 2 tbsp olive oil
- 1 tsp ground cumin
- Salt and pepper as needed
- Lemon wedges (for serving)

Instructions:

1. Over medium heat, warm the olive oil in a big pot. Sauté the onion and garlic after being added up to they are tender.

2. Cook for another min after adding the cumin.
3. When the spinach has wilted, add it to the stew and stir.
4. Chickpeas and vegetable broth Must be added to the pot. After bringing to a boil, turn down the heat, and let the Mixture simmer for about 20 mins.
5. Add salt and pepper as needed when preparing the soup.
6. With a squeeze of fresh lemon juice on top, serve the soup hot.

NUTRITION INFO (per serving):

Cals: 180

Protein: 8g

Fat: 7g

Carbs: 23g

Fiber: 7g

142. Egyptian Chicken and Egg Tagine with Green Peas

Time: 1 hr

Servings: 4

Ingredients:

- 4 chicken thighs, bone-in and skin-on
- 1 onion, chop-up
- 3 cloves of garlic, chop-up
- 1 cup of refrigerate green peas
- 4 eggs
- 2 tbsp olive oil
- 1 tsp ground cumin
- 1 tsp ground paprika
- 1/2 tsp ground turmeric
- 1/4 tsp ground cinnamon
- Salt and pepper as needed
- Fresh parsley, chop-up (for garnish)

Instructions:

1. Over medium heat, warm the olive oil in a sizable saucepan or tagine. Brown the chicken thighs all over after adding them.
2. Chicken Must be taken out of the pot and placed aside. Add the onion and garlic to the same saucepan and cook, stirring occasionally, up to tender.
3. Add the salt, pepper, cinnamon, paprika, turmeric, and cumin after stirring.
4. Put the chicken back in the pot and cover it with water. When the chicken is cooked through, bring to a boil, then lower the heat and simmer for about 40 mins.
5. Cook the green peas for a further five mins after adding them to the pot.
6. Make sure to evenly space the eggs as you cautiously crack them into the kettle. Cook the eggs for a further five mins, covered, or up to they are done to your preference.
7. Serve the tagine hot with fresh parsley as a garnish.

NUTRITION INFO (per serving):

Cals: 360

Protein: 28g

Fat: 24g

Carbs: 8g

Fiber: 2g

143. Egyptian Rice and Vermicelli Soup with Cilantro

Time: 45 mins

Servings: 6

Ingredients:

- 1 cup of long-grain rice
- 1/2 cup of vermicelli, broken into mini pieces
- 1 onion, chop-up
- 3 cloves of garlic, chop-up
- 4 cups of vegetable broth
- 2 tbsp olive oil
- 1/4 cup of fresh cilantro, chop-up
- Salt and pepper as needed
- Lemon wedges (for serving)

Instructions:

1. Olive oil Must be heated in a sizable pot over medium heat. Sauté the onion and garlic after being added up to they are tender.
2. Vermicelli Must be added to the stew and cooked up to golden brown.
3. Rice and veggie broth Must be combined. Once it starts to boil, turn the heat down, cover, and simmer for 20 to 25 mins, or up to the rice is done.
4. Add the fresh cilantro and season as needed with salt and pepper.
5. With a squeeze of fresh lemon juice on top, serve the soup hot.

NUTRITION INFO (per serving):

Cals: 220

Protein: 4g

Fat: 6g

Carbs: 39g

Fiber: 1g

144. Egyptian Stuffed Bell Peppers with Rice and Lentils

Time: 1 hr 15 mins

Servings: 4

Ingredients:

- 4 bell peppers (any color), tops take outd and seeds take outd
- 1 cup of cooked rice
- 1 cup of cooked lentils
- 1 onion, chop-up
- 3 cloves of garlic, chop-up
- 2 tomatoes, diced
- 2 tbsp olive oil
- 1 tsp ground cumin
- 1 tsp ground coriander
- 1/2 tsp ground cinnamon
- Salt and pepper as needed
- Fresh parsley, chop-up (for garnish)

Instructions:

1. Set the oven's temperature to 375°F (190°C).
2. The bell peppers Must be blanched for 5 mins in a big pot of boiling water. Drain, then set apart.
3. Olive oil Must be heated in a different pan over medium heat. Sauté the onion and garlic after being added up to they are tender.
4. Add the salt, pepper, cinnamon, cumin, and coriander.
5. Cooked rice, lentils, and tomatoes Must all be added to the pan. To blend, thoroughly stir.
6. Place the rice and lentil Mixture inside the bell peppers. Put them inside a baking pan.
7. Bake for 30 mins with the foil covering the baking dish. When the peppers are soft and slightly browned, take out the foil and bake for a further 10-15 mins.
8. Serve the filled bell peppers hot with fresh parsley added as a garnish.

NUTRITION INFO (per serving):

Cals: 280

Protein: 10g

Fat: 7g

Carbs: 47g

Fiber: 9g

145. Egyptian Lamb Tagine with Almonds and Raisins

Time: 2 hrs

Servings: 4

Ingredients:

- 1 lb (450g) lamb, cubed
- 1 onion, chop-up
- 3 cloves of garlic, chop-up
- 1 cup of beef or lamb broth
- 1/2 cup of raisins
- 1/2 cup of slivered almonds
- 2 tbsp olive oil
- 2 tsp ground cumin
- 1 tsp ground coriander
- 1 tsp ground cinnamon
- 1/2 tsp ground ginger
- Salt and pepper as needed
- Fresh mint leaves, chop-up (for garnish)

Instructions:

1. Heat the olive oil in a sizable saucepan or tagine over medium heat. Add the lamb, then sear it thoroughly.
2. Lamb Must be taken out of the saucepan and placed aside. Add the onion and garlic to the same saucepan and cook, stirring occasionally, up to tender.
3. Add the salt, pepper, cinnamon, ginger, cumin, and coriander.
4. Add the beef or lamb broth to the pot and add the lamb back. Bring to a boil, lower the heat, cover, and simmer for about one and a half hrs, or up to the lamb is fork-tender.
5. Add the raisins and almond slivers after simmering for another 15 mins.
6. Warm lamb tagine Must be served with fresh mint leaves on top.

NUTRITION INFO (per serving):

Cals: 410

Protein: 23g

Fat: 26g

Carbs: 23g

Fiber: 5g

146. Egyptian Stuffed Zucchini with Rice

Time: 1 hr
Servings: 4

Ingredients:

- 4 medium zucchini
- 1 cup of rice
- 1/2 cup of diced onions
- 2 cloves garlic, chop-up
- 1/2 cup of diced tomatoes
- 1/4 cup of chop-up fresh parsley
- 1/4 cup of chop-up fresh dill
- 1/4 cup of chop-up fresh mint
- 1/4 cup of olive oil
- Salt and pepper as needed
- Lemon wedges for serving

Instructions:

1. Set the oven's temperature to 375°F (190°C).
2. Slice off the zucchini's tops and take out the pulp, leaving a shell.
3. Rice, onions, garlic, tomatoes, parsley, dill, mint, olive oil, salt, and pepper Must all be combined in a bowl. Combine thoroughly.
4. Place the stuffed zucchini shells in a baking tray. Fill the zucchini shells with the rice Mixture.
5. When the rice and zucchini are cooked, cover the dish with foil and bake for 40 mins.
6. With lemon slices, serve hot.

NUTRITION INFO (per serving):
Cals: 220
Protein: 4g
Fat: 10g
Carbs: 30g
Fiber: 3g

147. Egyptian Lamb and Cauliflower Tagine with Potatoes

Time: 2 hrs
Servings: 6

Ingredients:

- 1.5 lbs lamb Muster, cubed
- 1 medium cauliflower, slice into florets
- 3 medium potatoes, peel off and cubed
- 1 onion, chop-up
- 3 cloves garlic, chop-up
- 2 tbsp olive oil
- 1 tsp ground cumin
- 1 tsp ground coriander
- 1/2 tsp ground turmeric
- 1/2 tsp ground cinnamon
- 1/4 tsp cayenne pepper (non-compulsory for spice)
- 1 cup of chicken broth
- Salt and pepper as needed
- Chop-up fresh cilantro for garnish

Instructions:

1. In a tagine or big pot, heat the olive oil over medium-low heat.
2. Add the lamb and cook it up to it is well-browned all over. Take out of the pot and reserve.
3. Add the onions and garlic to the same pot. till transparent, sauté.
4. Cumin, coriander, turmeric, cinnamon, cayenne, salt, and pepper Must be added. The spices Must be thoroughly combined with the onions and garlic.
5. Add the potatoes, cauliflower, and chicken broth to the saucepan along with adding the meat back in.
6. When the lamb is tender and the veggies are fully cooked, boil the Mixture with the lid on for 1.5 to 2 hrs.
7. Before serving, garnish with fresh cilantro.

NUTRITION INFO (per serving):
Cals: 380
Protein: 24g
Fat: 18g
Carbs: 30g
Fiber: 6g

148. Egyptian Spinach and Chickpea Salad with Tahini Dressing

Time: 20 mins
Servings: 4

Ingredients:

- 6 cups of fresh spinach leaves
- 1 cup of cooked chickpeas
- 1/2 cup of cherry tomatoes, halved
- 1/4 cup of chop-up red onion
- 1/4 cup of chop-up fresh parsley
- 1/4 cup of chop-up fresh mint
- 2 tbsp tahini

- 2 tbsp lemon juice
- 2 tbsp water
- 1 clove garlic, chop-up
- Salt and pepper as needed

Instructions:

1. The spinach, chickpeas, cherry tomatoes, red onion, parsley, and mint Must all be combined in a big bowl.
2. To create the dressing, combine the tahini, lemon juice, water, garlic, salt, and pepper in a separate mini bowl.
3. The dressing Must be poured over the salad and thoroughly combined in.
4. Serve right away.

NUTRITION INFO (per serving):

Cals: 160

Protein: 8g

Fat: 7g

Carbs: 19g

Fiber: 6g

149. Egyptian Chicken and Egg Tagine with Bell Peppers

Time: 1 hr

Servings: 4

Ingredients:

- 4 chicken thighs, bone-in and skin-on
- 2 bell peppers, split
- 1 onion, split
- 4 eggs
- 3 cloves garlic, chop-up
- 2 tbsp olive oil
- 1 tsp ground cumin
- 1 tsp ground coriander
- 1/2 tsp ground turmeric
- 1/4 tsp cayenne pepper (non-compulsory for spice)
- Salt and pepper as needed
- Chop-up fresh cilantro for garnish

Instructions:

1. In a tagine or big skillet, heat the olive oil over medium heat.
2. Salt, pepper, cumin, coriander, turmeric, and cayenne pepper are used to season the chicken thighs.
3. The chicken Must be added to the tagine and cooked up to both sides are browned. Chicken Must be taken out of the tagine and placed aside.
4. Add the onions and garlic to the same tagine. The onions Must be transparent after sautéing.
5. The bell peppers Must be added to the tagine and cooked for a few mins, or up to they soften.
6. Place the chicken back in the tagine amid the bell peppers.
7. Over the chicken and bell peppers, crack the eggs.
8. Cook the eggs in the covered tagine for around 10 mins, or up to they are done to your preference.
9. Before serving, garnish with fresh cilantro.

NUTRITION INFO (per serving):

Cals: 320

Protein: 26g

Fat: 21g

Carbs: 7g

Fiber: 2g

150. Egyptian Rice and Vermicelli Pilaf with Raisins and Pine Nuts

Time: 30 mins

Servings: 4

Ingredients:

- 1 cup of long-grain rice
- 1/2 cup of vermicelli, broken into mini pieces
- 2 tbsp butter
- 2 cups of chicken or vegetable broth
- 1/4 cup of raisins
- 1/4 cup of pine nuts
- Salt as needed

Instructions:

1. Melt the butter in a Big skillet over medium heat.
2. Vermicelli Must be added and cooked up to golden brown while tossing constantly to avoid scorching.
3. Stir the vermicelli and butter into the rice after adding it to the skillet.
4. Bring to a boil after adding the chicken or veggie broth.
5. When the rice is done and the liquid has been absorbed, lower the heat to low, cover the skillet, and simmer for 15 to 20 mins.

6. The pine nuts Must be lightly toasted in a different mini skillet over medium heat up to golden brown.
7. When the rice is finished cooking, toss in the raisins and toasted pine nuts before fluffing it with a fork.
8. As needed, add salt to the dish.
9. Serve warm.

NUTRITION INFO (per serving):
Cals: 290
Protein: 5g
Fat: 11g
Carbs: 43g
Fiber: 2g

151. Egyptian Stuffed Bell Peppers with Rice and Spinach

Time: 1 hr
Servings: 4

Ingredients:

- 4 bell peppers (any color), tops take outd and seeds take outd
- 1 cup of cooked rice
- 1 cup of chop-up spinach
- 1/2 cup of diced tomatoes
- 1/4 cup of chop-up fresh parsley
- 1/4 cup of chop-up fresh dill
- 1/4 cup of chop-up fresh mint
- 1/4 cup of diced onions
- 2 cloves garlic, chop-up
- 2 tbsp olive oil
- Salt and pepper as needed

Instructions:

1. Set the oven's temperature to 375°F (190°C).
2. Cooked rice, chop-up spinach, tomatoes, parsley, dill, mint, onions, garlic, olive oil, salt, and pepper Must all be combined in a big bowl. Combine thoroughly.
3. Place the bell peppers in a baking tray after stuffing them with the rice and spinach Mixture.
4. Bake the dish, covered with foil, for 30-35 mins, or up to the peppers are soft and the filling is thoroughly heated.
5. Serve warm.

NUTRITION INFO (per serving):
Cals: 170
Protein: 3g
Fat: 7g
Carbs: 25g
Fiber: 4g

152. Egyptian Rice and Beef Stuffed Cabbage Leaves with Tomato Sauce

Time: 1 hr 30 mins
Servings: 4

Ingredients:

- 12 Big cabbage leaves
- 1 cup of cooked rice
- 1/2 lb ground beef
- 1/2 onion, lightly chop-up
- 2 cloves garlic, chop-up
- 1/4 cup of chop-up fresh parsley
- 1/4 tsp ground cinnamon
- Salt and pepper as needed
- 2 cups of tomato sauce
- 1 cup of water
- Juice of 1 lemon

Instructions:

1. The cabbage leaves Must be melted by briefly blanching them in boiling water. Drain, then set apart.
2. Cooked rice, ground beef, onion, garlic, parsley, cinnamon, salt, and pepper Must all be combined in a big bowl.
3. Place a dollop of the beef and rice Mixture in the middle of a cabbage leaf. As you roll it up, tuck the sides in. Repeat with the rest of the filling and leaves.
4. Spread tomato sauce across the bottom of a big pot. In the pot, arrange the packed cabbage leaves.
5. Over the cabbage rolls, add the remaining tomato sauce, water, and lemon juice.
6. For approximately an hr, or up to the cabbage leaves are soft and the flavors are well-balanced, simmer the Mixture in a covered pot over low heat.
7. With the tomato sauce on top, serve the stuffed cabbage leaves.

NUTRITION INFO: (per serving)
Cals: 320
Protein: 16g
Fat: 8g

Carbs: 45g

Fiber: 6g

153. Egyptian Stuffed Eggplant with Rice and Spinach

Time: 1 hr

Servings: 4

Ingredients:

- 4 Big eggplants
- 1 cup of cooked rice
- 1 cup of chop-up spinach
- 1/2 onion, lightly chop-up
- 2 cloves garlic, chop-up
- 1/4 cup of chop-up fresh dill
- 1/4 tsp ground cumin
- Salt and pepper as needed
- 1/4 cup of tomato sauce
- 1/4 cup of vegetable broth
- Juice of 1 lemon

Instructions:

1. Set the oven's temperature to 375°F (190°C).
2. Take out the eggplants' tops, then slice them in half lengthwise. Take out the flesh, leaving a 1/2-inch border behind.
3. The flesh of the take outd eggplant Must be chop-up and left aside.
4. The onion and garlic Must be sautéed till tender in a big pan. Add the chop-up flesh of the eggplant and simmer for a short while.
5. Add the cooked rice, spinach that has been chop-up, dill, cumin, salt, and pepper. additional 2 to 3 mins of cooking.
6. Place the rice and spinach Mixture inside the eggplant halves.
7. Combine the tomato sauce, vegetable broth, and lemon juice in a baking dish. In the dish, put the stuffed eggplants.
8. Bake the dish for about 40 mins, or up to the eggplants are soft. Cover the dish with foil.
9. Serve the stuffed eggplants with the baking dish's sauce.

NUTRITION INFO: (per serving)

Cals: 220

Protein: 5g

Fat: 1g

Carbs: 52g

Fiber: 10g

154. Egyptian Lamb and Potato Tagine with Carrots

Time: 2 hrs

Servings: 6

Ingredients:

- 2 lbs lamb Muster, slice into chunks
- 2 onions, chop-up
- 4 cloves garlic, chop-up
- 2 tbsp vegetable oil
- 2 tsp ground cumin
- 2 tsp ground coriander
- 1 tsp ground turmeric
- 1/2 tsp ground cinnamon
- Salt and pepper as needed
- 4 carrots, peel off and split
- 4 potatoes, peel off and diced
- 2 cups of vegetable broth
- 1/4 cup of chop-up fresh cilantro

Instructions:

1. In a sizable saucepan or tagine, heat the vegetable oil over medium-low heat.
2. Brown the lamb chunks all over after adding them. Lamb Must be taken out of the saucepan and placed aside.
3. The onions and garlic Must be cooked in the same pot up to they are tender and transparent.
4. Cumin, coriander, cinnamon, ginger, turmeric, and salt Must be added. The spices Must be thoroughly combined with the onions and garlic.
5. Add the carrots, potatoes, and vegetable stock to the saucepan with the lamb before covering.
6. Heat Must be turned down once the Mixture comes to a boil. When the lamb is cooked and the flavors are well-balanced, simmer the dish with the lid on for about 1 1/2 to 2 hrs.
7. Before serving, top with fresh cilantro.

NUTRITION INFO: (per serving)

Cals: 420

Protein: 24g

Fat: 15g

Carbs: 46g

Fiber: 8g

155. Egyptian Spinach and Lentil Salad with Mint

Time: 30 mins

Servings: 4

Ingredients:

- 2 cups of cooked lentils
- 4 cups of fresh spinach leaves
- 1/4 cup of chop-up fresh mint
- 1/2 red onion, thinly split
- 1 tomato, diced
- Juice of 1 lemon
- 2 tbsp olive oil
- Salt and pepper as needed

Instructions:

1. The cooked lentils, spinach, mint, red onion, and tomato Must all be combined in a big bowl.
2. Combine the lemon juice, olive oil, salt, and pepper in a mini bowl.
3. Over the salad, drizzle the dressing and toss to blend.
4. Before serving, let the salad sit for about 10 mins to let the flavors mingle.

NUTRITION INFO: (per serving)

Cals: 260

Protein: 14g

Fat: 8g

Carbs: 33g

Fiber: 12g

156. Egyptian Chicken and Okra Stew with Lemon

Time: 1 hr 30 mins

Servings: 6

Ingredients:

- 1 whole chicken, slice into pieces
- 2 onions, chop-up
- 4 cloves garlic, chop-up
- 2 tbsp vegetable oil
- 1 tsp ground cumin
- 1 tsp ground coriander
- 1/2 tsp groundturmeric
- Salt and pepper as needed
- 1 lb okra, trimmed
- Juice of 2 lemons
- 4 cups of chicken broth
- 2 tbsp chop-up fresh cilantro

Instructions:

1. Vegetable oil Must be heated in a sizable pot over medium heat. Brown the chicken pieces all over after adding them. Chicken Must be taken out of the pot and placed aside.
2. The onions and garlic Must be cooked in the same pot up to they are tender and transparent.
3. Salt, pepper, turmeric, coriander, and cumin Must be added. The spices Must be thoroughly combined with the onions and garlic.
4. Add the okra, lemon juice, and chicken stock to the saucepan along with the chicken back in it.
5. Heat Must be turned down once the Mixture comes to a boil. For approximately an hr, or up to the chicken is cooked through and soft, cover the saucepan and simmer.
6. Just before serving, stir in the chop-up cilantro.

NUTRITION INFO: (per serving)

Cals: 320

Protein: 28g

Fat: 14g

Carbs: 22g

Fiber: 5g

157. Egyptian Rice and Chicken Stuffed Grape Leaves with Dill

Time: 1 hr 30 mins

Servings: 4

Ingredients:

- 1 cup of long-grain rice
- 1/2 lb ground chicken
- 1/2 onion, lightly chop-up
- 2 cloves garlic, chop-up
- 1/4 cup of chop-up fresh dill
- 1/4 tsp ground cinnamon
- Salt and pepper as needed
- 24 grape leaves, rinsed and drained
- Juice of 1 lemon
- 2 tbsp olive oil
- 1 cup of chicken broth

Instructions:

1. Cook the rice in a medium saucepan as directed on the box/pkg. Set apart for cooling.
2. Cooked rice, ground chicken, onion, garlic, dill, cinnamon, salt, and pepper Must all be combined in a big bowl.

3. A grape leaf Must be placed vein side up on a flat surface. In the middle of the leaf, place a tbsp of the rice and chicken Mixture. Wrap the leaf tightly after folding the sides over the filling. Repetition is required with the remaining grape leaves and filling.
4. Place the packed grape leaves in a single layer in a big container.
5. Over the packed grape leaves, pour the chicken stock, lemon juice, and olive oil.
6. Once the grape leaves are soft and the flavors are well-balanced, simmer the Mixture with the lid on for about an hr over low heat.
7. Some of the cooking liquid Must be served with the packed grape leaves.

NUTRITION INFO: (per serving)
Cals: 270
Protein: 10g
Fat: 7g
Carbs: 45g
Fiber: 4g

158. Egyptian Lamb Tagine with Dates and Apricots

Time: 2 hrs
Servings: 4

Ingredients:

- 1.5 lbs (680g) lamb Muster, slice into chunks
- 1 onion, chop-up
- 3 cloves of garlic, chop-up
- 1 tsp ground cumin
- 1 tsp ground coriander
- 1/2 tsp ground cinnamon
- 1/2 tsp ground ginger
- 1/4 tsp ground turmeric
- 1 cup of pitted dates
- 1 cup of dried apricots
- 2 cups of chicken broth
- Salt and pepper as needed
- Fresh cilantro for garnish

Instructions:

1. Heat some oil in a sizable tagine or heavy-bottomed saucepan over medium heat. Add the lamb, then sear it thoroughly. Lamb Must be taken out of the saucepan and placed aside.
2. Add the chop-up garlic and onion to the same pot. Sauté the onion up to it turns translucent.
3. The pot Must now contain the ground cumin, coriander, cinnamon, ginger, and turmeric. The spices Must be thoroughly combined with the onion and garlic.
4. Back in the pot, add the browned lamb. Add the chicken broth, dried apricots, and pitted dates. As needed, add salt and pepper to the food.
5. When the lamb is cooked, simmer it for 1.5 to 2 hrs with the lid on over low heat.
6. Warm lamb tagine Must be served with fresh cilantro on top. It pairs well with rice or couscous.

NUTRITION INFO (per serving):
Cals: 450
Fat: 15g
Carbs: 46g
Protein: 35g

159. Egyptian Rice and Beef Stuffed Cabbage Leaves with Garlic Sauce

Time: 1 hr 30 mins
Servings: 6

Ingredients:

- 12 Big cabbage leaves
- 1 lb (450g) ground beef
- 1 cup of cooked rice
- 1 onion, lightly chop-up
- 2 cloves of garlic, chop-up
- 2 tbsp tomato paste
- 1/2 tsp ground allspice
- 1/2 tsp ground cinnamon
- 1/4 tsp ground nutmeg
- Salt and pepper as needed
- 2 cups of chicken broth
- Garlic Sauce:
- 1 cup of plain yogurt
- 2 cloves of garlic, chop-up
- 1 tbsp lemon juice
- Salt as needed

Instructions:

1. Bring water in a big pot to a boil. The cabbage leaves Must be added and blanched for a few mins up to they are supple and tender. Take the leaves off and place them somewhere to cool.
2. Ground beef, cooked rice, chop-up onion, chop-up garlic, tomato paste, allspice, cinnamon, nutmeg, salt, and pepper Must all be combined in

a combining dish. All the components Must be thoroughly combined.
3. A portion of the meat and rice combination Must be placed in the center of every cabbage leaf. As you tightly roll the leaf, fold the sides in. Repeat with the rest of the filling and leaves.
4. Place the packed cabbage leaves in a single layer in a big pot. Over the cabbage rolls, pour the chicken broth.
5. Once the cabbage leaves are cooked through and the filling is soft, cover the pot and simmer on low heat for about an hr.
6. Make the garlic sauce in the meantime by combining plain yogurt, chop-up garlic, lemon juice, and salt in a basin. Combine thoroughly.
7. Warm stuffed cabbage rolls with garlic sauce are served.

NUTRITION INFO (per serving):
Cals: 320
Fat: 14g
Carbs: 27g
Protein: 22g

160. Egyptian Stuffed Eggplant with Rice and Mushrooms

Time: 1 hr 30 mins
Servings: 4

Ingredients:
- 2 Big eggplants
- 1 cup of cooked rice
- 8 oz (225g) mushrooms, chop-up
- 1 onion, lightly chop-up
- 3 cloves of garlic, chop-up
- 1/4 cup of chop-up fresh parsley
- 1/4 cup of chop-up fresh mint
- 2 tbsp tomato paste
- 1 tsp ground cumin
- 1 tsp ground coriander
- 1/2 tsp paprika
- Salt and pepper as needed
- Olive oil for drizzling

Instructions:
1. Set the oven's temperature to 375°F (190°C).
2. Slice the eggplants in half lengthwise, take out the flesh, and leave a shell that is 1/2 inch thick. Put the flesh aside for later use.
3. Olive oil Must be heated in a pan over medium heat. Add the chop-up garlic and onion, both chop-up. Sauté the onion up to it turns translucent.
4. Add the mushrooms and the diced flesh of the eggplant to the pan. Cook up to their fluids are released and they are tender.
5. Add the cooked rice, tomato paste, chop-up parsley, chop-up mint, ground cumin, ground coriander, paprika, salt, and pepper. Stir to combine. To thoroughly incorporate all ingredients, stir well.
6. The rice and mushroom combination Must be placed within the eggplant shells. Over the top, drizzle some olive oil.
7. In a baking dish, place the packed eggplants, and cover with foil. Bake the eggplants in the preheated oven for about 40 mins, or up to they are soft.
8. Hot stuffed eggplants can be served as a side dish or as a main course.

NUTRITION INFO (per serving):
Cals: 250
Fat: 8g
Carbs: 40g
Protein: 8g

161. Egyptian Lamb and Potato Tagine with Onions

Time: 2 hrs
Servings: 4

Ingredients:
- 1.5 lbs (680g) lamb Muster, slice into chunks
- 2 Big onions, thinly split
- 3 cloves of garlic, chop-up
- 1 tsp ground cumin
- 1 tsp ground coriander
- 1/2 tsp ground cinnamon
- 1/2 tsp ground turmeric
- 1/4 tsp cayenne pepper (non-compulsory for heat)
- 4 medium potatoes, peel off and slice into chunks
- 2 cups of chicken broth
- Salt and pepper as needed
- Fresh cilantro for garnish

Instructions:

1. Heat some oil in a sizable tagine or heavy-bottomed saucepan over medium heat. Add the lamb, then sear it thoroughly. Lamb Must be taken out of the saucepan and placed aside.
2. Add the chop-up garlic and onion slices to the same pot. Onions Must be sautéed up to they are tender and transparent.
3. Cumin, coriander, cinnamon, turmeric, and cayenne pepper (if using) Must all be added to the pot. The spices Must be thoroughly combined with the onions and garlic.
4. Back in the pot, add the browned lamb. Chicken broth and potato cubes Must be added. As needed, add salt and pepper to the food.
5. For around 1.5 to 2 hrs, or up to the lamb is soft and the potatoes are cooked through, cover the saucepan and simmer it on low heat.
6. Serve the hot lamb and potato tagine with fresh cilantro on top. It goes great with bread or rice.

NUTRITION INFO (per serving):
Cals: 480
Fat: 20g
Carbs: 40g
Protein: 35g

162. Egyptian Spinach and Lentil Soup with Cumin and Coriander

Time: 45 mins
Servings: 6

Ingredients:

- 1 cup of dried green or brown lentils, rinsed
- 1 onion, chop-up
- 3 cloves of garlic, chop-up
- 1 tsp ground cumin
- 1 tsp ground coriander
- 1/2 tsp ground turmeric
- 6 cups of vegetable broth or water
- 1 lb (450g) fresh spinach, washed and roughly chop-up
- Juice of 1 lemon
- Salt and pepper as needed
- Olive oil for drizzling

Instructions:

1. Lentils, chop-up onion, chop-up garlic, ground cumin, ground coriander, and ground turmeric Must all be combined in a sizable pot.
2. Add the water or vegetable broth, and then bring to a boil. When the lentils are ready, turn the heat down to low, cover the pot, and simmer for about 30 mins.
3. Cook the spinach for an additional 5 mins, or up to it wilts, after adding the chop-up spinach to the pot.
4. Puree the soup in a normal or immersion blender up to it is silky and creamy. If using a standard blender, blend the soup in mini batches and use caution because it will be hot.
5. Add the lemon juice after seasoning as needed with salt and pepper.
6. Olive oil Must be drizzled over the hot bowl of lentil and spinach soup.

NUTRITION INFO (per serving):
Cals: 200
Fat: 4g
Carbs: 32g
Protein: 12g

163. Egyptian Chicken and Okra Stew with Cilantro

Time: 1 hr
Servings: 4

Ingredients:

- 4 chicken thighs, bone-in and skin-on
- 1 onion, chop-up
- 3 cloves of garlic, chop-up
- 1 tsp ground cumin
- 1 tsp ground coriander
- 1/2 tsp ground turmeric
- 1/4 tsp cayenne pepper (non-compulsory for heat)
- 1 lb (450g) okra, ends trimmed
- 2 cups of chicken broth
- Juice of 1 lemon
- Salt and pepper as needed
- Fresh cilantro for garnish

Instructions:

1. Heat some oil in a big saucepan on a medium heat. Brown the chicken thighs on both sides after adding them, skin side down. Chicken Must be taken out of the pot and placed aside.
2. Add the chop-up garlic and onion to the same pot. Sauté the onion up to it turns translucent.

3. The pot Must now contain the ground cumin, coriander, turmeric, and cayenne pepper (if using). The spices Must be thoroughly combined with the onion and garlic.
4. The pot Must now contain the browned chicken thighs. Add the chicken broth and the trimmed okra. As needed, add salt and pepper to the food.
5. The okra Must be soft and the chicken Must be cooked through after about 40 mins of simmering on low heat with the lid on.
6. Add the lemon juice and, if necessary, taste and adjust the seasoning.
7. Serve the hot chicken and okra stew with fresh cilantro on top. It pairs well with bread or rice.

NUTRITION INFO (per serving):
Cals: 380
Fat: 18g
Carbs: 20g
Protein: 35g

164. Egyptian Rice and Chicken Stuffed Grape Leaves with Yogurt Sauce:

Time: 1 hr 30 mins
Servings: 4

Ingredients:
- 1 cup of long-grain rice
- 1 cup of chicken breast, cooked and shredded
- 24-30 grape leaves (preserved or fresh)
- 1 onion, lightly chop-up
- 2 tbsp olive oil
- 2 tbsp lemon juice
- 2 cloves garlic, chop-up
- 1 tsp ground cumin
- 1 tsp ground coriander
- Salt and pepper as needed

Instructions:
1. Rice, diced chicken, onion, olive oil, lemon juice, garlic, cumin, coriander, salt, and pepper Must all be combined in a big bowl. Combine thoroughly.
2. Use cold water to rinse any preserved grape leaves to get rid of the excess salt. When using fresh grape leaves, blanch them briefly in boiling water before rinsing under cold water.
3. Place roughly one tbsp of the rice and chicken Mixture in the middle of every grape leaf, one at a time.
4. Similar to rolling a burrito, fold the leaf's sides over the filling before tightly rolling it from the bottom to the top.
5. With the remaining grape leaves and filling, repeat the procedure.
6. Seam side down, arrange the packed grape leaves in a single layer in a pot. The grape leaves Must be covered with water.
7. In order to prevent the grape leaves from unraveling while cooking, put a heavy plate on top of them.
8. Once the rice is done and the grape leaves are soft, cover the saucepan and let it simmer on low heat for about an hr.
9. The yogurt sauce can be made by combining plain yogurt, chop-up garlic, lemon juice, and salt in a mini basin while you wait. Combine thoroughly.
10. Whether hot or cold, serve the stuffed grape leaves with the yogurt sauce on the side.

NUTRITION INFO (per serving):
Cals: 320
Fat: 8g
Carbs: 48g
Protein: 16g
Fiber: 3g

165. Egyptian Stuffed Zucchini with Rice and Lentils:

Time: 1 hr
Servings: 6

Ingredients:
- 6 zucchinis
- 1 cup of rice
- 1/2 cup of lentils
- 1 onion, lightly chop-up
- 2 cloves garlic, chop-up
- 2 tbsp olive oil
- 2 tbsp tomato paste
- 1 tsp ground cumin
- 1 tsp ground coriander
- 1 tsp dried mint
- Salt and pepper as needed
- Lemon wedges for serving

Instructions:

1. The zucchini's tops Must be take outd before hollowing them out with a spoon, making sure to leave a thin layer of flesh inside.
2. Rice and lentils Must be rinsed in cold water.
3. Olive oil Must be heated in a pan over medium heat. Sauté the chop-up garlic and onion up to they are transparent after being added.
4. Stir the rice and lentils for a few mins after adding them to the pan.
5. Salt, pepper, dried mint, cumin, coriander, and tomato paste Must all be combined. one more min of cooking.
6. After removing the pan from the heat, let the Mixture to gradually cool.
7. Fill every hollowed-out zucchini with a substantial amount of the rice and lentil Mixture.
8. Place the packed zucchinis closely together in a saucepan and cover with water.
9. When the water is boiling, turn the heat down to low and let the Mixture simmer for 30 to 40 mins, or up to the rice is done and the zucchinis are soft.
10. Serve the hot stuffed zucchinis with lemon wedges and fresh mint as an accompaniment.

NUTRITION INFO (per serving):
Cals: 250
Fat: 6g
Carbs: 43g
Protein: 8g
Fiber: 6g

166. Egyptian Lamb and Cauliflower Tagine with Chickpeas and Tomatoes:

Time: 2 hrs
Servings: 4

Ingredients:

- 1 lb lamb, slice into cubes
- 1 cauliflower, slice into florets
- 1 can chickpeas, drained and rinsed
- 2 tomatoes, diced
- 1 onion, lightly chop-up
- 3 cloves garlic, chop-up
- 2 tbsp olive oil
- 1 tsp ground cumin
- 1 tsp ground coriander
- 1 tsp ground turmeric
- 1/2 tsp ground cinnamon
- Salt and pepper as needed
- Fresh cilantro for garnish

Instructions:

1. Over medium heat, warm the olive oil in a sizable saucepan or tagine.
2. Add the chop-up garlic and diced onion, and sauté up to aromatic and tender.
3. Cubes of lamb Must be added to the stew and cooked up to browned all over.
4. Add the ground cumin, coriander, cinnamon, turmeric, and salt and pepper after stirring. one more min of cooking.
5. Chickpeas, chop-up tomatoes, and cauliflower florets Must all be added to the saucepan. Combine thoroughly.
6. Fill the saucepan with water so that it covers the contents.
7. The Mixture Must be brought to a boil, then simmer for 1.5 to 2 hrs, covered, up to the lamb is fork-tender and the flavors are well-balanced.
8. Serve the hot lamb and cauliflower tagine with fresh cilantro on top.

NUTRITION INFO (per serving):
Cals: 380
Fat: 18g
Carbs: 22g
Protein: 32g
Fiber: 7g

167. Egyptian Spinach and Chickpea Soup with Turmeric and Ginger:

Time: 40 mins
Servings: 6

Ingredients:

- 1 lb fresh spinach, washed and chop-up
- 1 can chickpeas, drained and rinsed
- 1 onion, lightly chop-up
- 2 cloves garlic, chop-up
- 1-inch piece of fresh ginger, finely grated
- 2 tbsp olive oil
- 1 tsp ground turmeric
- 1/2 tsp ground cumin
- 4 cups of vegetable broth
- Salt and pepper as needed

- Lemon wedges for serving

Instructions:

1. Over medium heat, warm the olive oil in a big pot.
2. To the pot, add the chop-up garlic, finely grated ginger, and the diced onion. Sauté up to they are aromatic and tender.
3. Add the ground cumin and turmeric. one more min of cooking.
4. Cook the spinach up to it wilts by adding the chop-up spinach to the pot.
5. Chickpeas and vegetable broth Must be added to the pot. The Mixture Must boil.
6. To enable the flavors to merge, turn the heat down to low, cover the pot, and simmer for around 20 to 25 mins.
7. Add salt and pepper as needed when preparing the soup.
8. Serve the hot spinach and chickpea soup with a squeeze of lemon juice as a garnish.

NUTRITION INFO (per serving):

Cals: 180
Fat: 6g
Carbs: 24g
Protein: 10g
Fiber: 8g

168. Egyptian Chicken and Egg Tagine with Moroccan Spices:

Time: 1 hr
Servings: 4

Ingredients:

- 4 chicken thighs, bone-in and skin-on
- 4 eggs
- 1 onion, lightly chop-up
- 2 cloves garlic, chop-up
- 2 tbsp olive oil
- 1 tsp ground cumin
- 1 tsp ground coriander
- 1 tsp ground paprika
- 1/2 tsp ground cinnamon
- Salt and pepper as needed
- Fresh parsley for garnish

Instructions:

1. In a deep skillet or tagine, warm the olive oil over medium heat.
2. To the tagine, add the chop-up garlic and diced onion. Sauté up to they are transparent and supple.
3. Put the skin-side down chicken thighs in the tagine. Cook up to they are well-browned all over.
4. The chicken thighs Must be covered with the ground cumin, coriander, paprika, cinnamon, salt, and pepper. Combine thoroughly.
5. Fill the tagine with water up to the chicken thighs are only half submerged. For about 30 to 40 mins, or up to the chicken is cooked through and soft, cover and boil the chicken.
6. Place the eggs in the tagine carefully, distributing them equally among the chicken thighs.
7. Once more covering the tagine, simmer it for a further 5-7 mins, or up to the eggs are done to your preference.
8. Hot chicken and egg tagine Must be served with fresh parsley on top.

NUTRITION INFO (per serving):

Cals: 360
Fat: 24g
Carbs: 5g
Protein: 30g
Fiber: 1g

169. Egyptian Rice and Vermicelli Soup with Mint and Lemon:

Time: 30 mins
Servings: 4

Ingredients:

- 1 cup of vermicelli noodles, broken into mini pieces
- 1 cup of long-grain rice
- 4 cups of vegetable broth
- 1 onion, lightly chop-up
- 2 tbsp olive oil
- 2 tbsp lemon juice
- 2 tbsp fresh mint leaves, chop-up
- Salt and pepper as needed

Instructions:

1. Over medium heat, warm the olive oil in a big pot.
2. Vermicelli noodles Must be added to the pot and cooked up to golden brown, turning constantly to avoid burning.

3. The chop-up onion Must be added to the pot and sautéed up to tender and transparent.
4. Add the rice with a stir, then boil it for a few mins to coat it with oil.
5. Then, add the veggie broth, and bring everything to a boil.
6. When the rice is cooked and soft, lower the heat to low, cover the pan, and simmer for about 15 to 20 mins.
7. Lemon juice and fresh mint leaves Must be combined. As needed, add salt and pepper to the food.
8. Serve the hot soup of rice and vermicelli.

NUTRITION INFO (per serving):

Cals: 280

Fat: 8g

Carbs: 47g

Protein: 5g

Fiber: 2g

170. Egyptian Chicken and Okra Stew with Garlic and Paprika:

Time: 1 hr 30 mins

Servings: 4

Ingredients:

- 4 chicken thighs, bone-in
- 1 lb okra, trimmed and halved
- 1 onion, lightly chop-up
- 4 cloves garlic, chop-up
- 2 tbsp olive oil
- 2 tbsp tomato paste
- 1 tsp paprika
- 1 tsp ground cumin
- 1/2 tsp ground coriander
- Salt and pepper as needed
- 4 cups of chicken broth
- Fresh cilantro, chop-up (for garnish)

Instructions:

1. Olive oil Must be heated in a sizable pot over medium heat. Brown the chicken thighs on every sides after adding them. Chicken Must be taken out of the pot and placed aside.
2. Add the onion and garlic to the same pot. Sauté the onion up to it turns translucent.
3. Add the salt, pepper, paprika, cumin, coriander, and tomato paste after stirring. For 1-2 mins, cook.
4. Add the chicken broth and put the chicken thighs back in the pot. Boil for a few mins, then turn down the heat, cover the pot, and simmer for 45 mins.
5. Okra Must be tender after an additional 15 mins of cooking after being added to the saucepan.
6. Serve the stew hot with fresh cilantro on top.

NUTRITION INFO (per serving):

Cals: 350

Protein: 25g

Fat: 20g

Carbs: 20g

Fiber: 6g

171. Egyptian Rice and Chicken Stuffed Grape Leaves with Dill-Yogurt Sauce:

Time: 1 hr 30 mins

Servings: 6

Ingredients:

- 1 cup of long-grain rice
- 1 lb chicken breast, cooked and shredded
- 1/2 cup of fresh parsley, lightly chop-up
- 1/4 cup of fresh dill, lightly chop-up
- 1/4 cup of fresh mint, lightly chop-up
- 1/4 cup of lemon juice
- 2 tbsp olive oil
- 1 tsp ground cumin
- 1/2 tsp ground coriander
- Salt and pepper as needed
- 1 jar grape leaves, drained and rinsed
- Dill-Yogurt Sauce:
- 1 cup of Greek yogurt
- 2 tbsp fresh dill, lightly chop-up
- 1 clove garlic, chop-up
- Salt and pepper as needed

Instructions:

1. Cooked chicken, rice, parsley, dill, mint, lemon juice, extra virgin olive oil, cumin, coriander, salt, and pepper Must all be combined in a big bowl. Combine thoroughly.
2. A clean surface Must have a grape leaf on it. Place two tsp or so of the chicken and rice Mixture in the leaf's middle. Wrap the leaf tightly after folding the sides over the filling. Repetition is required with the remaining grape leaves and filling.

3. Place the packed grape leaves seam side down in a big pot. The grape leaves Must be covered with water. To weigh the grape leaves down while they cook, place a heatproof plate on top of them.
4. Heat the water to a rolling boil, then lower the heat, cover the pot, and simmer for one hr.
5. Combine the yogurt, dill, garlic, salt, and pepper in a bowl to make the dill-yogurt sauce in the interim. Combine thoroughly.
6. Serve the stuffed grape leaves hot with the dill-yogurt sauce on the side.

NUTRITION INFO (per serving):
Cals: 320
Protein: 22g
Fat: 8g
Carbs: 42g
Fiber: 4g

172. Egyptian Stuffed Zucchini with Rice and Chickpeas in Tomato Sauce:

Time: 1 hr 30 mins
Servings: 4

Ingredients:

- 4 Big zucchini
- 1 cup of long-grain rice
- 1 cup of canned chickpeas, drained and rinsed
- 1 onion, lightly chop-up
- 2 cloves garlic, chop-up
- 2 tbsp olive oil
- 1 can diced tomatoes (14 oz)
- 1 tsp ground cumin
- 1/2 tsp ground cinnamon
- 1/2 tsp ground coriander
- Salt and pepper as needed
- Fresh parsley, chop-up (for garnish)

Instructions:

1. Scoop out the meat of the zucchini after removing the tips, leaving the shell behind. Slice the flesh off the zucchini after scooping it out.
2. Olive oil Must be heated in a sizable skillet over medium heat. Sauté the onion and garlic up to the onion is transparent after adding them.
3. Cook the zucchini flesh in the skillet for two to three mins. Rice, chickpeas, diced tomatoes, cumin, cinnamon, coriander, salt, and pepper are all added while stirring. Cook for a further two mins.
4. Place the rice and chickpea Mixture inside the zucchini shells, carefully pushing the filling into place.
5. In a baking dish, spread the tomato sauce over the stuffed zucchini. The dish is covered with foil.
6. Bake the zucchini for 45 mins at 375°F (190°C) in an oven that has been prepared.
7. Hot stuffed zucchini Must be served with fresh parsley on top.

NUTRITION INFO (per serving):
Cals: 280
Protein: 8g
Fat: 8g
Carbs: 47g
Fiber: 7g

173. Egyptian Lamb and Cauliflower Tagine with Turmeric and Cardamom:

Time: 2 hrs
Servings: 6

Ingredients:

- 2 lbs lamb Muster, cubed
- 1 cauliflower, slice into florets
- 2 onions, lightly chop-up
- 4 cloves garlic, chop-up
- 2 tbsp olive oil
- 2 tsp ground turmeric
- 1 tsp ground cardamom
- 1 tsp ground cumin
- 1/2 tsp ground cinnamon
- Salt and pepper as needed
- 4 cups of chicken broth
- Fresh cilantro, chop-up (for garnish)

Instructions:

1. Heat the olive oil in a sizable saucepan or tagine over medium heat. Brown the lamb cubes all over after adding them. Lamb Must be taken out of the saucepan and placed aside.
2. Add the onions and garlic to the same pot. The onions Must be sautéed up to transparent and tender.
3. Add the salt, pepper, cumin, cinnamon, turmeric, and cardamom. For 1-2 mins, cook.
4. Add the cauliflower florets and the lamb back to the saucepan. Put some chicken broth in there.

Bring to a boil, lower the heat to a simmer, cover the pot, and cook for one hr and thirty mins, or up to the lamb is cooked.
5. Serve the tagine hot with fresh cilantro as a garnish.

NUTRITION INFO (per serving):

Cals: 420

Protein: 30g

Fat: 20g

Carbs: 30g

Fiber: 7g

174. Egyptian Spinach and Chickpea Soup with Harissa and Cilantro:

Time: 45 mins

Servings: 4

Ingredients:

- 1 tbsp olive oil
- 1 onion, lightly chop-up
- 2 cloves garlic, chop-up
- 1 tsp ground cumin
- 1/2 tsp ground coriander
- 1/2 tsp harissa paste
- 4 cups of vegetable broth
- 2 cups of packed fresh spinach leaves
- 1 can chickpeas, drained and rinsed
- Salt and pepper as needed
- Fresh cilantro, chop-up (for garnish)

Instructions:

1. Olive oil Must be heated in a sizable pot over medium heat. Once the onion is tender and transparent, add the garlic and continue to sauté.
2. Add the harissa paste, cumin, and coriander after stirring. For one min, cook.
3. The veggie broth Must be added and brought to a boil.
4. Add the chickpeas and spinach leaves to the saucepan. Cook the spinach for 5-7 mins, or up to it wilts.
5. Puree the soup using a standard blender or an immersion blender up to it is smooth.
6. As needed, add salt and pepper to the food.
7. Serve the soup hot with fresh cilantro on top.

NUTRITION INFO (per serving):

Cals: 180

Protein: 8g

Fat: 6g

Carbs: 25g

Fiber: 7g

175. Egyptian Chicken and Egg Tagine with Preserved Lemon and Olives:

Time: 1 hr 30 mins

Servings: 4

Ingredients:

- 4 chicken thighs, bone-in
- 1 onion, lightly chop-up
- 2 cloves garlic, chop-up
- 2 tbsp olive oil
- 1 tsp ground cumin
- 1/2 tsp ground coriander
- 1/2 tsp ground ginger
- 1/4 tsp ground cinnamon
- Salt and pepper as needed
- 2 cups of chicken broth
- 1 preserved lemon, pulp take outd and rind chop-up
- 1/2 cup of green olives
- 4 eggs
- Fresh parsley, chop-up (for garnish)

Instructions:

1. Heat the olive oil in a sizable saucepan or tagine over medium heat. Brown the chicken thighs on every sides after adding them. Chicken Must be taken out of the pot and placed aside.
2. Add the onion and garlic to the same pot. The onion Must be cooked up to tender and transparent.
3. Add the salt, pepper, ginger, cinnamon, cumin, and coriander. For 1-2 mins, cook.
4. Add the chicken broth and put the chicken thighs back in the pot. After bringing to a boil, turn down the heat, cover the pan, and simmer for one hr.
5. Cook for 15 more mins after adding the preserved lemon and olives.
6. Once the eggs are cracked into the saucepan, cover it and cook for 5-7 mins, depending on how done you like your eggs.
7. Serve the tagine hot with fresh parsley as a garnish.

NUTRITION INFO (per serving):

Cals: 400

Protein: 30g
Fat: 26g
Carbs: 8g
Fiber: 2g

176. Egyptian Stuffed Bell Peppers with Rice and Feta Cheese

Time: 1 hr 30 mins
Servings: 4

Ingredients:

- 4 Big bell peppers (any color)
- 1 cup of cooked rice
- 1/2 cup of cut up feta cheese
- 1/4 cup of chop-up fresh parsley
- 1/4 cup of chop-up fresh mint
- 1 mini onion, lightly chop-up
- 2 cloves garlic, chop-up
- 2 tbsp olive oil
- 1 tsp ground cumin
- 1/2 tsp ground cinnamon
- Salt and pepper as needed
- 1 cup of tomato sauce
- 1 cup of vegetable broth

Instructions:

1. Set the oven's temperature to 375°F (190°C).
2. The bell peppers' tops Must be slice off, and the seeds and membranes Must be take outd.
3. Cooked rice, feta cheese, parsley, mint, onion, garlic, olive oil, cumin, cinnamon, salt, and pepper Must all be combined in a big bowl. Combine thoroughly.
4. Place the bell peppers upright in a baking dish after stuffing them with the rice Mixture.
5. Combine the tomato sauce and vegetable broth in a different bowl. Over the filled peppers, pour the Mixture.
6. Bake for 45 mins with the foil covering the baking dish.
7. When the peppers are soft and the tops are just beginning to brown, take out the cover and bake for another 15 mins.
8. Serve warm.

NUTRITION INFO per serving:
Cals: 250
Fat: 10g
Carbs: 32g
Protein: 8g

177. Egyptian Lamb Tagine with Prunes and Cinnamon

Time: 2 hrs 30 mins
Servings: 6

Ingredients:

- 2 lbs lamb Muster, slice into cubes
- 1 Big onion, lightly chop-up
- 4 cloves garlic, chop-up
- 2 tbsp olive oil
- 1 tsp ground cumin
- 1 tsp ground cinnamon
- 1/2 tsp ground ginger
- 1/2 tsp ground turmeric
- 1/4 tsp cayenne pepper (non-compulsory)
- Salt and pepper as needed
- 1 cup of pitted prunes
- 1 cup of chicken broth
- 2 tbsp honey
- 2 tbsp toasted sesame seeds (for garnish)
- Chop-up fresh parsley (for garnish)

Instructions:

1. Heat the olive oil in a sizable saucepan or tagine over medium heat. Brown the lamb cubes all over after adding them.
2. To the pot, add the chop-up garlic and chop-up onion, and cook up to the onion is transparent.
3. Add the salt, pepper, cayenne pepper (if using), turmeric, ginger, cumin, and cinnamon. To toast the spices, cook for 1-2 mins.
4. Prune, chicken broth, and honey Must all be added to the pot. To blend, thoroughly stir.
5. When the lamb is cooked, stew it for two hrs with the lid on over low heat.
6. Warm lamb tagine Must be served with toasted sesame seeds and fresh parsley slice on top.

NUTRITION INFO per serving:
Cals: 380
Fat: 20g
Carbs: 20g
Protein: 30g

178. Egyptian Rice and Beef Stuffed Cabbage Leaves with Tomato-Pepper Sauce

Time: 1 hr 30 mins

Servings: 4

Ingredients:

- 1 Big head of cabbage
- 1 lb ground beef
- 1 cup of cooked rice
- 1/4 cup of chop-up fresh parsley
- 1/4 cup of chop-up fresh dill
- 1 mini onion, lightly chop-up
- 2 cloves garlic, chop-up
- 2 tbsp olive oil
- 1 tsp ground cumin
- 1/2 tsp ground cinnamon
- Salt and pepper as needed
- 1 cup of tomato sauce
- 1 cup of vegetable broth
- 1 bell pepper, split

Instructions:

1. Bring water in a big pot to a boil. For about 5 mins, or up to the outer leaves are melted and can be easily detached, add the entire head of cabbage. Take the cabbage out of the water, then let it to cool a little.
2. Ground beef, cooked rice, parsley, dill, onion, garlic, extra virgin olive oil, cumin, cinnamon, salt, and pepper Must all be combined in a big bowl. Combine thoroughly.
3. Peel the cabbage leaves off with care, then take out the rough stem ends.
4. Every cabbage leaf Must have a scoop of the beef and rice Mixture in the center. The leaf Must be tightly rolled up by tucking in the sides as you go.
5. Place the packed cabbage leaves in a single layer in a big pot. Over the cabbage rolls, pour the tomato sauce and vegetable broth.
6. To the pot, add the bell pepper slices.
7. Once the cabbage is cooked and the flavors are blended, simmer the dish with the lid on for 45 to 1 hr over low heat.
8. Serve the tomato-pepper sauce alongside the hot packed cabbage rolls.

NUTRITION INFO per serving:
Cals: 390
Fat: 18g
Carbs: 30g
Protein: 27g

179. Egyptian Stuffed Eggplant with Rice and Peas

Time: 1 hr 15 mins

Servings: 4

Ingredients:

- 2 Big eggplants
- 1 cup of cooked rice
- 1/2 cup of refrigerate peas, thawed
- 1/4 cup of chop-up fresh parsley
- 1/4 cup of chop-up fresh mint
- 1 mini onion, lightly chop-up
- 2 cloves garlic, chop-up
- 2 tbsp olive oil
- 1 tsp ground cumin
- 1/2 tsp ground cinnamon
- Salt and pepper as needed
- 1 cup of tomato sauce
- 1 cup of vegetable broth

Instructions:

1. Set the oven's temperature to 375°F (190°C).
2. Slice the eggplants in half lengthwise, take out the flesh, and leave a shell that is approximately 1/2 inch thick. Slice the flesh of the eggplant into tiny pieces.
3. Olive oil Must be heated in a sizable skillet over medium heat. Add the chop-up onion, garlic, and eggplant. Sauté the eggplant up to it's tender and just starting to color.
4. The skillet Must now contain the cooked rice, peas, parsley, mint, cumin, cinnamon, salt, and pepper. Blend thoroughly.
5. Place the rice and veggie Mixture inside the eggplant shells.
6. The stuffed eggplants Must be put in a baking dish.
7. Combine the tomato sauce and vegetable broth in a different bowl. Over the filled eggplants, pour the Mixture.
8. Bake for 45 mins with the foil covering the baking dish.
9. When the eggplants are soft and the tops are just beginning to brown, take out the cover and bake for another 15 mins.
10. Serve warm.

NUTRITION INFO per serving:

Cals: 280

Fat: 10g

Carbs: 40g

Protein: 8g

180. Egyptian Lamb and Potato Tagine with Carrots and Cumin

Time: 2 hrs

Servings: 6

Ingredients:

- 2 lbs lamb stew meat, cubed
- 1 Big onion, lightly chop-up
- 4 cloves garlic, chop-up
- 2 tbsp olive oil
- 1 tsp ground cumin
- 1/2 tsp ground cinnamon
- 1/2 tsp ground coriander
- 1/4 tsp cayenne pepper (non-compulsory)
- Salt and pepper as needed
- 4 carrots, peel off and slice into chunks
- 3 potatoes, peel off and slice into chunks
- 2 cups of chicken broth
- Chop-up fresh cilantro (for garnish)

Instructions:

1. Heat the olive oil in a sizable saucepan or tagine over medium heat. Brown the lamb cubes all over after adding them.
2. To the pot, add the chop-up garlic and chop-up onion, and cook up to the onion is transparent.
3. Add the salt, pepper, cayenne pepper (if using), cumin, cinnamon, and coriander. To toast the spices, cook for 1-2 mins.
4. To the pot, add the potatoes, carrots, and chicken broth. To blend, thoroughly stir.
5. Once the lamb is cooked and the flavors are well-balanced, simmer the dish with the lid on for 1 hr 30 mins over low heat.
6. Serve the hot lamb and potato tagine with fresh cilantro that has been chop-up.

NUTRITION INFO per serving:

Cals: 420

Fat: 20g

Carbs: 30g

Protein: 30g

181. Egyptian Spinach and Lentil Salad with Lemon-Tahini Dressing

Time: 30 mins

Servings: 4

Ingredients:

- 4 cups of fresh spinach leaves
- 1 cup of cooked lentils
- 1/2 cup of cherry tomatoes, halved
- 1/4 cup of chop-up red onion
- 2 tbsp chop-up fresh parsley
- 2 tbsp chop-up fresh mint
- 2 tbsp lemon juice
- 1 tbsp tahini
- 1 tbsp olive oil
- 1 clove garlic, chop-up
- Salt and pepper as needed

Instructions:

1. Combine the spinach, lentils, cherry tomatoes, red onion, parsley, and mint in a sizable bowl. Combine thoroughly by tossing.
2. To create the dressing, combine the lemon juice, tahini, olive oil, garlic, salt, and pepper in a mini bowl.
3. Toss the salad to uniformly coat the items with the dressing after pouring it over it.
4. Serve the lentil and spinach salad right away.

NUTRITION INFO per serving:

Cals: 180

Fat: 7g

Carbs: 20g

Protein: 10g

182. Egyptian Spinach and Lentil Salad with Pomegranate Dressing:

Time: 30 mins

Servings: 4

Ingredients:

- 2 cups of fresh spinach leaves
- 1 cup of cooked lentils
- 1/2 cup of pomegranate seeds
- 1/4 cup of chop-up red onion
- 1/4 cup of cut up feta cheese
- 1/4 cup of chop-up walnuts
- For the dressing:
- 2 tbsp pomegranate juice

- 1 tbsp lemon juice
- 1 tbsp olive oil
- 1 tsp honey
- Salt and pepper as needed

Instructions:

1. Combine the spinach, lentils, pomegranate seeds, red onion, feta cheese, and walnuts in a sizable salad dish.
2. The dressing is made by combining the pomegranate juice, lemon juice, olive oil, honey, salt, and pepper in a mini bowl.
3. Over the salad, drizzle the dressing, and combine to blend.
4. Enjoy the salad right away after serving it.

NUTRITION INFO (per serving):

Cals: 220
Protein: 12g
Carbs: 24g
Fat: 9g
Fiber: 7g

183. Egyptian Chicken and Okra Stew with Turmeric and Coriander:

Time: 1 hr
Servings: 6

Ingredients:

- 1.5 lbs chicken, slice into pieces
- 1 lb okra, stems trimmed
- 1 onion, chop-up
- 3 cloves garlic, chop-up
- 2 tomatoes, diced
- 2 tbsp tomato paste
- 2 tsp ground turmeric
- 1 tsp ground coriander
- 4 cups of chicken broth
- Salt and pepper as needed
- Fresh cilantro, chop-up (for garnish)

Instructions:

1. Combine the spinach, lentils, pomegranate seeds, red onion, feta cheese, and walnuts in a sizable salad dish.
2. The dressing is made by combining the pomegranate juice, lemon juice, olive oil, honey, salt, and pepper in a mini bowl.
3. Over the salad, drizzle the dressing, and combine to blend.
4. Enjoy the salad right away after serving it.

NUTRITION INFO (per serving):

Cals: 280
Protein: 26g
Carbs: 20g
Fat: 10g
Fiber: 5g

184. Egyptian Rice and Chicken Stuffed Grape Leaves with Mint-Yogurt Sauce:

Time: 1 hr 30 mins
Servings: 4

Ingredients:

- 1 cup of long-grain rice
- 1/2 lb ground chicken
- 1/4 cup of chop-up fresh parsley
- 2 tbsp chop-up fresh mint
- 1 tbsp chop-up fresh dill
- 1/2 tsp ground cinnamon
- 1/2 tsp ground allspice
- Salt and pepper as needed
- 24 grape leaves, drained if canned
- For the Mint-Yogurt Sauce:
- 1 cup of plain yogurt
- 2 tbsp chop-up fresh mint
- 1 tbsp lemon juice
- Salt and pepper as needed

Instructions:

1. Rice, ground chicken, parsley, mint, dill, cinnamon, allspice, salt, and pepper Must all be combined in a bowl. Combine thoroughly.
2. A grape leaf Must be placed glossy side down on a level surface. Place 1 tbsp or so of the rice and chicken Mixture in the leaf's middle.
3. The leaf is rolled up firmly by first folding the bottom over the contents and then the sides.
4. With the remaining grape leaves and filling, repeat the procedure.
5. Place the packed grape leaves in a single layer in a big container. The grape leaves Must be covered with water.
6. To keep the grape leaves in the water, place a plate on top of them. For roughly an hr, or up to the rice is cooked and the grape leaves are soft, cover the saucepan and simmer.
7. The Mint-Yogurt Sauce Must be made in the

meantime by blending yogurt, mint, lemon juice, salt, and pepper in a bowl. Combine thoroughly.

8. Serve the stuffed grape leaves with the mint-yogurt sauce hot or at room temperature.

NUTRITION INFO (per serving):
Cals: 330
Protein: 18g
Carbs: 43g
Fat: 8g
Fiber: 5g

185. Egyptian Rice and Vermicelli Pilaf with Pistachios and Saffron

Time: 45 mins
Servings: 4

Ingredients:

- 1 cup of long-grain rice
- 1/2 cup of vermicelli noodles, broken into mini pieces
- 2 tbsp butter
- 2 cups of chicken or vegetable broth
- 1/4 tsp saffron threads
- 1/4 cup of shelled pistachios, chop-up
- Salt, as needed

Instructions:

1. Rice Must be thoroughly rinsed in cold water up to the water is clear. Flow freely.
2. Melt the butter in a Big skillet over medium heat. While continuously stirring, add the vermicelli noodles and cook up to golden brown.
3. The rice Must be added to the skillet and cooked for a few mins while being stirred to evenly distribute the butter.
4. Bring the broth to a simmer in a separate mini pot. Add the saffron threads to the simmering soup after dissolving them in a tbsp of hot water.
5. Over the rice and vermicelli in the skillet, pour the broth Mixture. As needed, add salt to the dish. After bringing to a boil, turn down the heat. For 20 to 25 mins, or up to the rice is cooked through and the liquid has been absorbed, cover and simmer the rice.
6. After being taken off the heat, the pilaf Must sit covered for 5 mins. With a fork, fluff the rice.
7. Before serving, add some chop-up pistachios as a garnish.

NUTRITION INFO (per serving):
Cals: 280
Fat: 11g
Carbs: 39g
Protein: 6g

186. Egyptian Stuffed Bell Peppers with Rice and Herbs

Time: 1 hr
Servings: 6

Ingredients:

- 6 bell peppers (any color)
- 1 cup of long-grain rice
- 1 onion, lightly chop-up
- 2 cloves garlic, chop-up
- 2 tomatoes, diced
- 1/4 cup of fresh parsley, chop-up
- 1/4 cup of fresh mint, chop-up
- 1/4 cup of olive oil
- 1 tsp ground cumin
- 1/2 tsp ground coriander
- Salt and pepper, as needed
- Water, as needed

Instructions:

1. Set the oven's temperature to 350°F (175°C).
2. The bell peppers' tops Must be slice off, and the seeds and membranes Must be take outd. Place aside.
3. Rice, onion, garlic, tomatoes, parsley, mint, olive oil, cumin, coriander, salt, and pepper Must all be combined in a big bowl. Combine thoroughly.
4. Pack the rice Mixture tightly within the bell peppers.
5. In a baking dish, arrange the filled peppers vertically. Fill the dish with water up to it is about 1/4 inch deep.
6. Bake the dish in the oven for 40 to 45 mins, or up to the rice is done and the peppers are soft.
7. As a side dish or as a main course, serve hot.

NUTRITION INFO (per serving):
Cals: 240
Fat: 8g
Carbs: 38g
Protein: 4g

187. Egyptian Lamb Tagine with Almonds and Ras el Hanout

Time: 2 hrs 30 mins

Servings: 4

Ingredients:

- 1.5 lbs (700g) lamb Muster, slice into cubes
- 1 onion, lightly chop-up
- 3 cloves garlic, chop-up
- 2 tbsp olive oil
- 2 tsp ras el hanout spice blend
- 1 tsp ground cumin
- 1/2 tsp ground cinnamon
- 1/2 tsp ground ginger
- 1/4 tsp ground turmeric
- 1 cup of chicken or vegetable broth
- 1/2 cup of dried apricots, chop-up
- 1/2 cup of blanched almonds
- Salt and pepper, as needed
- Fresh cilantro, for garnish (non-compulsory)

Instructions:

1. Over medium heat, warm the olive oil in a sizable saucepan or tagine. Add the lamb cubes and sauté them up to evenly browned. Lamb Must be taken out of the saucepan and placed aside.
2. Add the chop-up garlic and onion to the same pot. Sauté the onion up to it becomes transparent and tender.
3. Add the ras el hanout, cumin, cinnamon, ginger, turmeric, salt, and pepper to the saucepan with the lamb once more. To evenly distribute the spices and lamb, stir thoroughly.
4. Add the chicken or vegetable broth, then boil the Mixture. Cook the lamb for about two hrs, covered, on low heat, or up to it is tender.
5. To the pot, add the chop-up blanched almonds and dried apricots. To blend, stir.
6. For the sauce to slightly thicken and the flavors to come together, simmer it for an additional 30 mins, uncovered.
7. If preferred, garnish the hot lamb tagine with fresh cilantro. It goes great with couscous or steaming rice.

NUTRITION INFO (per serving):
Cals: 460
Fat: 27g
Carbs: 20g
Protein: 36g

188. Egyptian Rice and Beef Stuffed Cabbage Leaves with Tamarind Sauce

Time: 1 hr 30 mins

Servings: 6

Ingredients:

- 12 Big cabbage leaves
- 1/2 lb (225g) ground beef
- 1/2 cup of long-grain rice
- 1 onion, lightly chop-up
- 2 cloves garlic, chop-up
- 1/4 cup of fresh parsley, chop-up
- 1/4 cup of fresh mint, chop-up
- 2 tbsp olive oil
- 1 tsp ground cumin
- 1/2 tsp ground cinnamon
- Salt and pepper, as needed
- Water, as needed
- Tamarind Sauce:
- 1/2 cup of tamarind pulp
- 1 cup of water
- 2 tbsp honey
- Salt, as needed

Instructions:

1. Bring water in a big pot to a boil. After adding, blanch the cabbage leaves for 2 mins, or up to they are soft. Drain, then set apart.
2. Ground beef, rice, onion, garlic, parsley, mint, olive oil, cumin, cinnamon, salt, and pepper Must all be combined in a bowl. Combine thoroughly.
3. Lay a cabbage leaf out on a spotless work area. Place some of the beef and rice Mixture in the leaf's middle. The leaf's sides Must be folded over the filling before being securely rolled. Repeat with the remaining filling and cabbage leaves.
4. In a big pot, put the stuffed cabbage rolls. The rolls Must be covered with water.
5. Using a medium heat, bring the pot to a simmer. For about 45 mins, or up to the rice is done and the cabbage is soft, simmer the dish covered.
6. Make the tamarind sauce while the cabbage rolls are cooking. The tamarind pulp and water Must be combined in a mini saucepan. After bringing to a boil, lower the heat, and simmer for 10 mins, or up to the tamarind pulp has broken down and the Mixture has somewhat thickened.
7. Add the salt and honey, and then taste and adjust the sweetness as desired.

8. Warm stuffed cabbage rolls with tamarind sauce are served.

NUTRITION INFO (per serving):
Cals: 280
Fat: 10g
Carbs: 34g
Protein: 14g

189. Egyptian Stuffed Eggplant with Rice and Tomato-Herb Sauce

Time: 1 hr 30 mins
Servings: 4

Ingredients:

- 2 Big eggplants
- 1 cup of long-grain rice
- 1 onion, lightly chop-up
- 2 cloves garlic, chop-up
- 2 tomatoes, diced
- 1/4 cup of fresh parsley, chop-up
- 1/4 cup of fresh mint, chop-up
- 2 tbsp olive oil
- 1 tsp ground cumin
- 1/2 tsp ground coriander
- Salt and pepper, as needed
- Tomato-Herb Sauce:
- 2 tbsp olive oil
- 1 onion, lightly chop-up
- 2 cloves garlic, chop-up
- 4 tomatoes, diced
- 1 tbsp tomato paste
- 1/4 cup of fresh parsley, chop-up
- 1/4 cup of fresh mint, chop-up
- 1 tsp ground cumin
- 1/2 tsp ground coriander
- Salt and pepper, as needed

Instructions:

1. Set the oven's temperature to 375°F (190°C).
2. The eggplants Must be split lengthwise. Making sure not to penetrate the skin, crisscross-score the flesh. To take out any bitterness, salt the slice sides and let them to sit for 10 mins. Towel dry after rinsing.
3. Put the slice-side-up eggplant halves on a baking sheet. Sprinkle with olive oil, then roast for about 30 mins, or up to the flesh is soft, in the preheated oven.
4. Prepare the stuffing while the eggplant is roasting. The rice Must be prepared as directed on the packaging.
5. Olive oil Must be heated in a skillet over medium heat. Add the chop-up garlic and onion, and cook up to the onion is transparent and tender.
6. The skillet Must now contain the diced tomatoes, parsley, mint, cumin, coriander, salt, and pepper. The tomatoes Must soften after a few mins of cooking.
7. Add the cooked rice and thoroughly incorporate it into the tomato sauce. Get rid of the heat.
8. After the eggplant has finished roasting, carefully take out the flesh, reserving a thin layer that is still adhered to the skin. Slice the flesh that was take outd and stir it into the rice Mixture. Combine thoroughly.
9. Pack the rice and tomato Mixture tightly inside the eggplant halves.
10. Warm up the olive oil in a pot over medium heat while you make the tomato-herb sauce. Add the chop-up garlic and onion, and cook up to the onion softens.
11. To the pot, add the chop-up tomatoes, tomato paste, parsley, mint, cumin, coriander, salt, and pepper. 10 mins Must pass while simmering for a modest sauce thickening.
12. Over the filled eggplants, pour the tomato-herb sauce. Bake the baking sheet again for an additional 15 to 20 mins.
13. Serve the tomato-herb sauce alongside the heated stuffed eggplants.

NUTRITION INFO (per serving):
Cals: 320
Fat: 10g
Carbs: 52g
Protein: 8g

190. Egyptian Lamb and Potato Tagine with Prunes and Ginger

Time: 2 hrs
Servings: 4

Ingredients:

- 1.5 lbs (700g) lamb stew meat, cubed
- 2 onions, lightly chop-up
- 3 cloves garlic, chop-up
- 2 tbsp olive oil
- 2 tsp ground cumin
- 1 tsp ground coriander

- 1 tsp ground ginger
- 1/2 tsp ground cinnamon
- Salt and pepper, as needed
- 4 potatoes, peel off and slice into chunks
- 1 cup of pitted prunes
- 1 cup of chicken or vegetable broth
- Fresh cilantro, for garnish (non-compulsory)

Instructions:

1. Over medium heat, warm the olive oil in a sizable saucepan or tagine. Add the lamb cubes and sauté them up to evenly browned. Lamb Must be taken out of the saucepan and placed aside.
2. Add the chop-up garlic and onion in the same pot. The onions Must be sautéed up to transparent and tender.
3. Add the ground cumin, ground coriander, ground ginger, ground cinnamon, salt, and pepper to the saucepan with the lamb once more. To evenly distribute the spices and lamb, stir thoroughly.
4. Add the chicken or vegetable broth to the pot along with the potatoes and prunes. To blend, stir.
5. Simmer the Mixture for a short while. Cook the potatoes and lamb covered in the pot over low heat for about 1 hr 30 mins, or up to the potatoes are soft.
6. If preferred, garnish the hot lamb and potato tagine with fresh cilantro. It goes great with crusty bread or couscous.

NUTRITION INFO (per serving):

Cals: 480

Fat: 14g

Carbs: 52g

Protein: 38g

191. Egyptian Stuffed Zucchini with Rice and Dill in Lemon Sauce

Time: 1 hr

Servings: 4

Ingredients:

- 8 mini zucchini
- 1 cup of rice
- 1/2 cup of chop-up fresh dill
- 2 tbsp olive oil
- 1 onion, lightly chop-up
- 2 garlic cloves, chop-up
- 1 tsp ground cumin
- 1 tsp ground coriander
- Salt and pepper as needed
- Juice of 2 lemons
- 2 cups of vegetable broth

Instructions:

1. Scoop out the meat of the zucchini after removing the tips, leaving the shell behind. Place aside.
2. The olive oil Must be heated in a saucepan over medium heat. Saute the onion and garlic till transparent after adding them.
3. To the pot, incorporate the rice, lightly split zucchini flesh, dill, cumin, coriander, salt, and pepper. While constantly stirring, cook for 2 to 3 mins.
4. Place the rice Mixture within the zucchini skins.
5. In a big pot, put the stuffed zucchini. Lemon juice and vegetable broth Must be added. The zucchini must be submerged in the liquid.
6. When the rice and zucchini are cooked, turn the heat down to low and let the Mixture simmer for 30 to 40 mins.
7. Place the lemon sauce on top of the filled zucchini before serving.

NUTRITION INFO (per serving):

Cals: 220

Fat: 7g

Carbs: 36g

Protein: 5g

192. Egyptian Lamb and Cauliflower Tagine with Saffron and Cinnamon

Time: 2 hrs

Servings: 6

Ingredients:

- 2 lbs lamb, slice into cubes
- 1 cauliflower, slice into florets
- 1 onion, chop-up
- 4 garlic cloves, chop-up
- 2 tbsp olive oil
- 2 tsp ground cumin
- 1 tsp ground cinnamon
- 1/2 tsp saffron threads
- Salt and pepper as needed
- 2 cups of vegetable broth
- 1/4 cup of chop-up fresh parsley

Instructions:

1. Over medium heat, warm the olive oil in a sizable saucepan or tagine. Add the lamb and cook it up to it is well-browned all over.
2. The onion and garlic Must be added to the stew and cooked up to tender.
3. Add the salt, pepper, saffron, cumin, and cinnamon.
4. Vegetable broth and cauliflower florets Must be added to the pot. When the lamb is tender, simmer for 1.5 to 2 hrs over low heat after bringing to a boil.
5. Serve the tagine hot with chop-up parsley as a garnish.

NUTRITION INFO (per serving):
Cals: 380
Fat: 23g
Carbs: 10g
Protein: 32g

193. Egyptian Spinach and Chickpea Soup with Lemon and Cumin

Time: 40 mins
Servings: 4

Ingredients:

- 1 onion, chop-up
- 2 garlic cloves, chop-up
- 2 tbsp olive oil
- 4 cups of fresh spinach leaves
- 1 can chickpeas, drained and rinsed
- 4 cups of vegetable broth
- Juice of 1 lemon
- 1 tsp ground cumin
- Salt and pepper as needed

Instructions:

1. Over medium heat, warm the olive oil in a big pot. Add the onion and garlic, then cook up to they are tender.
2. Cook the spinach leaves in the pot up to they are completely wilted.
3. Add the chickpeas, vegetable broth, cumin, salt, and pepper. Stir in the lemon juice. Once it has boiled, turn down the heat, cover, and simmer for 20 mins.
4. Pour the soup into a blender or use an immersion blender to puree it.
5. With a drizzle of olive oil and a dusting of cumin, serve the soup hot.

NUTRITION INFO (per serving):
Cals: 180
Fat: 7g
Carbs: 23g
Protein: 8g

194. Egyptian Chicken and Egg Tagine with Harissa and Paprika

Time: 1 hr
Servings: 4

Ingredients:

- 4 chicken thighs, bone-in and skin-on
- 1 onion, lightly chop-up
- 2 garlic cloves, chop-up
- 2 tbsp olive oil
- 2 tsp harissa paste
- 1 tsp paprika
- Salt and pepper as needed
- 4 eggs
- Chop-up fresh cilantro for garnish

Instructions:

1. Over medium heat, warm the olive oil in a sizable saucepan or tagine. Add the chicken thighs and sauté them up to they are evenly browned. Take out and reserve the chicken.
2. The onion and garlic Must be added to the same saucepan and sautéed up to tender.
3. Add salt, pepper, paprika, harissa paste, and other seasonings.
4. Add enough water to the pot to cover the chicken before adding it back. Boil for a few mins, then turn down the heat and simmer for 30 mins.
5. Make sure the eggs are equally spread in the tagine before carefully cracking them. Once the eggs are cooked to your preference, continue cooking them covered for an additional 5-7 mins.
6. Serve hot and garnish with chop-up cilantro.

NUTRITION INFO (per serving):
Cals: 320
Fat: 22g
Carbs: 4g
Protein: 26g

195. Egyptian Rice and Vermicelli Soup with Chickpeas and Parsley

Time: 30 mins
Servings: 6

Ingredients:

- 1 cup of rice
- 1/2 cup of vermicelli noodles, broken into mini pieces
- 1 onion, chop-up
- 2 garlic cloves, chop-up
- 2 tbsp olive oil
- 4 cups of vegetable broth
- 1 can chickpeas, drained and rinsed
- 1/4 cup of chop-up fresh parsley
- Salt and pepper as needed

Instructions:

1. Olive oil Must be heated in a sizable pot over medium heat. Vermicelli noodles Must be added and cooked up to golden brown.
2. Sauté the onion and garlic in the pot up to they are tender.
3. Add salt, pepper, chickpeas, vegetable broth, and rice to the dish. Bring to a boil, then lower the heat to a simmer, covering the pot, and cook the rice for 15 to 20 mins.
4. Serve hot after adding the parsley.

NUTRITION INFO (per serving):
Cals: 250
Fat: 7g
Carbs: 42g
Protein: 8g

196. Egyptian Stuffed Bell Peppers with Rice and Tomato-Pepper Sauce

Time: 1 hr 30 mins
Servings: 4

Ingredients:

- 4 bell peppers (any color)
- 1 cup of long-grain rice
- 1 onion, lightly chop-up
- 2 cloves garlic, chop-up
- 1 tomato, diced
- 1/4 cup of chop-up fresh parsley
- 1/4 cup of chop-up fresh mint
- 2 tbsp olive oil
- 1 tsp ground cumin
- 1 tsp ground coriander
- 1/2 tsp salt
- 1/4 tsp black pepper
- 1 cup of vegetable broth
- For the tomato-pepper sauce:
- 1 tbsp olive oil
- 1 onion, lightly chop-up
- 2 cloves garlic, chop-up
- 1 red bell pepper, diced
- 1 green bell pepper, diced
- 1 can (14 ozs) crushed tomatoes
- 1 tsp ground cumin
- 1 tsp ground coriander
- 1/2 tsp salt
- 1/4 tsp black pepper

Instructions:

1. Set the oven's temperature to 375°F (190°C).
2. Take out the bell peppers' tops, then scoop out the seeds and membranes. Place aside.
3. Rice, chop-up onion, chop-up garlic, diced tomato, parsley, mint, olive oil, cumin, coriander, salt, and black pepper Must all be combined in a big bowl. Combine thoroughly.
4. Place the bell peppers in a baking dish after stuffing them with the rice Mixture.
5. Fill the baking dish's bottom with the veggie broth.
6. Bake for 45 mins with the foil covering the baking dish.
7. Make the tomato-pepper sauce while the peppers are baking. In a pan over medium heat, warm the olive oil.
8. To the pan, add the chop-up garlic and diced onion, and cook up to the ingredients are tender.
9. Cook for 5 mins after adding the diced red and green bell peppers to the pan.
10. Add the cumin, coriander, salt, and black pepper along with the crushed tomatoes. Cook for ten mins.
11. Serve the stuffed peppers with the tomato-pepper sauce after taking them out of the oven.

Nutrition (per serving):
Cals: 278 Fat: 8g Carbs: 48g Protein: 6g Fiber: 6g

197. Egyptian Lamb Tagine with Apricots and Ras el Hanout

Time: 2 hrs 30 mins
Servings: 6

Ingredients:

- 2 lbs boneless lamb Muster, slice into chunks
- 2 tbsp olive oil
- 1 onion, lightly chop-up
- 3 cloves garlic, chop-up
- 2 tsp ras el hanout spice blend
- 1 tsp ground cumin
- 1 tsp ground coriander
- 1/2 tsp ground cinnamon
- 1/2 tsp ground ginger
- 1/2 tsp ground turmeric
- 1/4 tsp cayenne pepper (non-compulsory, for heat)
- 1 cup of dried apricots
- 1 cup of chicken broth
- 2 tbsp honey
- Salt and pepper, as needed
- Chop-up fresh cilantro, for garnish

Instructions:

1. Over medium heat, warm the olive oil in a big pot or Dutch oven. Brown the lamb chunks all over after adding them. Lamb Must be taken out of the saucepan and placed aside.
2. Add the chop-up garlic and onion to the same pot. up to melted, sauté.
3. Add the ras el hanout, cumin, coriander, cinnamon, ginger, turmeric, and cayenne pepper to the saucepan with the lamb once more. Stirring helps the spices adhere to the lamb.
4. Honey, chicken broth, and dried apricots Must all be added to the stew. Add salt and pepper as needed.
5. After bringing the Mixture to a simmer, lower the heat. For two hrs, or up to the lamb is cooked, simmer the Mixture with the lid on.
6. Serve the hot lamb tagine with fresh cilantro that has been chop-up on top. It goes great with rice or couscous.

Nutrition (per serving):
Cals: 408 Fat: 20g Carbs: 29g Protein: 29g Fiber: 4g

198. Egyptian Rice and Beef Stuffed Cabbage Leaves with Mint-Yogurt Sauce

Time: 1 hr 30 mins
Servings: 6

Ingredients:

- 12 Big cabbage leaves
- 1 lb ground beef
- 1 cup of cooked rice
- 1 onion, lightly chop-up
- 2 cloves garlic, chop-up
- 1 tomato, diced
- 1/4 cup of chop-up fresh parsley
- 1/4 cup of chop-up fresh mint
- 2 tbsp olive oil
- 1 tsp ground cumin
- 1 tsp ground coriander
- 1/2 tsp salt
- 1/4 tsp black pepper
- For the mint-yogurt sauce:
- 1 cup of plain yogurt
- 2 tbsp chop-up fresh mint
- 1 clove garlic, chop-up
- 1 tbsp lemon juice
- Salt and pepper, as needed

Instructions:

1. Bring water in a big pot to a boil. After adding, blanch the cabbage leaves for 2 to 3 mins, or up to they are tender. Drain, then set apart.
2. Combine the ground beef, cooked rice, diced tomato, parsley, mint, olive oil, cumin, coriander, salt, and black pepper in a sizable bowl. Combine thoroughly.
3. Place a spoonful of the beef and rice Mixture in the middle of every cabbage leaf as you go. Wrap the leaf tightly after folding the sides over the filling. Repeat with the remaining filling and cabbage leaves.
4. Seam side down, arrange the stuffed cabbage rolls in a single layer in a big pot or Dutch oven.
5. Fill the pot with water so that the cabbage rolls are only slightly submerged. After bringing to a boil, turn down the heat. For 45 mins, simmer the saucepan with the lid on.
6. Make the mint-yogurt sauce while the cabbage rolls cook. Combine the plain yogurt, chop-up garlic, chop-up mint, lemon juice, salt, and pepper in a mini bowl. Combine thoroughly.
7. Serve the heated stuffed cabbage rolls with the mint-yogurt sauce poured over them.

Nutrition (per serving):
Cals: 348 Fat: 18g Carbs: 24g Protein: 24g Fiber: 4g

199. Egyptian Stuffed Eggplant with Rice and Chickpeas in Herb Sauce

Time: 1 hr 30 mins
Servings: 4

Ingredients:

- 2 Big eggplants
- 1 cup of cooked rice
- 1 can (15 ozs) chickpeas, drained and rinsed
- 1 onion, lightly chop-up
- 2 cloves garlic, chop-up
- 1 tomato, diced
- 1/4 cup of chop-up fresh parsley
- 1/4 cup of chop-up fresh mint Continuation of Recipe 4: Egyptian Stuffed Eggplant with Rice and Chickpeas in Herb Sauce
- Ingredients (continued):
- 2 tbsp olive oil
- 1 tsp ground cumin
- 1 tsp ground coriander
- 1/2 tsp salt
- 1/4 tsp black pepper
- For the herb sauce:
- 1 cup of plain yogurt
- 2 tbsp chop-up fresh parsley
- 2 tbsp chop-up fresh mint
- 1 clove garlic, chop-up
- 1 tbsp lemon juice
- Salt and pepper, as needed

Instructions:

1. Set the oven's temperature to 375°F (190°C).
2. Slice the eggplants in half lengthwise, scoop out the meat, and trim the edges to leave a 1/2 inch border. Slice the flesh from the scooped-out eggplant and set it aside.
3. Olive oil Must be heated in a sizable skillet over medium heat. Sauté up to melted after adding the chop-up garlic and diced onion.
4. Cook the chop-up flesh of the eggplant in the skillet for 5 mins.
5. Add the cooked rice, chickpeas, diced tomato, parsley, mint, cumin, coriander, salt, and black pepper after stirring everything together. Combine thoroughly.
6. The rice and chickpea filling Must be placed inside every eggplant half. The stuffed eggplants Must be put in a baking dish.
7. Bake for 45 mins with the foil covering the baking dish.
8. Prepare the herb sauce while the eggplants are baking. Combine the plain yogurt, chop-up garlic, chop-up parsley, chop-up mint, and salt & pepper in a mini bowl. Combine thoroughly.
9. Serve the hot stuffed eggplants with the herb sauce after removing them from the oven.

Nutrition (per serving):
Cals: 328 Fat: 11g Carbs: 49g Protein: 12g Fiber: 11g

200. Egyptian Lamb and Potato Tagine with Turmeric and Cumin

Time: 2 hrs
Servings: 4

Ingredients:

- 2 lbs boneless lamb Muster, slice into chunks
- 2 tbsp olive oil
- 1 onion, lightly chop-up
- 3 cloves garlic, chop-up
- 2 tsp ground turmeric
- 1 tsp ground cumin
- 1 tsp ground coriander
- 1/2 tsp ground cinnamon
- 1/4 tsp cayenne pepper (non-compulsory, for heat)
- 4 medium potatoes, peel off and slice into chunks
- 2 cups of chicken broth
- Salt and pepper, as needed
- Chop-up fresh cilantro, for garnish

Instructions:

1. Over medium heat, warm the olive oil in a big pot or Dutch oven. Brown the lamb chunks all over after adding them. Lamb Must be taken out of the saucepan and placed aside.
2. Add the chop-up garlic and onion to the same pot. up to melted, sauté.
3. Add the ground turmeric, cumin, coriander, cinnamon, and cayenne pepper to the pot with the lamb once more. Stirring helps the spices adhere to the lamb.
4. Pour the chicken broth into the pot along with the potato chunks. Add salt and pepper as needed.
5. Heat Must be turned down once the Mixture comes to a boil. The lamb and potatoes Must be

cooked after 1 hr and 30 mins of simmering under cover.
6. Serve the hot lamb and potato tagine with fresh cilantro that has been chop-up. It goes great with bread or rice.

Nutrition (per serving):
Cals: 508 Fat: 27g Carbs: 31g Protein: 37g Fiber: 4g

201. Egyptian Spinach and Lentil Salad with Orange Dressing

Time: 30 mins
Servings: 4

Ingredients:

- 2 cups of fresh spinach leaves
- 1 cup of cooked lentils
- 1 orange, segmented
- 1/4 cup of chop-up red onion
- 1/4 cup of chop-up fresh parsley
- 2 tbsp olive oil
- 1 tbsp orange juice
- 1 tbsp lemon juice
- Salt and pepper as needed

Instructions:

1. The spinach, lentils, orange segments, red onion, and parsley Must all be combined in a big bowl.
2. Combine the olive oil, orange juice, lemon juice, salt, and pepper in a separate mini bowl.
3. After adding the dressing, carefully toss the salad to blend.
4. Salad can be served cold or at room temperature.

NUTRITION INFO (per serving):
Cals: 180
Protein: 8g
Fat: 7g
Carbs: 23g
Fiber: 6g

202. Egyptian Chicken and Okra Stew with Tomato and Coriander

Time: 1 hr
Servings: 6

Ingredients:

- 1.5 lbs chicken pieces (such as thighs or drumsticks)
- 1 lb fresh okra, trimmed
- 1 onion, chop-up
- 3 cloves garlic, chop-up
- 1 can diced tomatoes (14 oz)
- 1 tbsp tomato paste
- 1 tsp ground cumin
- 1 tsp ground coriander
- 1/2 tsp ground turmeric
- Salt and pepper as needed
- Fresh coriander leaves for garnish

Instructions:

1. Heat some oil in a big saucepan on a medium heat. Add the chicken pieces and sauté them up to they are evenly browned.
2. The onion and garlic Must be added to the stew and cooked up to tender.
3. Add the tomato paste, cumin, coriander, turmeric, salt, and pepper along with the diced tomatoes. The chicken Must be covered with water.
4. Heat Must be turned down once the Mixture comes to a boil. For 30 mins, simmer the saucepan with the cover on.
5. When the chicken is thoroughly cooked and the okra is tender, return the okra to the saucepan and simmer for an additional 15 to 20 mins.
6. Serve the stew hot with fresh coriander leaves as a garnish.

NUTRITION INFO (per serving):
Cals: 290
Protein: 25g
Fat: 12g
Carbs: 19g
Fiber: 6g

203. Egyptian Rice and Chicken Stuffed Grape Leaves with Tzatziki Sauce

Time: 1 hr 30 mins
Servings: 8

Ingredients:

- 1 cup of long-grain rice
- 1 lb ground chicken
- 1 onion, lightly chop-up
- 1/4 cup of chop-up fresh parsley
- 1/4 cup of chop-up fresh mint
- 1/4 cup of chop-up fresh dill
- 1/4 cup of lemon juice

- 1/4 cup of olive oil
- 1 tsp ground cumin
- 1/2 tsp ground cinnamon
- Salt and pepper as needed
- 40-50 grape leaves (rinsed and drained)
- Tzatziki sauce for serving

Instructions:

1. Rice, ground chicken, onion, parsley, mint, dill, lemon juice, olive oil, cumin, cinnamon, salt, and pepper Must all be combined in a big bowl. Combine thoroughly.
2. A grape leaf Must be placed shining side down on a spotless work area. Onto the leaves at the stem end, add about 1 tbsp of the rice and chicken Mixture.
3. Wrap the leaf tightly after folding the sides over the filling. Repetition is required with the remaining grape leaves and filling.
4. Seam side down, arrange the packed grape leaves in a single layer in a big container. The grape leaves Must be covered with water.
5. To weigh down the grape leaves and keep them from unraveling, place a heatproof plate on top of them.
6. Heat the water up to it boils, then turn the heat down to low. The rice Must be cooked and soft after about an hr of simmering under cover.
7. Take the stuffed grape leaves out of the pot and serve them with tzatziki sauce warm or at room temperature.

NUTRITION INFO (per serving):

Cals: 280
Protein: 15g
Fat: 10g
Carbs: 33g
Fiber: 3g

204. Egyptian Stuffed Zucchini with Rice and Tomato-Herb Sauce

Time: 1 hr 30 mins
Servings: 6

Ingredients:

- 6 medium zucchini
- 1 cup of long-grain rice
- 1 onion, lightly chop-up
- 2 cloves garlic, chop-up
- 1/4 cup of chop-up fresh parsley
- 1/4 cup of chop-up fresh dill
- 1/4 cup of chop-up fresh mint
- 2 tbsp olive oil
- 1 can diced tomatoes (14 oz)
- 1 tsp ground cumin
- 1 tsp ground coriander
- Salt and pepper as needed

Instructions:

1. Using a spoon or a zucchini corer, take out the zucchini's tops and leave behind shells that are about 1/4-inch thick. The flesh from the zucchini Must be saved.
2. Rice, onion, garlic, parsley, dill, mint, salt, and pepper Must all be combined in a big bowl. Combine thoroughly before adding the reserved zucchini flesh.
3. Place a little amount of rice Mixture inside every zucchini shell, leting room at the top for the rice to expand while cooking.
4. Olive oil Must be heated in a sizable pot over medium heat. Salt, pepper, cumin, coriander, and diced tomatoes Must all be added. Several mins of cooking will help the flavors blend.
5. Put the filled zucchini in the pot with the tomato sauce surrounding them. Add just enough water to the zucchini to barely cover it.
6. After bringing the liquid to a boil, turn down the heat. The rice and zucchini Must be soft after about an hr of simmering under cover.
7. Serve the hot stuffed zucchini while still hot and cover it with some of the tomato-herb sauce.

NUTRITION INFO (per serving):

Cals: 200
Protein: 5g
Fat: 6g
Carbs: 34g
Fiber: 4g

205. Egyptian Spinach and Chickpea Soup with Ginger and Turmeric

Time: 45 mins
Servings: 4

Ingredients:

- 2 tbsp olive oil
- 1 onion, chop-up
- 2 cloves garlic, chop-up
- 1 tsp ground ginger
- 1 tsp ground turmeric
- 1/2 tsp ground cumin
- 4 cups of vegetable broth
- 1 can (15 ozs) chickpeas, drained and rinsed
- 1 bunch spinach, chop-up
- Salt and pepper as needed
- Fresh lemon juice (non-compulsory, for serving)

Instructions:

1. Over medium heat, warm the olive oil in a big pot. The onion and garlic Must be added and sautéed up to tender.
2. Cook for an additional min after stirring in the ground ginger, turmeric, and cumin.
3. The veggie broth Must be added and brought to a boil. For fifteen mins, simmer over low heat.
4. For an additional 10 mins, up to the spinach wilts, add the chickpeas and spinach to the saucepan.
5. As needed, add salt and pepper to the food. Before serving, if preferred, squeeze some fresh lemon juice over the soup.

NUTRITION INFO (per serving):
Cals: 210
Fat: 8g
Carbs: 28g
Protein: 9g
Fiber: 7g

206. Egyptian Chicken and Egg Tagine with Cumin and Paprika

Time: 1 hr 30 mins
Servings: 4

Ingredients:

- 4 chicken thighs
- Salt and pepper as needed
- 2 tbsp olive oil
- 1 onion, chop-up
- 2 cloves garlic, chop-up
- 1 tsp ground cumin
- 1 tsp paprika
- 1 can (14 ozs) diced tomatoes
- 1 cup of chicken broth
- 4 eggs
- Fresh parsley, chop-up (for garnish)

Instructions:

1. Chicken thighs Must be salted and peppered. In a tagine or big skillet, heat the olive oil over medium heat. Brown the chicken thighs on every sides after adding them. Chicken Must be taken out of the pan and put aside.
2. Add the chop-up garlic and onion to the same pan. Sauté the onion up to it turns translucent.
3. After one min, add the ground cumin and paprika and stir.
4. Add the chicken stock, diced tomatoes, and their juice to the pan. Simmer for a while.
5. After 30 mins, add the chicken thighs back to the pan, cover, and continue to simmer.
6. Crack an egg into every of the four little wells you created in the sauce. Up to the eggs are done to your preference, heat the skillet with a lid for an additional 5-7 mins.
7. Before serving, garnish with fresh parsley.

NUTRITION INFO (per serving):
Cals: 320
Fat: 21g
Carbs: 10g
Protein: 24g
Fiber: 2g

207. Egyptian Rice and Vermicelli Pilaf with Pine Nuts and Saffron

Time: 25 mins
Servings: 4

Ingredients:

- 1 cup of long-grain white rice
- 1/2 cup of vermicelli noodles, broken into mini pieces
- 2 tbsp butter
- 2 cups of chicken broth
- Pinch of saffron threads
- Salt as needed
- 1/4 cup of pine nuts, toasted

Instructions:

1. Rice Must be thoroughly rinsed in cold water up to the water is clear. Drain, then set apart.
2. Melt the butter in a Big pot over medium heat.

Vermicelli noodles Must be added and cooked up to golden brown.
3. Stir in the vermicelli after adding the rinsed rice to the pan.
4. Dissolve the saffron threads in a tbsp of boiling water in a separate mini basin. Place the pot with this Mixture inside.
5. Salt as needed, along with the chicken broth. When the rice is tender and the liquid has been absorbed, simmer for 15 mins with the heat on low and the lid on. Bring to a boil.
6. Take the pilaf off the heat, cover it, and let it sit for five mins.
7. With a fork, fluff the rice, then, just before serving, top with toasted pine nuts.

NUTRITION INFO (per serving):
Cals: 280
Fat: 12g
Carbs: 39g
Protein: 6g
Fiber: 2g

208. Egyptian Stuffed Bell Peppers with Rice and Lentils in Spicy Sauce

Time: 1 hr 30 mins
Servings: 4

Ingredients:

- 4 bell peppers (any color)
- 1/2 cup of basmati rice
- 1/2 cup of brown lentils
- 1 tbsp olive oil
- 1 onion, chop-up
- 2 cloves garlic, chop-up
- 1 tsp ground cumin
- 1 tsp ground coriander
- 1/2 tsp paprika
- 1/4 tsp cayenne pepper (non-compulsory, for extra spice)
- 1 can (14 ozs) diced tomatoes
- 1 cup of vegetable broth
- Salt and pepper as needed
- Fresh parsley, chop-up (for garnish)

Instructions:

1. Set the oven's temperature to 375°F (190°C).
2. The bell peppers' tops Must be slice off, and the seeds and membranes Must be take outd. Peppers Must be placed in a baking dish and left to bake.
3. According to the directions on the packaging, prepare the basmati rice and lentils. Take out any extra water, then set it aside.
4. Olive oil Must be heated in a sizable skillet over medium heat. Sauté up to melted after adding the chop-up garlic and diced onion.
5. Cook for an additional min after adding the ground cumin, coriander, paprika, and cayenne pepper (if using).
6. Add the vegetable broth, diced tomatoes, and their juice to the skillet. Cook for 10 mins after bringing to a simmer. As needed, add salt and pepper to the food.
7. Combine the cooked rice and lentils with the hot tomato sauce in a combining basin. Combine thoroughly till coated.
8. Fill the prepared bell peppers to the brim with the rice and lentil Mixture.
9. Bake for 45 mins with the foil covering the baking dish. Once the peppers are soft and somewhat browned, take out the foil and bake for a further 10-15 mins.
10. Before serving, garnish with fresh parsley.

NUTRITION INFO (per serving):
Cals: 290
Fat: 4g
Carbs: 56g
Protein: 12g
Fiber: 11g

209. Egyptian Lamb Tagine with Almonds and Moroccan Spices

Time: 2 hrs 30 mins
Servings: 6

Ingredients:

- 2 lbs lamb Muster, slice into chunks
- Salt and pepper as needed
- 2 tbsp olive oil
- 1 onion, chop-up
- 3 cloves garlic, chop-up
- 1 tsp ground cumin
- 1 tsp ground coriander
- 1/2 tsp ground cinnamon
- 1/4 tsp ground ginger
- 1/4 tsp ground turmeric
- 1 can (14 ozs) diced tomatoes

- 2 cups of vegetable broth
- 1/2 cup of dried apricots, chop-up
- 1/2 cup of blanched almonds
- Fresh cilantro, chop-up (for garnish)

Instructions:

1. Salt and pepper the lamb chunks as desired. In a tagine or big pot, heat the olive oil over medium-low heat. Add the lamb, then sear it thoroughly. Lamb Must be taken out of the saucepan and placed aside.
2. Add the chop-up garlic and onion to the same pot. Sauté the onion up to it turns translucent.
3. Cook for one more min after adding the ground cumin, coriander, cinnamon, ginger, and turmeric.
4. Pour in the vegetable broth, diced tomatoes with juice, chop-up apricots, and blanched almonds to the pot. Simmer for a while.
5. When the lamb is tender, add it back to the pot, cover it, and simmer for another two hrs on low heat.
6. To decrease the sauce, simmer without the lid for an additional 15 mins.
7. Before serving, garnish with fresh cilantro.

NUTRITION INFO (per serving):

Cals: 420
Fat: 25g
Carbs: 15g
Protein: 35g
Fiber: 4g

210. Egyptian Chicken and Okra Stew with Cilantro and Garlic

Time: 1 hr
Servings: 4

Ingredients:

- 4 chicken thighs, bone-in and skin-on
- 1 onion, lightly chop-up
- 4 cloves of garlic, chop-up
- 1 lb (450g) okra, ends trimmed
- 2 tomatoes, diced
- 1 tbsp tomato paste
- 1 tsp ground cumin
- 1 tsp ground coriander
- 1/2 tsp ground turmeric
- 1/4 tsp cayenne pepper (non-compulsory)
- Salt and pepper as needed
- Fresh cilantro leaves, chop-up, for garnish

Instructions:

1. Over medium heat, warm some oil in a big pot. Brown the chicken thighs all over after adding them. Chicken Must be taken out of the pot and placed aside.
2. Add the onion and garlic to the same pot. Sauté the onion up to it turns translucent.
3. Okra, tomatoes, tomato paste, cumin, coriander, turmeric, cayenne (if using), salt, and pepper are all ingredients that Must be included. To blend, thoroughly stir.
4. Put the chicken thighs back in the pot and cover everything with water. Bring to a boil, then lower the heat, cover, and simmer for 45 mins, or up to the okra is soft and the chicken is cooked through.
5. If necessary, taste and adjust the seasoning. Serve the stew hot with fresh cilantro leaves as a garnish.

NUTRITION INFO:

Cals: 350 per serving
Fat: 16g
Protein: 28g
Carbs: 25g
Fiber: 8g

211. Egyptian Rice and Chicken Stuffed Grape Leaves with Tomato-Herb Sauce

Time: 1 hr 30 mins
Servings: 6

Ingredients:

- 1 cup of long-grain rice
- 1 lb (450g) ground chicken
- 1 onion, lightly chop-up
- 2 cloves of garlic, chop-up
- 1/4 cup of chop-up fresh parsley
- 1/4 cup of chop-up fresh dill
- 1/4 cup of chop-up fresh mint
- Juice of 1 lemon
- Salt and pepper as needed
- 1 jar of grape leaves in brine (about 60 leaves)
- Tomato-Herb Sauce:
- 1 can (14 oz) diced tomatoes
- 2 tbsp tomato paste
- 1/4 cup of chop-up fresh parsley
- 1/4 cup of chop-up fresh dill

- 1/4 cup of chop-up fresh mint
- Juice of 1 lemon
- Salt and pepper as needed

Instructions:

1. Rice Must be thoroughly rinsed in cold water up to the water is clear. Flow freely.
2. Ground chicken, onion, garlic, parsley, dill, mint, lemon juice, salt, and pepper Must all be combined in a big bowl. Combine thoroughly.
3. Place a tiny portion of the chicken and rice Mixture in the center of every grape leaf before folding the sides inward. To create a stuffed grape leaf, tightly roll the leaf. Repeat with the rest of the Mixture and leaves.
4. Seam-side down, arrange the packed grape leaves in a single layer in a pot.
5. The tomato-herb sauce is made by blending diced tomatoes, tomato paste, parsley, dill, mint, lemon juice, salt, and pepper in a separate bowl. Pour the sauce over the packed grape leaves after thoroughly combining.
6. Fill the pot with water so that the packed grape leaves are submerged. To retain the leaves in the liquid, place a heatproof plate on top of them.
7. To cook the rice and combine the flavors, bring the saucepan to a boil, then turn the heat down to low and simmer for about an hr.
8. With some of the tomato-herb sauce spooned on top, serve the hot stuffed grape leaves.

NUTRITION INFO:

Cals: 280 per serving
Fat: 9g
Protein: 19g
Carbs: 32g
Fiber: 4g

212. Egyptian Stuffed Zucchini with Rice and Chickpeas in Garlic Sauce

Time: 1 hr 15 mins
Servings: 4

Ingredients:

- 4 Big zucchini
- 1 cup of long-grain rice
- 1 can (15 oz) chickpeas, drained and rinsed
- 1 onion, lightly chop-up
- 4 cloves of garlic, chop-up
- 1/4 cup of chop-up fresh parsley
- 1/4 cup of chop-up fresh dill
- Juice of 1 lemon
- Salt and pepper as needed
- Garlic Sauce:
- 4 cloves of garlic, chop-up
- 2 tbsp olive oil
- Juice of 1 lemon
- Salt as needed

Instructions:

1. Take out the zucchini's tops and use a spoon to scoop out the meat, leaving a hollow shell behind. Keep the zucchini flesh aside.
2. Rice, chickpeas, onion, reserved zucchini flesh, garlic, parsley, dill, lemon juice, salt, and pepper Must all be combined in a bowl. Combine thoroughly.
3. Pack the rice and chickpea Mixture tightly inside the zucchini shells.
4. Place the filled zucchini in a single layer in a big pot. Cover the zucchini with water, then add more.
5. The zucchini Must simmer for about 45 mins, or up to the rice is done and the zucchini is soft, after bringing the water to a boil.
6. Garlic cloves that have been chop-up Must be cooked in olive oil up to golden brown. Add the salt and lemon juice after removing from the heat.
7. Serve the heated filled zucchini with the garlic sauce poured over top.

NUTRITION INFO:

Cals: 320 per serving
Fat: 8g
Protein: 9g
Carbs: 56g
Fiber: 8g

213. Egyptian Lamb and Cauliflower Tagine with Turmeric and Cardamom

Time: 2 hrs
Servings: 6

Ingredients:

- 2 lbs (900g) lamb Muster, slice into cubes
- 1 onion, lightly chop-up
- 4 cloves of garlic, chop-up
- 1 tsp ground turmeric

- 1 tsp ground cumin
- 1/2 tsp ground cardamom
- 1/4 tsp ground cinnamon
- 1/4 tsp ground nutmeg
- Salt and pepper as needed
- 1 head of cauliflower, slice into florets
- 2 tbsp olive oil
- 1 cup of vegetable or chicken broth
- Juice of 1 lemon
- Chop-up fresh parsley, for garnish

Instructions:

1. Olive oil Must be heated in a sizable pot over medium heat. Brown the lamb cubes all over after adding them. Lamb Must be taken out of the saucepan and placed aside.
2. Add the onion and garlic to the same pot. Sauté the onion up to it turns translucent.
3. Add the salt, pepper, cinnamon, nutmeg, turmeric, cumin, and cardamom. The spices Must be thoroughly combined with the onion and garlic.
4. Add the cauliflower florets and the lamb back to the saucepan. To blend, stir.
5. Add the lemon juice and chicken or vegetable broth. Bring to a boil, then lower the heat to a simmer, cover the pot, and cook for 1.5 to 2 hrs, or up to the lamb is fork-tender and the flavors are well-balanced.
6. If necessary, taste and adjust the seasoning. Serve the hot lamb and cauliflower tagine with fresh parsley on top.

NUTRITION INFO:

Cals: 420 per serving

Fat: 25g

Protein: 32g

Carbs: 16g

Fiber: 5g

214. Egyptian Spinach and Chickpea Soup with Harissa and Lemon

Time: 40 mins

Servings: 4

Ingredients:

- 1 tbsp olive oil
- 1 onion, lightly chop-up
- 2 cloves of garlic, chop-up
- 1 tsp ground cumin
- 1/2 tsp ground coriander
- 1/4 tsp ground cinnamon
- 4 cups of vegetable or chicken broth
- 1 can (15 oz) chickpeas, drained and rinsed
- 1 lb (450g) fresh spinach leaves
- 2 tbsp harissa paste
- Juice of 1 lemon
- Salt and pepper as needed

Instructions:

1. Olive oil Must be heated in a sizable pot over medium heat. Add the garlic and onion. Sauté the onion up to it turns translucent.
2. Cinnamon, coriander, and cumin Must be added. The spices Must be thoroughly combined with the onion and garlic.
3. Add the chicken or vegetable broth, then bring to a boil.
4. Add the spinach leaves and chickpeas. Up to the spinach wilts, stir occasionally while letting the soup simmer for about 10 mins.
5. Add the lemon juice and harissa paste after combining. As needed, add salt and pepper to the food.
6. Take the soup off the stove. Blend the soup up to it's smooth using an immersion blender or a countertop blender.
7. If preferred, top the hot spinach and chickpea soup with a dash of harissa and a drizzle of extra virgin olive oil.

NUTRITION INFO:

Cals: 180 per serving

Fat: 5g

Protein: 10g

Carbs: 25g

Fiber: 9g

215. Egyptian Lamb and Potato Tagine with Turmeric and Cumin

Time: 2 hrs

Servings: 4

Ingredients:

- 1.5 lbs lamb Muster, cubed
- 2 tbsp vegetable oil
- 1 Big onion, chop-up
- 4 garlic cloves, chop-up
- 1 tsp ground turmeric
- 1 tsp ground cumin

- 1 tsp ground coriander
- 1 tsp paprika
- 1/2 tsp ground cinnamon
- Salt and pepper as needed
- 3 Big potatoes, peel off and slice into chunks
- 2 cups of vegetable broth
- Fresh cilantro, chop-up (for garnish)

Instructions:

1. In a sizable saucepan or tagine, heat the vegetable oil over medium-low heat. Brown the lamb cubes all over after adding them. Lamb Must be taken out of the saucepan and placed aside.
2. Add the chop-up garlic and onion to the same pot. Sauté the onion up to it turns translucent.
3. Spice up the dish with the turmeric, cumin, coriander, paprika, cinnamon, salt, and pepper. The spices Must be thoroughly combined with the onions and garlic.
4. Add the potatoes and lamb back to the pot. Bring the Mixture to a boil after adding the veggie broth.
5. For about 1.5 to 2 hrs, or when the lamb is soft and the potatoes are cooked through, reduce the heat to low, cover the pot, and let it simmer.
6. Serve the tagine hot with fresh cilantro as a garnish.

NUTRITION INFO: (per serving)
Cals: 480
Protein: 27g
Carbs: 34g
Fat: 26g
Fiber: 5g

216. Egyptian Rice and Beef Stuffed Cabbage Leaves with Lemon-Tahini Sauce

Time: 1.5 hrs
Servings: 6

Ingredients:

- 12 Big cabbage leaves
- 1 lb ground beef
- 1 cup of cooked rice
- 1 mini onion, lightly chop-up
- 2 garlic cloves, chop-up
- 1/4 cup of chop-up fresh parsley
- 2 tbsp tomato paste
- 1 tsp ground cumin
- 1 tsp ground coriander
- Salt and pepper as needed
- 1 can (14 ozs) diced tomatoes, undrained
- 1/4 cup of lemon juice
- 2 tbsp tahini
- Chop-up fresh mint (for garnish)

Instructions:

1. Big saucepan of salted water Must be brought to a boil. The cabbage leaves Must be blanched for 2–3 mins or up to they are soft. Take them out of the pot and place them aside.
2. Ground beef, cooked rice, chop-up onion, chop-up garlic, parsley, tomato paste, cumin, coriander, salt, and pepper Must all be combined in a bowl. Combine thoroughly.
3. Every cabbage leaf Must have a scoop of the beef and rice Mixture in the center. Wrap the leaf tightly after folding the sides over the filling.
4. Place the stuffed cabbage leaves in a single layer in a Big skillet. Over the cabbage rolls, pour the diced tomatoes and their liquid. For around 45 mins, simmer the skillet with the cover on.
5. To prepare the sauce, combine the tahini and lemon juice in a mini bowl.
6. Serve the heated stuffed cabbage rolls with the lemon-tahini sauce poured over top and fresh mint leaves slice on the side.

NUTRITION INFO: (per serving)
Cals: 290
Protein: 17g
Carbs: 23g
Fat: 15g
Fiber: 5g

217. Egyptian Stuffed Eggplant with Rice and Peppers in Tomato Sauce

Time: 1 hr 30 mins
Servings: 4

Ingredients:

- 2 Big eggplants
- 1 cup of cooked rice
- 1 red bell pepper, chop-up
- 1 green bell pepper, chop-up
- 1 mini onion, lightly chop-up
- 2 garlic cloves, chop-up
- 2 tbsp olive oil

- 1 tsp ground cumin
- 1 tsp ground coriander
- 1/2 tsp paprika
- Salt and pepper as needed
- 1 can (14 ozs) diced tomatoes, undrained
- Fresh parsley, chop-up (for garnish)

Instructions:

1. Set the oven's temperature to 375°F (190°C).
2. Slice the eggplants in half lengthwise, take out the flesh, and then discard the shell. Slice the flesh of the eggplant into tiny pieces.
3. Olive oil Must be heated in a sizable skillet over medium heat. Add the chop-up onion, bell peppers, chop-up garlic, and eggplant. Sauté the vegetables up to they are soft.
4. Add the cooked rice along with the salt, pepper, paprika, cumin, and coriander powders. Let the flavors to meld for an additional 2 to 3 mins of cooking.
5. Place the rice and veggie Mixture inside the eggplant shells. Put them inside a baking pan.
6. Over the filled eggplants, pour the diced tomatoes and their liquid.
7. Bake for 45 mins with the foil covering the baking dish. When the eggplants are soft and the tops are just beginning to brown, take out the cover and bake for another 10-15 mins.
8. Hot filled eggplants Must be served with fresh parsley on top.

NUTRITION INFO: (per serving)
Cals: 250
Protein: 5g
Carbs: 35g
Fat: 11g
Fiber: 8g

218. Egyptian Lamb and Potato Tagine with Carrots and Ras el Hanout

Time: 2 hrs
Servings: 4

Ingredients:

- 1.5 lbs lamb stew meat, cubed
- 2 tbsp olive oil
- 1 Big onion, chop-up
- 3 garlic cloves, chop-up
- 2 tsp ras el hanout spice blend
- 1 tsp ground ginger
- 1 tsp ground cinnamon
- Salt and pepper as needed
- 4 carrots, peel off and slice into chunks
- 3 Big potatoes, peel off and slice into chunks
- 1 cup of vegetable broth
- Chop-up fresh parsley (for garnish)

Instructions:

1. Heat the olive oil in a sizable saucepan or tagine over medium heat. Brown the lamb cubes all over after adding them. Lamb Must be taken out of the saucepan and placed aside.
2. Add the chop-up garlic and onion to the same pot. Sauté the onion up to it turns translucent.
3. Salt, pepper, ground ginger, ground cinnamon, and the ras el hanout spice Mixture to the saucepan. The spices Must be thoroughly combined with the onions and garlic.
4. Add the carrots, potatoes, and vegetable stock to the saucepan with the lamb before covering. The Mixture Must boil.
5. When the lamb is soft and the vegetables are fully cooked, turn the heat down to low, cover the pot, and let it simmer for 1.5 to 2 hrs.
6. Hot tagine Must be served with freshly chop-up parsley on top.

NUTRITION INFO: (per serving)
Cals: 480
Protein: 27g
Carbs: 34g
Fat: 26g
Fiber: 5g

219. Egyptian Spinach and Lentil Salad with Yogurt Dressing and Mint

Time: 30 mins
Servings: 4

Ingredients:

- 4 cups of fresh spinach leaves, washed and chop-up
- 1 cup of cooked lentils
- 1/2 cup of cherry tomatoes, halved
- 1/4 cup of red onion, thinly split
- 2 tbsp chop-up fresh mint leaves
- 1/4 cup of plain yogurt
- 1 tbsp lemon juice
- 1 tbsp olive oil
- Salt and pepper as needed

Instructions:

1. Chop the spinach and add with the cooked lentils, cherry tomatoes, red onion, and chop-up mint in a big bowl.
2. To create the dressing, combine the plain yogurt, lemon juice, olive oil, salt, and pepper in a separate mini bowl.
3. Over the spinach and lentil Mixture, drizzle the dressing. To evenly coat the salad, thoroughly toss.
4. Serve the lentil and spinach salad cold.

NUTRITION INFO: (per serving)

Cals: 150
Protein: 8g
Carbs: 22g
Fat: 4g
Fiber: 8g

220. Egyptian Chicken and Egg Tagine with Preserved Lemon and Paprika

Time: 1 hr
Servings: 4

Ingredients:

- 4 chicken thighs, bone-in and skin-on
- 2 tbsp olive oil
- 1 onion, thinly split
- 3 cloves garlic, chop-up
- 1 tsp ground cumin
- 1 tsp ground coriander
- 1 tsp paprika
- 1 preserved lemon, rinsed and split
- 4 eggs
- Salt and pepper as needed
- Fresh cilantro or parsley for garnish

Instructions:

1. In a tagine or Big pan, heat the olive oil over medium heat. Add the chicken thighs and sauté them up to both sides are browned. Take out and reserve the chicken.
2. Add the chop-up garlic and onion to the same pan. Cook up to melted and just beginning to brown.
3. To the pan, add the ground cumin, coriander, and paprika. The spices Must be thoroughly combined with the onions and garlic.
4. Put the chicken back in the pan and cover it with just enough water to barely cover it. Simmering while covered. For 30 mins, cook.
5. Slices of preserved lemon Must be added to the tagine and stirred gently. One egg Must be cracked into every of the four sauce wells. Once the eggs are cooked to your preference, heat the tagine with the lid on for an extra 10-15 mins.
6. As needed, add salt and pepper to the food. Before serving, garnish with fresh cilantro or parsley.

NUTRITION INFO (per serving):

Cals: 420
Fat: 26g
Carbs: 9g
Protein: 38g

221. Egyptian Rice and Vermicelli Soup with Mint and Chickpeas

Time: 45 mins
Servings: 6

Ingredients:

- 1 cup of vermicelli noodles
- 2 tbsp butter
- 1 cup of long-grain rice
- 4 cups of chicken or vegetable broth
- 1 cup of cooked chickpeas
- 2 tbsp chop-up fresh mint leaves
- Salt and pepper as needed

Instructions:

1. Melt the butter in a Big pot over medium heat. As you stir regularly to prevent burning, add the vermicelli noodles and cook up to they are golden brown.
2. Stir the rice in the pot to evenly distribute the butter throughout the grains. Cook for a further two mins.
3. Bring to a boil after adding the chicken or veggie broth. For 15-20 mins, or up to the rice is cooked and soft, lower the heat, cover the pot, and simmer.
4. Add chop-up mint and cooked chickpeas to the soup. Stir thoroughly and add salt and pepper as needed.
5. The chickpeas must cook for an extra five mins to reheat. Serve warm.

NUTRITION INFO *(per serving):*
Cals: 300
Fat: 6g
Carbs: 54g
Protein: 8g

222. Egyptian Stuffed Bell Peppers with Rice and Herbs in Spicy Sauce

Time: 1 hr 30 mins
Servings: 6

Ingredients:

- 6 bell peppers (any color), tops take outd and seeded
- 1 cup of long-grain rice
- 1 onion, lightly chop-up
- 2 tomatoes, diced
- 1/2 cup of chop-up fresh herbs (such as parsley, cilantro, and dill)
- 2 tbsp olive oil
- 2 cloves garlic, chop-up
- 1 tsp ground cumin
- 1/2 tsp ground cinnamon
- 1/2 tsp ground coriander
- 1/4 tsp cayenne pepper (adjust as needed)
- Salt and pepper as needed
- 2 cups of vegetable broth
- Lemon wedges for serving

Instructions:

1. Set the oven's temperature to 350°F (175°C).
2. Rice, diced onion, diced tomatoes, chop-up herbs, olive oil, chop-up garlic, ground cumin, ground cinnamon, ground coriander, cayenne pepper, salt, and pepper Must all be combined in a big bowl. Combine thoroughly.
3. Fill every bell pepper about three-quarters of the way with the rice Mixture. The filled peppers Must be put in a baking dish.
4. Around the stuffed peppers in the baking dish, pour the vegetable broth.
5. Bake the dish in the preheated oven for 45 mins with the foil covering it. Once the foil has been take outd, bake for a further 10-15 mins, or up to the rice is done and the peppers are soft.
6. Hot bell peppers with the stuffing and lemon wedges on the side Must be served.

NUTRITION INFO *(per serving):*
Cals: 230
Fat: 6g
Carbs: 42g
Protein: 5g

223. Egyptian Lamb Tagine with Prunes and Cinnamon-Saffron Sauce

Time: 2 hrs
Servings: 4

Ingredients:

- 1.5 lbs (700g) lamb Muster, slice into chunks
- 2 tbsp olive oil
- 1 onion, lightly chop-up
- 3 cloves garlic, chop-up
- 1 tsp ground cumin
- 1 tsp ground coriander
- 1 tsp ground cinnamon
- 1/2 tsp ground ginger
- 1/4 tsp saffron threads, soaked in 2 tbsp warm water
- 1 cup of beef or vegetable broth
- 1 cup of pitted prunes
- Salt and pepper as needed
- Fresh cilantro for garnish

Instructions:

1. Over medium heat, warm the olive oil in a big tagine or Dutch oven. Brown the lamb chunks all over after adding them. Lamb take outd; place aside.
2. Add the chop-up garlic and onion to the same pot. Cook the onion up to it becomes transparent and tender.
3. Add the ground cumin, coriander, cinnamon, ginger, saffron threads that have been soaked (together with the soaking water), beef or vegetable broth, and pitted prunes to the saucepan with the lamb once more. To blend, thoroughly stir.
4. As needed, add salt and pepper to the food. As soon as the Mixture comes to a boil, turn the heat down to low and cover the pan.
5. Up to the lamb is soft and the flavors are well-balanced, simmer for 1.5 to 2 hrs.
6. Before serving, garnish with fresh cilantro.

NUTRITION INFO (per serving):
Cals: 480
Fat: 28g
Carbs: 32g
Protein: 29g

224. Egyptian Rice and Beef Stuffed Cabbage Leaves with Tomato-Garlic Sauce

Time: 1 hr 30 mins
Servings: 6

Ingredients:
- 12 Big cabbage leaves
- 1 lb (450g) ground beef
- 1 cup of cooked rice
- 1 onion, lightly chop-up
- 2 cloves garlic, chop-up
- 1/4 cup of chop-up fresh parsley
- 1 tsp ground cumin
- 1/2 tsp ground cinnamon
- Salt and pepper as needed
- 2 cups of tomato sauce
- 1 cup of water
- 2 cloves garlic, chop-up
- 2 tbsp olive oil
- Juice of 1 lemon
- Salt and pepper as needed

Instructions:
1. Bring water in a big pot to a boil. The cabbage leaves Must be blanched for 3 to 5 mins, or up to they are soft. Drain, then set apart.
2. Ground beef, cooked rice, chop-up onion, chop-up garlic, chop-up parsley, ground cumin, ground cinnamon, salt, and pepper Must all be combined in a bowl. Combine thoroughly.
3. Place some of the beef and rice Mixture in the center of a cabbage leaf. Wrap the leaf tightly after folding the sides over the filling. Repeat with the remaining filling and cabbage leaves.
4. Tomato sauce, water, chop-up garlic, olive oil, lemon juice, salt, and pepper Must all be combined in a big pot. To combine, thoroughly stir.
5. Seam side down, add the stuffed cabbage rolls to the pot. Ensure that they are firmly packed.
6. Over a medium heat, simmer the sauce. Cook the cabbage rolls under cover for 45–1 hr, or up to they are soft and cooked through.
7. With some of the sauce spooned on top, serve the stuffed cabbage rolls hot.

NUTRITION INFO (per serving):
Cals: 320
Fat: 12g
Carbs: 33g
Protein: 20g

225. Egyptian Stuffed Eggplant with Rice and Tomato-Pepper Sauce

Time: 1 hr 30 mins
Servings: 4

Ingredients:
- 4 mini eggplants
- 1 cup of long-grain rice
- 1 onion, lightly chop-up
- 2 cloves garlic, chop-up
- 1/4 cup of chop-up fresh parsley
- 2 tbsp olive oil
- 1 tsp ground cumin
- 1/2 tsp ground cinnamon
- 1/2 tsp paprika
- Salt and pepper as needed
- 1 cup of tomato sauce
- 1 cup of vegetable broth
- 1 red bell pepper, split
- Fresh mint leaves for garnish

Instructions:
1. Set the oven's temperature to 375°F (190°C).
2. The eggplants Must have their tops take outd before being split lengthwise. Take out the flesh, leaving a 1/2-inch border all the way around. Slice the take outd flesh and set it aside.
3. Olive oil is heated in a pan over medium heat. Include the split flesh of the eggplant as well as the chop-up garlic and onion. Cook up to the eggplant is cooked and the onion is translucent.
4. Rice, parsley that has been chop-up, cumin, cinnamon, paprika, salt, and pepper Must all be added to the pan. After thoroughly combining, cook for another 2 mins.
5. With the rice Mixture, fill the hollowed-out eggplant halves, pressing it firmly in place.
6. Combine tomato sauce and vegetable broth in a baking dish. In the dish, arrange the filled eggplants in a single layer. On top, scatter the red bell pepper slices.

7. Bake the dish in the preheated oven for 45 mins with the foil covering it. When the rice is cooked and the eggplants are soft, take out the cover and bake for an additional 15 mins.
8. Before serving, garnish with fresh mint leaves.

NUTRITION INFO (per serving):

Cals: 280
Fat: 7g
Carbs: 52g
Protein: 6g

226. Egyptian Lamb and Potato Tagine with Carrots and Moroccan Spices

Time: 2 hrs
Servings: 4

Ingredients:

- 1 kg lamb Muster, slice into chunks
- 4 medium potatoes, peel off and quartered
- 3 carrots, peel off and split
- 1 onion, lightly chop-up
- 3 garlic cloves, chop-up
- 2 tsp ground cumin
- 2 tsp ground coriander
- 1 tsp ground cinnamon
- 1 tsp ground turmeric
- 1 tsp paprika
- 1 can (400g) diced tomatoes
- 2 cups of chicken or vegetable broth
- Salt and pepper as needed
- Fresh cilantro leaves, for garnish

Instructions:

1. Heat some oil in a sizable tagine or heavy-bottomed saucepan over medium heat. Add the lamb, then sear it thoroughly. Lamb Must be taken out of the saucepan and placed aside.
2. Add the onions and garlic to the same pot. The onions Must be sautéed up to transparent and tender.
3. Cumin, coriander, cinnamon, turmeric, and paprika Must be added. The spices Must be thoroughly combined into the onions and garlic.
4. Potatoes, carrots, diced tomatoes, and stock Must all be added to the saucepan along with the lamb. Add salt and pepper as needed.
5. Heat Must be turned down once the Mixture comes to a boil. For about 1.5 to 2 hrs, or up to the lamb is soft and the flavors are well-balanced, simmer the Mixture in a covered saucepan.
6. Serve the tagine hot with fresh cilantro leaves as a garnish. Enjoy!

227. Egyptian Spinach and Lentil Salad with Lemon-Tahini Dressing and Pomegranate

Time: 30 mins
Servings: 4

Ingredients:

- 2 cups of baby spinach leaves
- 1 cup of cooked lentils
- 1/2 cup of pomegranate seeds
- 1/4 cup of chop-up fresh parsley
- 1/4 cup of chop-up fresh mint
- 1/4 cup of chop-up red onion
- 1/4 cup of chop-up cucumber
- 1/4 cup of chop-up cherry tomatoes
- 2 tbsp lemon juice
- 2 tbsp tahini
- 1 tbsp olive oil
- 1 clove garlic, chop-up
- Salt and pepper as needed

Instructions:

1. Baby spinach, cooked lentils, pomegranate seeds, parsley, mint, red onion, cucumber, and cherry tomatoes Must all be combined in a sizable salad bowl.
2. Lemon juice, tahini, olive oil, chop-up garlic, salt, and pepper Must all be thoroughly combined in a mini basin.
3. Toss the salad carefully to evenly distribute the dressing over all of the ingredients.
4. Salad Must be served right away. Enjoy!

228. Egyptian Chicken and Okra Stew with Garlic and Paprika

Time: 1 hr 30 mins

Servings: 6

Ingredients:

- 1 kg chicken thighs, bone-in and skin-on
- 500g okra, ends trimmed
- 1 onion, lightly chop-up
- 4 garlic cloves, chop-up
- 1 tsp ground cumin
- 1 tsp ground paprika
- 1/2 tsp ground coriander
- 1/2 tsp ground turmeric
- 1/4 tsp cayenne pepper (non-compulsory for spice)
- 2 tbsp olive oil
- 2 cups of chicken broth
- Salt and pepper as needed
- Chop-up fresh cilantro, for garnish

Instructions:

1. Olive oil Must be heated in a sizable pot over a medium-high heat. Cook the chicken thighs up to browned after adding them skin-side down. Chicken Must be taken out of the pot and placed aside.
2. Add the chop-up garlic and onion to the same pot. The onion Must be cooked up to tender and transparent.
3. Add the turmeric, cumin, paprika, coriander, and cayenne (if using). The spices Must be thoroughly combined into the onions and garlic.
4. Add the chicken and any accumulated liquids back to the pot. Add the chicken broth and the okra. Add salt and pepper as needed.
5. Heat Must be turned down once the Mixture comes to a boil. For about an hr, or up to the chicken is cooked through and tender, simmer the Mixture covered.
6. Serve the stew hot with fresh cilantro on top. Enjoy!

229. Egyptian Rice and Chicken Stuffed Grape Leaves with Dill-Yogurt Sauce

Time: 1 hr 30 mins
Servings: 4

Ingredients:

- 1 cup of long-grain rice
- 1/2 cup of diced cooked chicken breast
- 1/4 cup of chop-up fresh dill
- 1/4 cup of chop-up fresh parsley
- 2 tbsp chop-up fresh mint
- 2 tbsp lemon juice
- 1 tbsp olive oil
- 1/2 tsp ground cumin
- 1/2 tsp ground coriander
- 1/4 tsp ground cinnamon
- Salt and pepper as needed
- 20-25 grape leaves (canned or fresh)
- 1 cup of plain yogurt
- 1 clove garlic, chop-up
- 1 tbsp chop-up fresh dill
- 1 tbsp lemon juice
- Salt as needed

Instructions:

1. Rice, diced chicken, chop-up dill, parsley, mint, lemon juice, olive oil, cumin, coriander, cinnamon, salt, and pepper Must all be combined in a bowl. Combine thoroughly.
2. A grape leaf Must be placed vein-side up on a flat surface. Place a spoonful or more of the rice Mixture in the leaf's middle.
3. The grape leaf is folded over the filling on both sides before being tightly rolled into a cigar shape. Repetition is required with the remaining grape leaves and filling.
4. Seam-side down, arrange the packed grape leaves in a single layer in a pot. Grape leaves Must be covered with water, and then a plate or lid Must be placed on top to weigh them down.
5. Heat the water up to it boils, then turn the heat down to low. For about 45 mins, or up to the rice is done and the grape leaves are soft, cover the saucepan and simmer the grape leaves.
6. Combine the plain yogurt, chop-up garlic, dill, lemon juice, and salt in a mini bowl.
7. With the dill-yogurt sauce poured on top, serve the stuffed grape leaves hot or at room temperature. Enjoy!

230. Egyptian Stuffed Zucchini with Rice and Chickpeas in Tomato-Herb Sauce

Time: 1 hr 30 mins
Servings: 6

Ingredients:

- 6 medium zucchini
- 1 cup of cooked rice
- 1 cup of cooked chickpeas
- 1/4 cup of chop-up fresh parsley

- 1/4 cup of chop-up fresh dill
- 1/4 cup of chop-up fresh mint
- 1 onion, lightly chop-up
- 2 garlic cloves, chop-up
- 1 can (400g) diced tomatoes
- 1 tbsp tomato paste
- 1 tsp ground cumin
- 1 tsp ground coriander
- 1/2 tsp ground cinnamon
- 1/2 tsp sugar
- 2 tbsp olive oil
- Salt and pepper as needed

Instructions:

1. Take out the zucchini's tops and scoop out the flesh, leaving a hollow shell behind. Hold onto the flesh.
2. Cooked rice, cooked chickpeas, parsley, dill, mint, onion, garlic, salt, and pepper are all combined in a bowl. Combine thoroughly.
3. Firmly push the rice and chickpea Mixture into the hollowed-out zucchini.
4. Olive oil Must be heated in a sizable pot over medium heat. Add the diced tomatoes, tomato paste, cumin, coriander, cinnamon, sugar, salt, and pepper along with the reserved zucchini flesh. Stir thoroughly.
5. In the tomato-herb sauce, nestle the stuffed zucchini in the pot.
6. Heat Must be turned down when the sauce comes to a boil. Up to the zucchini is soft, let the Mixture boil with the lid on for about 45 mins.
7. With the tomato-herb sauce spooned over them, serve the hot stuffed zucchini. Enjoy!

231. Egyptian Lamb and Cauliflower Tagine with Turmeric and Cardamom

Time: 2 hrs
Servings: 4

Ingredients:

- 1 kg lamb Muster, slice into chunks
- 1 mini cauliflower, slice into florets
- 1 onion, lightly chop-up
- 4 garlic cloves, chop-up
- 2 tsp ground turmeric
- 1 tsp ground cumin
- 1 tsp ground coriander
- 1/2 tsp ground cardamom
- 1/4 tsp ground cinnamon
- 1 can (400g) diced tomatoes
- 2 cups of chicken or vegetable broth
- 2 tbsp olive oil
- Salt and pepper as needed
- Chop-up fresh cilantro, for garnish

Instructions:

1. Heat some oil in a sizable tagine or heavy-bottomed saucepan over medium heat. Add the lamb, then sear it thoroughly. Lamb Must be taken out of the saucepan and placed aside.
2. Add the onions and garlic to the same pot. The onions Must be sautéed up to transparent and tender.
3. Add the cinnamon, cardamom, cardamom, cumin, and turmeric. The spices Must be thoroughly combined into the onions and garlic.
4. Add the cauliflower florets, diced tomatoes, and stock to the pot with the meat. Add salt and pepper as needed.
5. Heat Must be turned down once the Mixture comes to a boil. For about 1.5 to 2 hrs, or up to the lamb is soft and the cauliflower is cooked, simmer the Mixture with the lid on.
6. Serve the tagine hot with fresh cilantro leaves as a garnish. Enjoy!

132. Egyptian Stuffed Eggplant with Rice and Tomato-Herb Sauce

Time: 1 hr
Servings: 4

Ingredients:

- 4 Big eggplants
- 1 cup of long-grain rice
- 1 onion, lightly chop-up
- 2 tomatoes, diced
- 2 cloves of garlic, chop-up
- 1/4 cup of chop-up fresh parsley
- 1/4 cup of chop-up fresh mint
- 1/4 cup of chop-up fresh dill
- 2 tbsp olive oil
- Salt and pepper as needed

Instructions:

1. Set the oven's temperature to 375°F (190°C).
2. Slice the eggplants in half lengthwise, take out the flesh, and then discard the shell.
3. Slice the flesh of the eggplant into mini pieces and place it aside.

4. The olive oil Must be heated in a saucepan over medium heat. Cook the onion and garlic after being added up to tender.
5. Rice, parsley, mint, dill, split tomatoes, and pepper Must all be added. While intermittently stirring, cook for 5 mins.
6. Place the stuffed eggplant shells in a baking dish. Fill the eggplant shells with the rice Mixture.
7. Combine tomato sauce and water in a different bowl. Over the filled eggplants, pour the sauce.
8. Bake for 40 mins with the foil covering the baking dish.
9. When the eggplants are cooked, take out the foil and bake for a further 10 mins.
10. Serve hot and garnish with more herbs.

NUTRITION INFO (per serving):

Cals: 280
Protein: 6g
Carbs: 51g
Fat: 7g
Fiber: 9g

233. Egyptian Lamb and Potato Tagine with Prunes and Ginger

Time: 2 hrs
Servings: 6

Ingredients:

- 2 lbs lamb Muster, slice into chunks
- 4 medium potatoes, peel off and quartered
- 1 cup of pitted prunes
- 1 onion, chop-up
- 3 cloves of garlic, chop-up
- 2 tbsp finely grated fresh ginger
- 1 tsp ground cinnamon
- 1 tsp ground cumin
- 1 tsp ground coriander
- 1/2 tsp turmeric
- 2 tbsp olive oil
- Salt and pepper as needed
- Chop-up fresh cilantro for garnish

Instructions:

1. Heat the olive oil in a sizable saucepan or tagine over medium heat. Cook up to melted after adding the chop-up garlic and diced onion.
2. Brown the lamb Muster chunks all over in the pot after adding them.
3. Add the salt, pepper, turmeric, coriander, cumin, and finely grated ginger after stirring. Cook up to aromatic for one min.
4. Cover the pot with just enough water to cover the meat, then simmer for an hr.
5. Once the lamb is soft and the potatoes are cooked through, stir in the quartered potatoes and pitted prunes. Cook for an additional 30 to 40 mins.
6. If necessary, adjust the seasoning.
7. Serve the tagine hot with fresh cilantro that has been chop-up on top.

NUTRITION INFO (per serving):

Cals: 420
Protein: 28g
Carbs: 37g
Fat: 16g
Fiber: 6g

234. Egyptian Spinach and Lentil Salad with Pomegranate Dressing

Time: 30 mins
Servings: 4

Ingredients:

- 8 cups of fresh spinach leaves
- 1 cup of cooked green lentils
- 1/2 cup of pomegranate seeds
- 1/4 cup of cut up feta cheese
- 1/4 cup of chop-up walnuts
- 2 tbsp extra-virgin olive oil
- 1 tbsp pomegranate molasses
- 1 tbsp lemon juice
- Salt and pepper as needed

Instructions:

1. Fresh spinach leaves, cooked lentils, pomegranate seeds, cut up feta cheese, and chop-up walnuts Must all be combined in a big salad bowl.
2. Make the dressing by combining the olive oil, pomegranate molasses, lemon juice, salt, and pepper in a mini bowl.
3. Over the salad, drizzle the dressing and give it a gentle toss to coat.
4. Serve the lentil and spinach salad right away.

NUTRITION INFO (per serving):
Cals: 250

Protein: 11g
Carbs: 26g
Fat: 12g
Fiber: 6g

235. Egyptian Chicken and Okra Stew with Turmeric and Coriander

Time: 1 hr 30 mins
Servings: 6

Ingredients:

- 2 lbs chicken pieces (legs, thighs, or breasts)
- 2 cups of fresh okra, trimmed
- 1 onion, chop-up
- 3 cloves of garlic, chop-up
- 2 tomatoes, diced
- 2 tbsp tomato paste
- 2 tsp ground turmeric
- 1 tsp ground coriander
- 1/2 tsp ground cumin
- 4 cups of chicken broth
- 2 tbsp olive oil
- Salt and pepper as needed
- Chop-up fresh cilantro for garnish

Instructions:

1. Olive oil Must be heated in a sizable pot over medium heat. Cook up to melted after adding the chop-up garlic and diced onion.
2. Brown the chicken pieces all over in the pot after adding them.
3. Add the salt, pepper, ground cumin, ground coriander, and ground turmeric. Cook up to aromatic for one min.
4. Chicken stock, tomato paste, and diced tomatoes Must all be added to the saucepan. Boil for a few mins, then turn down the heat, cover the pot, and simmer for 45 mins.
5. When the chicken is thoroughly cooked and the okra is tender, add the fresh okra to the saucepan and simmer for an additional 15 mins.
6. If necessary, adjust the seasoning.
7. Serve the hot chicken and okra stew with fresh cilantro that has been chop-up.

NUTRITION INFO (per serving):
Cals: 320
Protein: 28g
Carbs: 12g
Fat: 18g

Fiber: 4g

236. Kushari (Egyptian Rice and Lentil Dish)

Time: 1 hr
Servings: 6

Ingredients:

- 1 cup of white rice
- 1 cup of brown lentils
- 1 cup of elbow macaroni
- 1 onion, thinly split
- 4 cloves of garlic, chop-up
- 2 tbsp vegetable oil
- 1 tbsp ground cumin
- 1 tbsp ground coriander
- 1/2 tsp cayenne pepper (non-compulsory)
- Salt and pepper as needed

For the tomato sauce:

- 2 tbsp vegetable oil
- 1 onion, lightly chop-up
- 2 cloves of garlic, chop-up
- 1 can (14 ozs) crushed tomatoes
- 1 tbsp tomato paste
- 1 tsp ground cumin
- 1 tsp ground coriander
- Salt and pepper as needed

For the garnish:

- Fried onions
- Chop-up fresh parsley
- Vinegar (non-compulsory)

Instructions:

1. Rice, lentils, and macaroni Must all be rinsed separately with cold water.
2. Bring 4 cups of water to a boil in a big pot. Cook the rice till soft after adding it. Drain, then set apart.
3. Bring 4 cups of water to a boil in another pot. When the lentils are ready, add them. Drain, then set apart.
4. As directed on the box/pkg, prepare the macaroni up to it is al dente. Drain, then set apart.
5. Vegetable oil Must be heated in a sizable skillet over medium heat. Add the chop-up garlic and onion slices. Cook till crispy and golden. The

onions Must be taken out of the skillet and reserved for garnish.
6. Add the cooked rice, lentils, macaroni, cumin, coriander, cayenne pepper (if using), salt, and pepper to the same skillet. Gently blend and heat through while stirring.
7. In a another skillet over medium heat, warm 2 tbsp of vegetable oil for the tomato sauce. Add the chop-up garlic and lightly diced onion. Cook for softening.
8. To the skillet, add the crushed tomatoes, tomato paste, cumin, coriander, salt, and pepper. Simmer for ten to fifteen mins, stirring once and then.
9. Pour the rice, lentil, and macaroni Mixture onto every person's plate or bowl before serving. Add tomato sauce on top. Add fried onions and freshly slice parsley as a garnish. Add a vinegar drizzle, if desired.
10. Cheers to your Kushari!

NUTRITION INFO (per serving):
Cals: 470
Protein: 15g
Carbs: 77g
Fat: 14g
Fiber: 9g

237. Molokhia Soup (Jute Leaf Soup)

Time: 1 hr
Servings: 4

Ingredients:
- 1 lb refrigerate or fresh molokhia leaves
- 4 cups of chicken or vegetable broth
- 2 cloves of garlic, chop-up
- 1 onion, lightly chop-up
- 2 tbsp vegetable oil
- 1 tsp ground coriander
- 1/2 tsp ground cumin
- Juice of 1 lemon
- Salt and pepper as needed
- For serving (non-compulsory):
- Cooked rice or vermicelli
- Grilled chicken or beef

Instructions:
1. Follow the directions on the packaging to defrost refrigerate molokhia leaves. Wash the molokhia leaves well if using fresh ones.
2. Vegetable oil Must be heated in a sizable pot over medium heat. Add the chop-up garlic and onion, both chop-up. Cook for softening.
3. Cook the molokhia leaves in the pot for about 5 mins, stirring occasionally.
4. Add the vegetable or chicken broth. Add the salt, pepper, ground cumin, and ground coriander. The Mixture Must be heated up to it boils, then it Must be simmered for 30 mins.
5. Smoothen the soup using a standard blender or an immersion blender. If using a standard blender, blend the soup in mini batches and use caution because it will be hot.
6. Add the lemon juice and then put the soup back in the pot. Stir thoroughly, and seasoning as necessary.
7. Pour the molokhia soup into dishes to serve. If preferred, top with grilled chicken or beef and serve with cooked rice or vermicelli on the side.

NUTRITION INFO (per serving):
Cals: 160
Protein: 3g
Carbs: 9g
Fat: 13g
Fiber: 5g

238. Egyptian Spinach and Chickpea Soup with Harissa and Cilantro

Time: 45 mins
Servings: 4

Ingredients:
- 2 tbsp olive oil
- 1 onion, lightly chop-up
- 3 cloves garlic, chop-up
- 1 tsp ground cumin
- 1 tsp ground coriander
- 1/2 tsp ground turmeric
- 1/4 tsp cayenne pepper (non-compulsory)
- 4 cups of vegetable broth
- 1 can (15 ozs) chickpeas, drained and rinsed
- 4 cups of fresh spinach, chop-up
- 2 tbsp harissa paste
- Salt and pepper, as needed
- Fresh cilantro leaves, for garnish

Instructions:
1. Over medium heat, warm the olive oil in a big

pot. Sauté the onion and garlic up to fragrant and melted after being added.
2. Add the cayenne pepper (if using), turmeric, cumin, and coriander after stirring. The spices Must be cooked for one more min to toast them.
3. Add the chickpeas and vegetable broth to the pot. Once it has boiled, turn down the heat, cover, and simmer for 15 mins.
4. Cook the spinach for about 5 mins, up to it has wilted.
5. Add the harissa paste after seasoning as needed with salt and pepper. Simmer for a further five mins.
6. Serve the soup hot with fresh cilantro leaves as a garnish.

NUTRITION INFO (per serving):
Cals: 230
Fat: 9g
Carbs: 30g
Protein: 9g
Fiber: 8g

239. Egyptian Chicken and Egg Tagine with Preserved Lemon and Olives

Time: 1 hr 30 mins
Servings: 4

Ingredients:
- 1 whole chicken, slice into pieces
- 2 tbsp olive oil
- 1 onion, lightly chop-up
- 3 cloves garlic, chop-up
- 1 tsp ground cumin
- 1 tsp ground coriander
- 1/2 tsp ground cinnamon
- 1/4 tsp ground ginger
- 1/4 tsp cayenne pepper (non-compulsory)
- Salt and pepper, as needed
- 1 preserved lemon, flesh discarded, rind rinsed and lightly chop-up
- 1/2 cup of green olives, pitted
- 1/4 cup of chop-up fresh cilantro, for garnish

Instructions:
1. In a sizable tagine or Dutch oven, heat the olive oil over medium heat. Brown the chicken pieces all over after adding them. Chicken Must be taken out of the pot and placed aside.
2. Add the chop-up garlic and onion to the same pot. Sauté the onion up to it becomes transparent and tender.
3. Add the salt, pepper, ginger, cinnamon, cumin, and cayenne pepper (if using). The spices Must be thoroughly combined with the onions and garlic.
4. Put the chicken back in the pot and cover it with just enough water to cover. Bring to a boil, then lower the heat, cover the pan, and simmer the chicken for one hr, or up to it is cooked through and soft.
5. Olives and lemon preserves are now added. Simmer for a further five mins.
6. Serve the chicken tagine hot with chop-up cilantro as a garnish. It goes great with couscous or rice.

NUTRITION INFO (per serving):
Cals: 390
Fat: 22g
Carbs: 8g
Protein: 38g
Fiber: 2g

240. Egyptian Rice and Vermicelli Pilaf with Pistachios and Saffron

Time: 30 mins
Servings: 4

Ingredients:
- 1 cup of basmati rice
- 1/2 cup of vermicelli noodles, broken into mini pieces
- 2 tbsp unsalted butter
- 2 cups of chicken or vegetable broth
- 1/4 tsp saffron threads
- 1/4 cup of shelled pistachios, chop-up
- Salt, as needed

Instructions:
1. Rice Must be thoroughly rinsed in cold water up to the water is clear. Drain, then set apart.
2. Melt the butter in a Big pot over medium heat. As you stir regularly to prevent burning, add the vermicelli noodles and cook up to they are golden brown.
3. Stir in the vermicelli noodles after adding the rinsed rice to the pan.

4. Saffron threads Must be dissolved in 2 tbsp of boiling water in a separate mini bowl. Stir well after adding the saffron water to the saucepan.
5. Salt the broth, whether it's made of chicken or vegetables. Bring to a boil, lower the heat to a simmer, cover the pot, and cook for 15 to 20 mins, or up to the rice is cooked through and the liquid has been absorbed.
6. After being taken off the heat, the pilaf Must sit covered for 5 mins. Before serving, fluff the rice with a fork.
7. Before serving, add some chop-up pistachios as a garnish.

NUTRITION INFO (per serving):
Cals: 310
Fat: 11g
Carbs: 48g
Protein: 6g
Fiber: 2g

241. Egyptian Stuffed Bell Peppers with Rice and Herbs

Time: 1 hr
Servings: 4

Ingredients:

- 4 bell peppers (any color), tops take outd and seeds discarded
- 1 cup of basmati rice
- 1 mini onion, lightly chop-up
- 2 cloves garlic, chop-up
- 1/4 cup of chop-up fresh parsley
- 1/4 cup of chop-up fresh dill
- 1/4 cup of chop-up fresh mint
- 2 tbsp olive oil
- 1 tsp ground cumin
- 1 tsp ground coriander
- Salt and pepper, as needed
- 1 cup of vegetable broth

Instructions:

1. Set the oven's temperature to 375°F (190°C).
2. Rice, chop-up onion, chop-up garlic, chop-up parsley, dill, and mint Must all be combined in a big bowl. Combine thoroughly.
3. Over medium heat, warm the olive oil in a skillet. Salt, pepper, coriander, cumin, and more. The spices Must cook for one min to toast.
4. Stir the rice Mixture while adding the seasoned oil, then pour it in.
5. Pack the rice and herb Mixture tightly within the bell peppers.
6. In a baking dish, arrange the filled peppers vertically. Fill the dish's bottom with the veggie broth.
7. Bake the dish for 45 mins, or up to the rice is done and the peppers are soft, with the foil covering.
8. In order to lightly brown the peppers' tops, take out the foil and bake the peppers for an additional 5 mins.
9. The filled bell peppers Must be served hot.

NUTRITION INFO (per serving):
Cals: 280
Fat: 8g
Carbs: 48g
Protein: 5g
Fiber: 5g

242. Egyptian Lamb Tagine with Almonds and Ras el Hanout

Time: 2 hrs
Servings: 4

Ingredients:

- 1.5 lbs lamb Muster, slice into cubes
- 2 tbsp olive oil
- 1 onion, lightly chop-up
- 3 cloves garlic, chop-up
- 1 tsp ground cumin
- 1 tsp ground coriander
- 1 tsp ground ginger
- 1 tsp ground cinnamon
- 1 tsp ras el hanout spice blend
- Salt and pepper, as needed
- 2 cups of chicken or vegetable broth
- 1/2 cup of dried apricots, chop-up
- 1/2 cup of blanched almonds
- Fresh cilantro leaves, for garnish

Instructions:

1. In a sizable tagine or Dutch oven, heat the olive oil over medium heat. Brown the lamb cubes all

over after adding them. Lamb Must be taken out of the saucepan and placed aside.
2. Add the chop-up garlic and onion to the same pot. Sauté the onion up to it becomes transparent and tender.
3. Add the salt, pepper, ras el hanout, ginger, cumin, and coriander. The spices Must be thoroughly combined with the onions and garlic.
4. Add the chicken or vegetable broth to the pot and add the lamb back in. When the lamb is cooked, simmer for 1.5 to 2 hrs with the heat reduced, the lid on.
5. Add the blanched almonds and chop-up dried apricots after stirring. Simmer for a further ten mins.
6. Warm lamb tagine Must be served with fresh cilantro leaves on top. It goes great with bread or couscous.

NUTRITION INFO (per serving):
Cals: 480
Fat: 29g
Carbs: 23g
Protein: 33g
Fiber: 6g

243. Egyptian Rice and Beef Stuffed Cabbage Leaves with Tamarind Sauce

Time: 1 hr 30 mins
Servings: 4

Ingredients:
- 8 Big cabbage leaves
- 1/2 lb ground beef
- 1/2 cup of cooked rice
- 1 mini onion, lightly chop-up
- 2 cloves garlic, chop-up
- 1/4 cup of chop-up fresh parsley
- 1/4 cup of chop-up fresh mint
- 2 tbsp olive oil
- 1 tsp ground cumin
- 1 tsp ground coriander
- Salt and pepper, as needed
- 1 can (14 ozs) crushed tomatoes
- 2 tbsp tamarind paste
- 1 tbsp honey
- 1 cup of water

Instructions:
1. Bring water in a big pot to a boil. After adding, blanch the cabbage leaves for two to three mins, or up to they are tender. The leaves Must be taken out of the container and put aside.
2. Ground beef, cooked rice, chop-up onion, chop-up garlic, chop-up parsley, chop-up mint, olive oil, cumin, coriander, salt, and pepper Must all be combined in a bowl. Combine thoroughly.
3. Every cabbage leaf Must have a scoop of the beef and rice Mixture in the center. As you tightly roll the leaf, fold the sides in.
4. The tamarind paste, honey, water, and crushed tomatoes Must all be combined in a different pan. After bringing to a boil, turn down the heat.
5. In the pot with the tamarind sauce, add the stuffed cabbage rolls. Once the flavors are blended and the cabbage is soft, simmer the dish covered for 45 to 1 hr.
6. With the tamarind sauce spooned over them, serve the stuffed cabbage rolls hot.

NUTRITION INFO (per serving):
Cals: 320
Fat: 12g
Carbs: 35g
Protein: 18g
Fiber: 6g

244. Foul Medames (Egyptian Fava Beans):

Time: 8 hrs (includes soaking and cooking time)
Servings: 4

Ingredients:
- 2 cups of dried fava beans
- Water for soaking and cooking
- 4 cloves garlic, chop-up
- 1/4 cup of lemon juice
- 1/4 cup of olive oil
- Salt, as needed
- Non-compulsory toppings: chop-up parsley, chop-up tomatoes, chop-up onions, olive oil

Instructions:
1. The dried fava beans Must be rinsed before being put in a big bowl. Leave them in the water overnight or for at least eight hrs.
2. The beans Must be drained and rinsed. Put them in a pot and fill it with clean water. Bring to a boil, lower the heat, and simmer the Mixture for one

to two hrs, or up to the beans are cooked through.
3. While retaining some of the cooking liquid, drain the beans.
4. Use a fork or a potato masher to mash the cooked beans in a big basin up to they have a gritty texture.
5. Olive oil, lemon juice, salt, and chop-up garlic are all added to the mashed beans. Combine thoroughly, if necessary adding a little of the conserved cooking liquid to achieve a creamy consistency.
6. To your liking, adjust the seasoning.
7. Serve the Foul Medames warm, drizzled with extra virgin olive oil, and topped with chop-up parsley, tomatoes, and onions as desired.

NUTRITION INFO (per serving):
Cals: 250
Protein: 12g
Carbs: 35g
Fat: 8g
Fiber: 10g

145. Koshari Pizza (Egyptian Street Food Pizza):

Time: 1 hr
Servings: 4-6

Ingredients:

- 1 prepared pizza dough
- 1 cup of cooked rice
- 1 cup of cooked lentils
- 1 cup of cooked pasta (such as macaroni or penne)
- 1 cup of tomato sauce
- 1 tsp ground cumin
- 1 tsp ground coriander
- 1/2 tsp ground cinnamon
- Salt and pepper, as needed
- 1/4 cup of olive oil
- Non-compulsory toppings: chop-up onions, chop-up tomatoes, chop-up parsley, hot sauce

Instructions:

1. As directed on the pizza dough packet, preheat your oven.
2. The pizza dough Must be rolled out to the required thickness on a lightly dusted surface.
3. Roll out the dough and place it on a pizza stone or baking sheet.
4. Combine the tomato sauce, salt, pepper, ground cumin, coriander, and cinnamon in a mini bowl.
5. Over the pizza crust, evenly distribute the spicy tomato sauce.
6. Cooked pasta, lentils, and rice Must all be combined with olive oil and salt & pepper in separate bowls.
7. Distribute the cooked pasta, lentils, and rice equally over the pizza crust.
8. Add non-compulsory garnishes such chop-up parsley, tomatoes, and onions.
9. Pizza Must be baked in a preheated oven for 15 to 20 mins, or up to the crust is crispy and golden.
10. Before slicing and serving, take it out of the oven and let it to cool somewhat.
11. Serve hot sauce on the side, if desired.

NUTRITION INFO (per serving):
Cals: 400
Protein: 10g
Carbs: 50g
Fat: 16g
Fiber: 5g

246. Hawawshi (Egyptian Meat Pie):

Time: 1 hr
Servings: 4-6

Ingredients:

- 1 lb ground beef or lamb
- 1 onion, lightly chop-up
- 2 cloves garlic, chop-up
- 1 tsp ground cumin
- 1 tsp ground coriander
- 1/2 tsp paprika
- Salt and pepper, as needed
- 1/4 cup of chop-up fresh parsley
- 1/4 cup of chop-up fresh cilantro
- 6 pita bread rounds

Instructions:

1. Turn on the oven to 400 °F (200 °C).
2. Ground beef or lamb, chop-up onion, chop-up garlic, cumin, coriander, paprika, salt, pepper, chop-up parsley, and cilantro Must all be combined in a sizable combining basin. All the components Must be thoroughly combined.

3. Every pita bread round Must be slice up in half to make two pockets.
4. Put a fair amount of the meat Mixture inside every pita bread pocket and press it down to fill it all the way.
5. The stuffed pita breads Must be baked for 20 to 25 mins in the preheated oven, or up to the meat is thoroughly cooked and the pita bread is crunchy.
6. Before serving, take the hawawshi out of the oven and let it cool for a while.
7. Serve the hawawshi plain or with your preferred dipping sauce, such as tahini or yogurt.

NUTRITION INFO (per serving):
Cals: 450
Protein: 25g
Carbs: 30g
Fat: 25g
Fiber: 2g

247. Mahshi (Stuffed Vegetables)

Time: 2 hrs
Servings: 4

Ingredients:
- 4 medium-sized bell peppers (any color)
- 4 medium-sized tomatoes
- 2 medium-sized eggplants
- 2 medium-sized zucchinis
- 1 cup of rice
- 1/2 cup of chop-up fresh parsley
- 1/2 cup of chop-up fresh mint
- 1/2 cup of chop-up fresh dill
- 1/4 cup of olive oil
- 2 cloves garlic, chop-up
- Juice of 1 lemon
- Salt and pepper as needed

Instructions:
1. Set the oven's temperature to 375°F (190°C).
2. Trim the tomatoes' and bell peppers' tops. Make hollow tomato and bell pepper shells by scooping out the interiors and seeds. Put them apart.
3. Slice the zucchini and eggplants in half lengthwise after peeling. Every half Must be hollowed out once the flesh is take outd, much like bell peppers and tomatoes.
4. Slice the flesh from the zucchini and eggplants into pieces and reserve it.
5. Rice, chop-up eggplant, chop-up zucchini, parsley, mint, dill, olive oil, chop-up garlic, lemon juice, salt, and pepper Must all be combined in a big bowl. Combine thoroughly.
6. The rice Mixture Must be tightly packed inside every vegetable shell.
7. In a baking dish, place the filled vegetables. Add a little olive oil as a drizzle.
8. Bake the dish for an hr while it is covered with aluminum foil.
9. Take out the cover after an hr and continue baking for a further 30 mins, or up to the veggies are soft and the tops are golden.
10. For the main course, serve the Mahshi hot. Additionally, you can serve it with a side of tomato sauce or yogurt.

NUTRITION INFO (per serving):
Cals: 320
Fat: 11g
Carbs: 52g
Protein: 6g
Fiber: 7g

248. Ful Wa Ta'meya (Fava Bean and Falafel Wraps)

Time: 1 hr
Servings: 4

Ingredients:
- 1 cup of dried fava beans
- 1 onion, lightly chop-up
- 3 cloves garlic, chop-up
- 1/2 cup of fresh parsley, chop-up
- 1/2 cup of fresh cilantro, chop-up
- 1 tsp ground cumin
- 1 tsp ground coriander
- 1/2 tsp baking powder
- Salt and pepper as needed
- Vegetable oil for frying
- 4 pita breads
- Toppings (non-compulsory): diced tomatoes, chop-up lettuce, tahini sauce, hot sauce

Instructions:
1. Overnight, soak the dried fava beans in water. Rinse and drain them.
2. The soaked fava beans, chop-up onion, chop-up garlic, parsley, cilantro, cumin, coriander, baking powder, salt, and pepper Must all be combined in

a mixer. Once thoroughly combined but with some remaining chunks, pulse.
3. After transferring the Mixture to a bowl, give it 15 mins to cool in the refrigerator.
4. In a deep frying pan, heat vegetable oil over medium heat.
5. Create mini, golf ball-sized patties or balls out of the falafel Mixture.
6. The falafel patties Must be golden brown and crispy on both sides after being fried in hot oil. Every side will take roughly three to four mins.
7. Falafel Must be taken out of the oil and leted to drain on paper towels.
8. In the oven or toaster, reheat the pita breads.
9. Open the pita pockets after Cutting them in half.
10. Falafel, split tomatoes, chop-up lettuce, and any additional toppings that you choose Must go inside every pita pocket.
11. The Ful Wa Ta'meya wraps Must be served right away, with non-compulsory side servings of tahini sauce and spicy sauce.

NUTRITION INFO (per serving):
Cals: 380
Fat: 10g
Carbs: 60g
Protein: 14g
Fiber: 11g

249. Shakshuka (Egyptian Style)

Time: 40 mins
Servings: 4

Ingredients:

- 2 tbsp olive oil
- 1 onion, chop-up
- 2 cloves garlic, chop-up
- 1 red bell pepper, chop-up
- 1 yellow bell pepper, chop-up
- 1 tsp ground cumin
- 1 tsp ground paprika
- 1/2 tsp ground cayenne pepper (non-compulsory)
- 1 can (14 oz) diced tomatoes
- Salt and pepper as needed
- 4-6 Big eggs
- Fresh parsley, chop-up (for garnish)

Instructions:

1. Over medium heat, warm the olive oil in a sizable frying pan or skillet.
2. Garlic and onion Must be added to the pan and sautéed up to tender and transparent.
3. Red and yellow bell peppers, chop-up, Must be added to the skillet and cooked for about 5 mins, or up to they begin to soften.
4. Add the cayenne pepper (if using), paprika, and ground cumin. To enable the spices to release their flavors, cook for one additional min.
5. Salt and pepper the tomatoes before adding them to the pan. Cook the ingredients for 10 to 15 mins, or up to the sauce slightly thickens.
6. Create a few little wells in the sauce, then crack the eggs inside. For about 5-8 mins, with the pan covered, cook the eggs up to the whites are set but the yolks are still a little runny.
7. Add some chop-up parsley to the shakshuka and serve it hot, straight from the pan.

NUTRITION INFO (per serving):
Cals: 220
Fat: 14g
Carbs: 15g
Protein: 10g
Fiber: 4g

250. Kofta (Spiced Ground Meat Skewers)

Time: 30 mins
Servings: 4

Ingredients:

- 500 grams ground beef or lamb
- 1 mini onion, lightly chop-up
- 2 cloves garlic, chop-up
- 2 tbsp fresh parsley, chop-up
- 1 tsp ground cumin
- 1 tsp ground coriander
- 1/2 tsp paprika
- Salt and pepper as needed
- Wooden skewers, soaked in water

Instructions:

1. Ground beef, chop-up garlic, chop-up onion, parsley, cumin, coriander, paprika, salt, and pepper Must all be combined in a bowl. All the components Must be thoroughly combined.

2. Take a mini portion of the meat Mixture and roll it around a wooden skewer to resemble a sausage. Using the remaining Mixture and skewers, repeat.
3. A grill or grill pan Must be preheated to high heat. The skewers Must be grilled on the grill for 10 to 12 mins, turning them over once or twice, or up to the meat is thoroughly cooked and attractively browned.
4. With your choice of sides, like as pita bread, tzatziki sauce, or a crisp salad, serve the kofta skewers hot.

NUTRITION INFO:
Cals: 280
Fat: 18g
Carbs: 4g
Protein: 24g

251. Fiteer Meshaltet (Egyptian Pastry)

Time: 2 hrs
Servings: 8

Ingredients:
- 500 grams all-purpose flour
- 1 tsp instant yeast
- 1/2 tsp salt
- 1 tbsp sugar
- 1 cup of warm water
- 1 cup of butter, dilute
- 1/2 cup of vegetable oil
- Non-compulsory fillings: cheese, chop-up meat, or a sweet filling of your choice (e.g., Nutella, jam)

Instructions:
1. Combine the flour, yeast, salt, and sugar in a sizable basin. Add the warm water a little at a time while combining up to the dough comes together.
2. The dough has to be smooth and elastic after 5 mins of kneading on a floured surface. It Must double in size after being formed into a ball and let to rest for an hr in a greased dish while being covered with a clean kitchen towel.
3. Turn on the oven to 200 °C (400 °F).
4. The dough Must be slice up into 8 equal pieces. Make a thin circle out of one portion by rolling it out on a floured board.
5. Dilute butter Must be brushed over the dough's surface and some vegetable oil Must be sprinkled on top. The dough Must be folded into a rectangle and then rolled into a cylinder. With the remaining dough portions, repeat this process.
6. Roll the cylinders into a flattened shape and place them on a baking pan. For about 20 mins, or up to golden and crispy, bake in the preheated oven.
7. After removing from the oven, let the fiteer to cool for a while. Slice and serve with the filling of your choice.

NUTRITION INFO:
Cals: 400
Fat: 25g
Carbs: 40g
Protein: 6g

252. Sayadeya (Fish Pilaf)

Time: 1 hr 30 mins
Servings: 6

Ingredients:
- 500 grams white fish fillets (such as cod or haddock)
- 2 cups of long-grain rice
- 1 Big onion, lightly chop-up
- 3 cloves garlic, chop-up
- 2 tbsp vegetable oil
- 1 tsp ground cumin
- 1 tsp ground coriander
- 1 tsp paprika
- 1/2 tsp turmeric
- 1/4 tsp cayenne pepper (non-compulsory, for spice)
- 2 tbsp tomato paste
- 4 cups of fish or vegetable broth
- Salt and pepper as needed
- Fresh parsley, chop-up (for garnish)
- Lemon wedges (for serving)

Instructions:
1. Rice Must be thoroughly rinsed in cold water up to the water is clear. Drain the rice after soaking it for 20 to 30 mins in cool water.
2. Vegetable oil Must be heated in a sizable pot over medium heat. Add the chop-up garlic and onion, and cook up to golden brown.
3. Then, add the cayenne pepper (if using), paprika, turmeric, ground cumin, ground coriander, and

paprika to the pot. To toast the spices, stir them for one min.
4. Combine the onions, spices, and tomato paste all together in the pot.
5. On top of the onion Mixture in the pot, arrange the fish fillets. Fish Must be salted and peppered.
6. Pour the vegetable or fish broth in the pot after adding the drained rice. Gently whisk everything together.
7. Heat Must be turned down once the Mixture comes to a boil. For about 25 to 30 mins, or up to the rice is done and the fish is flaky, simmer the Mixture with the lid on.
8. To enable the flavors to mingle, turn off the heat and let the pot remain, covered, for an additional 10 mins.
9. Serve the sayadeya hot with lemon wedges and fresh parsley on the side.

NUTRITION INFO:
Cals: 380
Fat: 8g
Carbs: 56g
Protein: 20g

153. Kabab Wa Kofta (Combined Grill)

Time: 45 mins
Servings: 4

Ingredients:

- 500 grams lamb cubes
- 500 grams ground beef or lamb
- 1 onion, lightly chop-up
- 3 cloves garlic, chop-up
- 2 tbsp fresh parsley, chop-up
- 1 tsp ground cumin
- 1 tsp ground coriander
- 1/2 tsp paprika
- Salt and pepper as needed
- Wooden skewers, soaked in water

Instructions:

1. Lamb cubes, ground beef, chop-up garlic, chop-up onion, parsley, cumin, coriander, paprika, salt, and pepper Must all be combined in a bowl. All the components Must be thoroughly combined.
2. Grab a handful of the Mixture and roll it around a wooden skewer to resemble a sausage. Using the remaining Mixture and skewers, repeat.
3. A grill or grill pan Must be preheated to high heat. As the meat cooks to the appropriate doneness, turn the skewers once or twice during the 12 to 15 mins they are on the grill.
4. With hot rice, grilled veggies, and your preferred sauces, serve the kabab wa kofta.

NUTRITION INFO:
Cals: 460
Fat: 30g
Carbs: 4g
Protein: 40g

254. Sambousek (Savory Pastry)

Time: 1 hr
Servings: 12

Ingredients:
For the dough:

- 2 cups of all-purpose flour
- 1/2 tsp salt
- 1/2 cup of unsalted butter, dilute
- 1/2 cup of warm water

For the filling:

- 250 grams ground beef or lamb
- 1 mini onion, lightly chop-up- 2 cloves garlic, chop-up
- 1/4 cup of fresh parsley, chop-up
- 1 tsp ground cumin
- 1 tsp ground coriander
- 1/2 tsp paprika
- Salt and pepper as needed
- Vegetable oil for frying

Instructions:

1. The flour and salt Must be combined in a big bowl. Add the dilute butter gradually while combining the ingredients up to they form coarse crumbs.
2. Once the warm water has been added gradually, begin to knead the dough up to it comes together and is smooth. The dough Must be covered and rested for 30 mins.
3. Prepare the filling while waiting. A little vegetable oil Must be heated in a skillet over medium heat. Add the chop-up garlic and onion, and cook up to transparent.
4. Breaking up the ground meat with a spoon, add it to the skillet, and cook up to it is browned. Add

the salt, pepper, paprika, cumin, and coriander. Cook for a short while to let the flavors to mingle. Take the filling off the stove and let it to cool.
5. In a deep fryer or Big pot, heat vegetable oil to 180 °C (350 °F).
6. The dough Must be rolled out to a thickness of about 1/8 inch on a floured surface. Slice out circles from the dough using a glass or a round cookie sliceter.
7. Every dough circle Must have a tbsp of the meat filling in the middle. To create a half-moon shape and seal the sambousek, fold the dough over and firmly press the edges together.
8. Sambousek Must be crisp and golden brown after being fried in hot oil. Take out from the oil, then drain on a platter covered with paper towels.
9. Warm sambousek is best served as an appetizer or light snack.

NUTRITION INFO:
Cals: 200
Fat: 12g
Carbs: 15g
Protein: 7g

255. Basbousa (Semolina Cake with Syrup):

Time: 1 hr
Servings: 8

Ingredients:

- 1 cup of semolina
- 1/2 cup of all-purpose flour
- 1 cup of desiccated coconut
- 1 cup of sugar
- 1/2 cup of unsalted butter, dilute
- 1 cup of milk
- 1 tsp baking powder
- 1/4 tsp vanilla extract
- Slivered almonds or pistachios for garnish

Instructions:

1. Set your oven's temperature to 180 °C (350 °F).
2. Semolina, flour, coconut, sugar, dilute butter, milk, baking soda, and vanilla extract Must all be combined in a big basin. All the components Must be thoroughly combined.
3. Spread the Mixture evenly after pouring it into a prepared baking dish.
4. Slice square or diamond shapes into the Mixture's top using a sharp knife.
5. Top every piece with a slivered almond or pistachio.
6. Bake for 30 to 40 mins, or up to the top is golden brown, in the preheated oven.
7. Make the syrup while the basbousa is baking.
8. When the basbousa is finished baking, take it out of the oven and drizzle the syrup evenly over the warm cake.
9. Before serving, let the basbousa cool and absorb the syrup.

NUTRITION INFO (per serving):
Cals: 320
Fat: 17g
Carbs: 38g
Protein: 5g

256. Umm Ali (Egyptian Bread Pudding):

Time: 40 mins
Servings: 6

Ingredients:

- 4 cups of stale bread, torn into mini pieces
- 2 cups of milk
- 1/2 cup of heavy cream
- 1/2 cup of sugar
- 1/4 cup of raisins
- 1/4 cup of chop-up nuts (such as pistachios or almonds)
- 2 tbsp unsalted butter, dilute
- 1 tsp vanilla extract
- Ground cinnamon for sprinkling

Instructions:

1. Set your oven's temperature to 180 °C (350 °F).
2. The slices of bread, milk, heavy cream, sugar, raisins, nuts, dilute butter, and vanilla essence Must all be combined in a big bowl. Combine thoroughly.
3. Spread the Mixture evenly in a baking dish that has been buttered.
4. On top, sprinkle cinnamon powder.
5. Bake for 25 to 30 mins, or up to the top is crisp and golden brown, in the preheated oven.
6. Before serving, take it out of the oven and let it to cool for a while.

NUTRITION INFO (per serving):
Cals: 390

Fat: 20g
Carbs: 47g
Protein: 8g

257. Bamia (Okra Stew):

Time: 1 hr 30 mins
Servings: 4

Ingredients:

- 500g (about 1 lb) fresh okra, trimmed and rinsed
- 500g (about 1 lb) beef or lamb stew meat, cubed
- 1 Big onion, lightly chop-up
- 3 cloves garlic, chop-up
- 2 tbsp vegetable oil
- 2 tbsp tomato paste
- 2 cups of water
- 1 tsp ground cumin
- 1 tsp ground coriander
- 1/2 tsp ground turmeric
- Salt and pepper as needed
- Cooked rice or bread for serving

Instructions:

1. Vegetable oil Must be heated in a sizable pot over medium heat.
2. To the pot, add the chop-up garlic and diced onion, and sauté up to golden brown.
3. Brown the stew meat on all sides in the pot after adding it.
4. Add the tomato paste along with the salt, pepper, cumin, coriander, and turmeric. For a few mins, cook.
5. Bring the water to a boil in the pot after adding it.
6. When the beef is cooked, reduce the heat to low, cover the pot, and simmer it for about 45 mins.
7. Okra Must be added to the saucepan and simmered for a further 30 mins, or up to it is thoroughly cooked.
8. With warm bread or rice, serve the bamia.

NUTRITION INFO (per serving):
Cals: 350
Fat: 16g
Carbs: 24g
Protein: 28g

158. Roz Bil Laban (Egyptian Rice Pudding):

Time: 1 hr 30 mins
Servings: 6

Ingredients:

- 1 cup of medium-grain rice
- 4 cups of milk
- 1/2 cup of sugar
- 1/4 cup of raisins
- 1/4 cup of chop-up nuts (such as almonds or pistachios)
- 1/2 tsp vanilla extract
- Ground cinnamon for sprinkling

Instructions:

1. Rice Must be thoroughly rinsed in cold water up to the water is clear.
2. Over medium heat, bring the milk to a boil in a big pot.
3. Stir thoroughly after adding the rinsed rice to the pot.
4. Stirring occasionally, lower the heat to a simmer and cook the rice in the milk for approximately an hr, or up to the rice is cooked and the Mixture has thickened.
5. Add the vanilla extract, sugar, raisins, and chop-up nuts. Stir thoroughly.
6. 10 more mins of cooking are required, occasionally stirring.
7. Take it off the fire and give it a min to cool.
8. Place ground cinnamon on top of the rice pudding once you've transferred it to serving plates or a big dish.
9. Either warm or cold, serve the roz bil laban.

NUTRITION INFO (per serving):
Cals: 340
Fat: 9g
Carbs: 57g
Protein: 9g

259. Mulukhiyah with Chicken (Jute Leaf Stew):

Time: 1 hr 30 mins
Servings: 4

Ingredients:

- 500g (about 1 lb) boneless chicken breasts or thighs, slice into mini pieces
- 1 cup of dried mulukhiyah leaves (available at Middle Eastern grocery stores)
- 4 cups of chicken broth
- 1 Big onion, lightly chop-up
- 3 cloves garlic, chop-up

- 2 tbsp vegetable oil
- 1 tbsp ground coriander
- 1/2 tsp ground cumin
- Salt and pepper as needed
- Cooked rice or bread for serving

Instructions:

1. The dried mulukhiyah leaves Must be washed in cold water and then placed aside.
2. Vegetable oil Must be heated in a sizable pot over medium heat.
3. To the pot, add the chop-up garlic and diced onion, and sauté up to golden brown.
4. Cook the chicken pieces in the pot after adding them, stirring occasionally, up to evenly browned.
5. Add the salt, pepper, cumin, and ground coriander. For a few mins, cook.
6. Bring the chicken stock to a boil in the kettle after adding it.
7. When the chicken is cooked through and soft, turn the heat down to low and let the stew simmer for about 45 mins.
8. Cook the mulukhiyah leaves for an extra 10 to 15 mins after rinsing them.
9. If necessary, adjust the seasoning.
10. Over hot rice or on toast, serve the mulukhiyah with chicken.

NUTRITION INFO (per serving):
Cals: 280
Fat: 11g
Carbs: 12g
Protein: 32g

260. Samak Mafroum (Stuffed Baked Fish):

Time: 1 hr 15 mins
Servings: 4

Ingredients:

- 1 whole fish (such as sea bass or snapper), cleaned and scaled
- 1 Big onion, lightly chop-up
- 2 tomatoes, diced
- 3 cloves garlic, chop-up
- 1/4 cup of chop-up fresh parsley
- 1/4 cup of chop-up fresh cilantro
- 2 tbsp vegetable oil
- 2 tbsp lemon juice
- Salt and pepper as needed
- Cooking twine or toothpicks for securing the fish
- Lemon wedges for serving

Instructions:

1. Set your oven's temperature to 180 °C (350 °F).
2. The chop-up onion, diced tomatoes, chop-up garlic, chop-up parsley, chop-up cilantro, vegetable oil, lemon juice, salt, and pepper Must all be combined in a big bowl. The stuffing Must be thoroughly combined.
3. The fish Must be washed in cold water and dried with paper towels.
4. Put the prepared filling inside the cavity of the fish.
5. Use toothpicks or cooking twine to fasten the fish and stop the stuffing from escaping.
6. On a baking sheet, spread a thin layer of vegetable oil over the packed fish.
7. For about 40 to 45 mins, or up to the fish is cooked through and flakes readily with a fork, bake in the preheated oven.
8. Before serving, take it out of the oven and let it to cool for a while.
9. Samak mafroum Must be served with lemon wedges.

NUTRITION INFO (per serving):
Cals: 280
Fat: 10g
Carbs: 7g
Protein: 38g

261. Roz Maa'amar (Egyptian Spiced Rice)

Time: 45 mins
Servings: 4

Ingredients:

- 2 cups of basmati rice
- 1 onion, lightly chop-up
- 3 cloves garlic, chop-up
- 2 tbsp vegetable oil
- 1 tsp ground cumin
- 1 tsp ground coriander
- 1/2 tsp turmeric
- 1/4 tsp cinnamon
- 4 cups of chicken or vegetable broth
- Salt and pepper as needed
- Chop-up fresh cilantro for garnish

Instructions:

1. Basmati rice Must be well rinsed in cold water up to the water is clear. Drain, then set apart.
2. Vegetable oil Must be heated in a sizable pot over medium heat. Cook the chop-up garlic and diced onion up to they are tender and transparent.
3. To toast the spices, add the cumin, coriander, turmeric, and cinnamon to the pot and simmer for an additional min.
4. Stir the rice in the pot to evenly distribute the spices. 2 to 3 mins of cooking.
5. Add the chicken or vegetable broth and salt and pepper as needed. Bring to a boil, lower the heat to a simmer, cover the pan, and cook for 20 to 25 mins, or up to the rice is cooked through and the liquid has been absorbed.
6. With a fork, fluff the rice, then top with freshly chop-up cilantro. Serve warm.

NUTRITION INFO (per serving):
Cals: 320
Fat: 7g
Carbs: 57g
Protein: 6g

262. Kofta Bil Saniyah (Baked Meatballs)

Time: 1 hr
Servings: 6

Ingredients:

- 1 lb ground beef
- 1/2 cup of breadcrumbs
- 1 onion, lightly chop-up
- 2 cloves garlic, chop-up
- 1/4 cup of chop-up fresh parsley
- 1 tsp ground cumin
- 1 tsp ground coriander
- 1/2 tsp paprika
- Salt and pepper as needed
- 1 egg, beaten
- 1 can (14 ozs) diced tomatoes
- 1 cup of beef or vegetable broth
- Chop-up fresh cilantro for garnish

Instructions:

1. Set your oven's temperature to 375°F (190°C).
2. Combine the ground beef, breadcrumbs, chop-up garlic, chop-up onion, chop-up parsley, cumin, coriander, paprika, salt, and pepper in a sizable bowl. Combine thoroughly.
3. Then, blend the meat Mixture with the beaten egg completely.
4. Make meatballs out of the Mixture that are about an inch in diameter.
5. The diced tomatoes and liquid Must be added to the baking dish with the meatballs.
6. Bake in the preheated oven for 30 mins with the foil covering the baking dish.
7. When the meatballs are fully cooked and golden brown, take off the foil and bake for a further 15 mins.
8. Serve hot with fresh cilantro that has been chop-up.

NUTRITION INFO (per serving):
Cals: 280
Fat: 15g
Carbs: 14g
Protein: 22g

263. Fatteh (Layered Bread and Rice Dish)

Time: 1 hr 30 mins
Servings: 6

Ingredients:

- 3 cups of cooked rice
- 4 Big pita breads, toasted and torn into pieces
- 2 cups of plain yogurt
- 3 cloves garlic, chop-up
- 2 tbsp tahini
- 2 tbsp lemon juice
- 1/4 cup of dilute butter
- 1 cup of cooked chickpeas
- Salt and pepper as needed
- Chop-up fresh parsley for garnish

Instructions:

1. Spread half of the shredded pita bread pieces as the first layer in a sizable serving plate.
2. Combine the yogurt, dilute butter, tahini, lemon juice, chop-up garlic, salt, and pepper in a different bowl. Combine thoroughly.
3. Over the top of the initial layer of pita bread, spread half of the yogurt Mixture.
4. Over the yogurt Mixture, sprinkle half of the cooked rice.
5. With the remaining pita bread, yogurt Mixture, and rice, repeat the layering.

6. Chickpeas are added on top, and fresh parsley is slice as a garnish.
7. Serve right away.

NUTRITION INFO (per serving):
Cals: 380
Fat: 14g
Carbs: 52g
Protein: 12g

264. Basbousa Bil Laban (Semolina Dessert with Milk)

Time: 1 hr
Servings: 8

Ingredients:
- 2 cups of semolina
- 1 cup of all-purpose flour
- 1 cup of sugar
- 1 cup of dilute butter
- 1 cup of milk
- 1 tsp vanilla extract
- 1 tsp baking powder
- 1/2 cup of slivered almonds
- Syrup:
- 2 cups of sugar
- 2 cups of water
- 1 tbsp lemon juice
- 1 tsp rose water (non-compulsory)

Instructions:
1. Turn on the oven to 350 °F (175 °C).
2. Semolina, flour, sugar, dilute butter, milk, vanilla extract, and baking powder Must all be combined in a big basin. A smooth batter will form after thorough combining.
3. Spread the batter evenly after pouring it onto a prepared baking dish.
4. The batter Must be covered in the almond slivers.
5. Bake for 30 to 40 mins in a preheated oven, or up to a toothpick inserted in the center of the cake comes out clean.
6. Make the syrup while the basbousa is baking. Combine the sugar, water, lemon juice, and rose water (if using) in a saucepan. Bring to a boil, then lower the heat and let the Mixture simmer for 10 to 15 mins, or up to the syrup slightly thickens.
7. Once the basbousa has finished baking, take out it from the oven and cover it with the hot syrup right away. Let it to sit for at least 20 mins so the syrup can absorb.
8. Slice into squares or diamonds, and serve at room temperature.

NUTRITION INFO (per serving):
Cals: 480
Fat: 21g
Carbs: 68g
Protein: 7g

265. Fattoush (Combined Vegetable Salad)

Time: 20 mins
Servings: 4

Ingredients:
- 4 cups of torn lettuce or combined salad greens
- 1 cucumber, diced
- 2 tomatoes, diced
- 1 green bell pepper, diced
- 1 red onion, thinly split
- 1/2 cup of chop-up fresh parsley
- 1/4 cup of chop-up fresh mint leaves
- 1/2 cup of chop-up radishes
- 1/2 cup of chop-up green onions
- 1/4 cup of extra-virgin olive oil
- 2 tbsp lemon juice
- 1 tsp sumac (non-compulsory)
- Salt and pepper as needed
- Pita bread, toasted and broken into pieces (non-compulsory)

Instructions:
1. The torn lettuce or combined salad greens, diced cucumber, tomatoes, green bell pepper, thinly split red onion, fresh parsley, fresh mint leaves, chop-up radishes, and chop-up green onions Must all be combined in a big bowl.
2. Make the dressing by combining the extra virgin olive oil, lemon juice, sumac (if using), salt, and pepper in a mini bowl.
3. To uniformly coat all of the salad's ingredients, drizzle the dressing over it and toss.
4. Just before serving, scatter toasted and broken pita bread pieces over the salad if like.
5. Serve right away.

NUTRITION INFO (per serving):
Cals: 160
Fat: 12g

Carbs: 12g

Protein: 2g

266. Koshari Bites (Egyptian Rice and Lentil Appetizers)

Time: 45 mins

Servings: 4

Ingredients:

- 1 cup of short-grain rice
- 1 cup of lentils
- 1 onion, lightly chop-up
- 2 cloves garlic, chop-up
- 1 tbsp vegetable oil
- 1 tsp ground cumin
- 1 tsp ground coriander
- Salt, as needed
- Pepper, as needed
- 2 tbsp tomato paste
- 2 cups of vegetable broth
- 1 cup of elbow macaroni
- 1/4 cup of white vinegar
- 2 tbsp vegetable oil (for frying)

Instructions:

1. According to the directions on the packaging, prepare the rice and lentils separately. Place aside.
2. The chop-up onion and chop-up garlic Must be cooked in vegetable oil up to golden brown in a big pan.
3. Salt, pepper, ground coriander, ground cumin, and add to the pan. For a few mins, stir.
4. Add the tomato paste and vegetable broth after stirring. Once it has boiled, turn down the heat, cover, and let it simmer for ten mins.
5. Follow the directions on the box/pkg to prepare the elbow macaroni. Drain, then set apart.
6. Cooked rice, cooked lentils, and cooked macaroni Must all be combined in a combining bowl. Combine thoroughly.
7. Recombine the Mixture after adding the white vinegar.
8. Create tiny bite-sized balls out of the Mixture.
9. In a frying pan, heat vegetable oil over medium heat. The koshari bits Must be fried till golden brown.
10. Serve the koshari bites as appetizers.

Nutrition:

Cals: 300

Fat: 8g

Carbs: 50g

Protein: 10g

267. Hawawshi Sandwich (Egyptian Meat Sandwich)

Time: 1 hr 30 mins

Servings: 6

Ingredients:

- 1 lb ground beef
- 1 onion, lightly chop-up
- 2 cloves garlic, chop-up
- 1 green bell pepper, lightly chop-up
- 2 tomatoes, lightly chop-up
- 2 tbsp chop-up fresh parsley
- 2 tbsp chop-up fresh cilantro
- 1 tbsp ground cumin
- 1 tbsp ground coriander
- 1 tsp paprika
- Salt, as needed
- Pepper, as needed
- 6 pita breads

Instructions:

1. Set your oven's temperature to 375°F (190°C).
2. Ground beef, diced green bell pepper, diced tomatoes, diced green onion, chop-up garlic, fresh parsley, fresh cilantro, paprika, salt, and pepper Must all be combined in a Big combining dish. Combine thoroughly.
3. Every pita bread half Must be split open to create a pocket.
4. Fill every pita pocket with the meat Mixture, pressing it down evenly.
5. The loaded pita pockets Must be baked for about 30 mins in a preheated oven, or up to the meat is thoroughly cooked and the pita bread is crunchy.
6. After taking them out of the oven, give them some time to cool.
7. Hot hawawshi sandwiches Must be served.

Nutrition:

Cals: 400

Fat: 15g

Carbs: 40g

Protein: 25g

268. Molokhia Salad (Jute Leaf Salad)

Time: 30 mins

Servings: 4

Ingredients:

- 4 cups of fresh or refrigerate molokhia leaves
- 2 tbsp vegetable oil
- 4 cloves garlic, chop-up
- 1 onion, lightly chop-up
- 1 tsp ground coriander
- Salt, as needed
- Pepper, as needed
- 1 tbsp lemon juice
- 1 tomato, diced
- 1 cucumber, diced
- 2 tbsp chop-up fresh parsley

Instructions:

1. When using fresh molokhia leaves, be sure to properly wash them and slice off any woody stems. To thaw molokhia if using refrigerate, follow the directions on the box/pkg.
2. Vegetable oil Must be heated in a sizable pot over medium heat.
3. In the oil, cook the chop-up onion and chop-up garlic up to aromatic and browned.
4. Salt, pepper, and ground coriander Must all be added to the saucepan. For a few mins, stir.
5. While stirring occasionally, add the molokhia leaves to the pot and cook for approximately 10 mins.
6. Turn off the heat and let the molokhia Mixture to cool.
7. Add lemon juice, diced tomato, cucumber, and fresh parsley to the pot once it has cooled. Combine thoroughly.
8. The molokhia salad can be served cold or warm.

Nutrition:
Cals: 150
Fat: 6g
Carbs: 20g
Protein: 5g

269. Bamia Bil Lahm (Okra with Meat)

Time: 1 hr 30 mins

Servings: 4

Ingredients:

- 1 lb beef or lamb, slice into cubes
- 1 onion, lightly chop-up
- 2 cloves garlic, chop-up
- 2 tbsp vegetable oil
- 2 cups of fresh or refrigerate okra
- 2 tomatoes, diced
- 1 tbsp tomato paste
- 1 tsp ground coriander
- Salt, as needed
- Pepper, as needed
- 2 cups of water
- Cooked rice (for serving)

Instructions:

1. The chop-up onion and chop-up garlic Must be cooked in vegetable oil in a big pot up to golden brown.
2. Brown the pork cubes on both sides in the pot after adding them.
3. Okra, tomato paste, chop-up tomatoes, ground coriander, salt, and pepper Must all be added to the pot. Stir thoroughly.
4. Add the water, then bring the concoction to a boil. Once the beef is cooked and the flavors have combined, lower the heat to low, cover the pot, and let it stew for approximately an hr.
5. Serve cooked rice beside the bamia bil lahme.

Nutrition:
Cals: 350
Fat: 15g
Carbs: 15g
Protein: 35g

270. Konafa (Sweet Pastry with Cheese)

Time: 1 hr

Servings: 8

Ingredients:

- 1 lb konafa dough (shredded phyllo dough)
- 1 cup of unsalted butter, dilute
- 1 cup of sugar
- 1 cup of water
- 1 tsp rose water (non-compulsory)
- 1 cup of ricotta cheese
- 1 cup of shredded mozzarella cheese
- Chop-up pistachios (for garnish)

Instructions:

1. Turn on the oven to 350 °F (175 °C).

2. In a uniform layer, press down the bottom of a baking dish with half of the konafa dough.
3. Combine the ricotta cheese and shredded mozzarella cheese in a another bowl.
4. Overtop the konafa dough in the baking dish, evenly distribute the cheese Mixture.
5. The leftover konafa dough Must be used to cover the cheese layer, lightly pushing it down.
6. Dr7. Make sure to cover the entire top of the konafa with the dilute butter as you drizzle it on.
7. Bake the konafa in the baking dish in the preheated oven for 30 to 40 mins, or up to it is crisp and golden brown.
8. Make the syrup by combining the sugar and water in a saucepan while the konafa is baking. Bring to a boil, then simmer for 10 mins, or up to slightly thickened. Add the rose water (if using) after removing the pan from the heat.
9. After the konafa has finished baking, take it out of the oven and drizzle the hot pastry with the syrup evenly.
10. Before Cutting the konafa into squares or diamonds, let it cool for a few mins.
11. Add chop-up pistachios as a garnish.
12. The konafa can be served hot or cold.

Nutrition:
Cals: 400
Fat: 20g
Carbs: 50g
Protein: 10g

271. Fasulia (Green Bean Stew)

Time: 1 hr 30 mins

Servings: 4

Ingredients:

- 1 lb green beans, ends trimmed and slice into 1-inch pieces
- 2 tbsp olive oil
- 1 onion, lightly chop-up
- 3 cloves garlic, chop-up
- 1 tsp ground cumin
- 1 tsp ground coriander
- 1 can (14 ozs) diced tomatoes
- 1 cup of vegetable broth
- Salt and pepper as needed

Instructions:

1. In a big pot, warm up the olive oil over medium heat. Cook up to the onion is transparent after adding the chop-up onion and garlic.
2. Cook for another min after adding the cumin and coriander.
3. The pot Must now contain the green beans, diced tomatoes, and vegetable broth. Add salt and pepper as needed.
4. As soon as the Mixture comes to a boil, turn the heat down to low and cover the pan. Approximately 1 hr Must pass for the green beans to become tender.
5. Serve the food hot and adjust the seasoning as necessary.

NUTRITION INFO: (per serving)
Cals: 150
Fat: 7g
Carbs: 20g
Protein: 5g
Fiber: 6g

272. Salata Baladi (Egyptian Tomato and Cucumber Salad)

Time: 15 mins

Servings: 4

Ingredients:

- 2 Big tomatoes, diced
- 1 cucumber, peel off and diced
- 1 mini red onion, thinly split
- 1/4 cup of fresh parsley, chop-up
- 2 tbsp fresh mint, chop-up
- 2 tbsp lemon juice
- 2 tbsp olive oil
- Salt and pepper as needed

Instructions:

1. The diced tomatoes, cucumber, red onion, parsley, and mint Must all be combined in a big bowl.
2. Combine the lemon juice, olive oil, salt, and pepper in a separate mini bowl.
3. Combine the salad ingredients gently after adding the dressing.
4. Before serving, let the salad sit for about 10 mins to let the flavors mingle.

NUTRITION INFO: (per serving)
Cals: 80
Fat: 6g
Carbs: 7g
Protein: 1g
Fiber: 2g

273. Hawawshi Burger (Egyptian Meat Burger)

Time: 40 mins
Servings: 4

Ingredients:

- 1 lb ground beef
- 1 onion, lightly chop-up
- 2 cloves garlic, chop-up
- 2 tbsp fresh parsley, chop-up
- 1 tsp ground cumin
- 1 tsp ground coriander
- 1/2 tsp paprika
- Salt and pepper as needed
- 4 burger buns
- Lettuce, tomato, and onion slices (for serving)

Instructions:

1. Combine the ground beef, chop-up garlic, chop-up onion, parsley, cumin, coriander, paprika, salt, and pepper in a sizable bowl.
2. Make patties by dividing the ingredients into 4 equal pieces.
3. Heat a skillet or grill to medium-high heat. The burger patties Must be cooked for 4–5 mins on every side, or up to they are cooked to your preference.
4. After lightly toasting the burger buns, layer the patties with lettuce, tomato, and onion slices to create the finished burgers.
5. While the Hawawshi burgers are still warm, serve them.

NUTRITION INFO: (per serving)
Cals: 400
Fat: 18g
Carbs: 35g
Protein: 24g
Fiber: 2g

274. Roz Bel Shaban (Rice Pudding with Rosewater)

Time: 1 hr 30 mins
Servings: 6

Ingredients:

- 1 cup of white rice
- 4 cups of milk
- 1/2 cup of sugar
- 1/4 tsp salt
- 1/2 tsp rosewater
- Ground cinnamon for garnish

Instructions:

1. Rice Must be thoroughly rinsed in cold water up to the water is clear. Flow freely.
2. Rice, milk, sugar, and salt Must all be combined together in a big pot. Over medium heat, bring the Mixture to a boil while stirring occasionally.
3. Stirring constantly for approximately an hr, or when the rice is soft and the Mixture has thickened, reduce the heat to low.
4. Cook for an additional five mins after adding the rosewater.
5. The rice pudding Must be taken off the stove and leted to cool to room temperature. Next, chill in the fridge.
6. Serve the chilled Roz Bel Shaban pudding with a dash of ground cinnamon as a garnish.

NUTRITION INFO: (per serving)
Cals: 250
Fat: 4g
Carbs: 49g
Protein: 7g
Fiber: 1g

275. Ful Medames Dip (Fava Bean Dip)

Time: 10 mins
Servings: 6

Ingredients:

- 2 cans (15 ozs every) cooked fava beans, drained and rinsed
- 2 cloves garlic, chop-up
- 2 tbsp lemon juice
- 2 tbsp olive oil
- 1/2 tsp ground cumin
- Salt and pepper as needed
- Chop-up fresh parsley (for garnish)
- Olive oil (for drizzling)

Instructions:

1. Fava beans, chop-up garlic, lemon juice, olive oil, cumin, salt, and pepper Must all be combined in a mixer.
2. If necessary, add a little water to the Mixture as you process it to achieve the ideal smoothness and creaminess.
3. Place the dip in a serving basin and top with freshly chop-up parsley.
4. Over the top, drizzle some olive oil.
5. Serve pita bread or vegetable sticks alongside the Ful Medames dip.

NUTRITION INFO: (per serving)
Cals: 180
Fat: 7g
Carbs: 22g
Protein: 9g
Fiber: 7g

276. Fatteh Bil Lahm (Meat and Bread Casserole)

Time: 1 hr
Servings: 4

Ingredients:

- 500 grams lamb or beef, diced
- 4 pita breads, toasted and slice into mini pieces
- 2 cups of plain yogurt
- 3 cloves garlic, chop-up
- 1 tsp ground cumin
- 1 tsp ground paprika
- Salt and pepper as needed
- Chop-up parsley for garnish
- Olive oil for cooking

Instructions:

1. Olive oil Must be heated in a sizable pan at medium heat. Cook the beef diced till browned after adding.
2. Salt, pepper, paprika, cumin, and chop-up garlic to the pan. The spices Must be thoroughly combined into the meat.
3. Fill the pan with water so that it covers the meat. When the meat is tender, simmer for 30 to 40 mins after bringing to a boil.
4. Whisk the yogurt, chop-up garlic, salt, and pepper in a separate basin.
5. Place the slices of toasted pita bread in a serving dish. Over the bread, pour the yogurt Mixture.
6. Over the yogurt and bread, spoon the cooked beef and its broth.
7. Olive oil Must be drizzled over the dish before serving.
8. When the Fatteh Bil Lahm is still warm, serve it right away.

NUTRITION INFO (per serving):
Cals: 450
Protein: 30g
Carbs: 35g
Fat: 20g

277. Basbousa Bil Ashta (Semolina Dessert with Cream)

Time: 1 hr 30 mins
Servings: 8

Ingredients:
For the cake:

- 2 cups of semolina
- 1 cup of sugar
- 1 cup of unsalted butter, dilute
- 1 cup of plain yogurt
- 1 tsp baking powder
- 1/2 tsp vanilla extract
- Slivered almonds for garnish

For the cream:

- 2 cups of milk
- 1/2 cup of sugar
- 1/4 cup of cornstarch
- 1/2 tsp rose water

Instructions:

1. Set your oven's temperature to 180 °C (350 °F).
2. Semolina, sugar, dilute butter, yogurt, baking soda, and vanilla extract Must all be combined in a combining dish. Combine thoroughly up to batter is uniform.
3. Pour the batter into a baking dish that has been greased and spread it out evenly.
4. Bake for 30 to 40 mins, or up to the top is golden brown, in the preheated oven.
5. Make the cream by boiling the milk in a saucepan over medium heat while the cake bakes. The sugar and cornstarch Must be combined in a different bowl before being added to the warm milk.

6. Up up to the Mixture thickens and boils, stir frequently. Add the rose water after removing from the heat.
7. When the cake is finished baking, take it out of the oven and spread the hot cake with the cream.
8. Before slicing the cake into diamond or square shapes, let it cool fully.
9. Add slivered almonds as a garnish to every slice.
10. Basbousa Bil Ashta Must be served at room temperature.

NUTRITION INFO (per serving):

Cals: 420

Protein: 6g

Carbs: 45g

Fat: 24g

278. Kushari Salad (Egyptian Rice and Lentil Salad)

Time: 45 mins

Servings: 6

Ingredients:

- 1 cup of rice
- 1 cup of brown lentils
- 1 cup of elbow macaroni
- 1 can (400g) chickpeas, drained and rinsed
- 1 onion, thinly split
- 3 cloves garlic, chop-up
- 3 tbsp vegetable oil
- 2 tbsp white vinegar
- 2 tbsp tomato paste
- 1 tsp ground cumin
- Salt and pepper as needed
- Chop-up parsley for garnish

Instructions:

1. Separately prepare the rice, lentils, and macaroni per the directions on the packaging. Drain, then set apart.
2. Vegetable oil Must be heated in a sizable pan at medium heat. Add the chop-up garlic and onion, and cook up to golden brown.
3. To the pan, add tomato paste, cumin, salt, and pepper. The components Must be thoroughly combined.
4. Stir the cooked lentils and chickpeas into the tomato paste Mixture in the pan after adding them. Cook for a further 2 to 3 mins.
5. Layer the cooked rice, lentil Mixture, and macaroni in a sizable serving dish.
6. Garnish with chop-up parsley and a drizzle of white vinegar.
7. Kushari Salad can be served warm or at room temperature.

NUTRITION INFO (per serving):

Cals: 380

Protein: 15g

Carbs: 65g

Fat: 6g

279. Kofta Tagine (Spiced Meat Stew)

Time: 1 hr 30 mins

Servings: 4

Ingredients:

- 500 grams ground beef or lamb
- 1 onion, lightly chop-up
- 3 cloves garlic, chop-up
- 1/4 cup of breadcrumbs
- 2 tbsp chop-up parsley
- 1 tsp ground cumin
- 1 tsp ground paprika
- 1/2 tsp ground cinnamon
- Salt and pepper as needed
- 2 tbsp olive oil
- 1 can (400g) diced tomatoes
- 1 cup of beef or vegetable broth
- Chop-up cilantro for garnish

Instructions:

1. The ground meat, lightly chop-up onion, chop-up garlic, breadcrumbs, parsley, cumin, paprika, cinnamon, salt, and pepper Must all be combined in a big bowl. To thoroughly incorporate all ingredients, stir well.
2. Make tiny oval kofta balls out of the meat Mixture.
3. Olive oil Must be heated over medium heat in a tagine or big skillet. Add the kofta balls and heat them up to they are evenly browned. The kofta Must be taken out of the tagine and kept aside.
4. Add broth and diced tomatoes to the same tagine. To blend, thoroughly stir.

5. The kofta Must be added back to the tagine, covered, and simmered for 45–60 mins to fully cook the meat and meld the flavors.
6. Before serving, garnish with chop-up cilantro.
7. Include rice or toast with the kofta tagine.

NUTRITION INFO (per serving):
Cals: 420
Protein: 25g
Carbs: 15g
Fat: 30g

280. Shakshuka with Feta Cheese (Egyptian Style)

Time: 30 mins
Servings: 2

Ingredients:
- 4 Big eggs
- 1 onion, chop-up
- 1 red bell pepper, chop-up
- 2 cloves garlic, chop-up
- 2 tbsp olive oil
- 1 can (400g) diced tomatoes
- 1 tsp ground cumin
- 1 tsp ground paprika
- Salt and pepper as needed
- 100 grams fetacheese, cut up
- Chop-up parsley for garnish

Instructions:
1. A big skillet with medium heat is used to heat the olive oil. Add the chop-up garlic, bell pepper, and onion, all chop-up. Sauté the vegetables up to they are tender and slightly browned.
2. To the skillet, add the diced tomatoes, cumin, paprika, salt, and pepper. The components Must be thoroughly combined. To let the flavors to merge, let the Mixture boil for about 10 mins.
3. Create a few tiny holes in the tomato Mixture, then crack the eggs within. When the eggs are cooked to the desired doneness, cover the skillet and continue cooking for an additional 5-7 mins.
4. Shakshuka is garnished with chop-up parsley and feta cheese cut ups.
5. Hot crusty bread Must be served with the Shakshuka with Feta Cheese.

NUTRITION INFO (per serving):
Cals: 380
Protein: 20g
Carbs: 20g
Fat: 25g

281. Mulukhiyah with Lamb (Jute Leaf Stew with Lamb)

Time: 1 hr 30 mins
Servings: 4

Ingredients:
- 500 grams lamb, cubed
- 2 cups of chop-up mulukhiyah leaves (Jute leaves)
- 4 cloves garlic, chop-up
- 1 onion, chop-up
- 2 tbsp vegetable oil
- 1 tsp ground coriander
- 1 tsp ground cumin
- 1 tsp ground paprika
- Salt and pepper as needed
- 4 cups of chicken or vegetable broth
- Cooked rice for serving
- Lemon wedges for serving

Instructions:
1. Vegetable oil Must be heated over medium heat in a big pot. Add the chop-up garlic and onion, both chop-up. Sauté up to the garlic is aromatic and the onion is transparent.
2. Cubed lamb Must be added to the stew and cooked up to browned all over.
3. Salt, pepper, paprika, ground coriander, and cumin Must all be added to the pot. The spices Must be thoroughly combined in to coat the lamb.
4. Fill the pot with the chicken or veggie broth. Bring to a boil, lower the heat, and simmer the lamb for an hr, or up to it is cooked.
5. Cook for an additional 10 mins after adding the chop-up mulukhiyah leaves.
6. Over heated rice, plate the Mulukhiyah with lamb. Over every plate, squeeze some lemon juice.

NUTRITION INFO (per serving):
Cals: 450
Protein: 30g
Carbs: 15g
Fat: 30g

282. Alexandrian Liver (Egyptian Liver Dish)

Time: 30 mins

Servings: 4

Ingredients:

- 500 grams of liver, split
- 2 onions, lightly chop-up
- 2 garlic cloves, chop-up
- 1 tsp ground cumin
- 1 tsp ground coriander
- 1/2 tsp ground chili powder
- Salt and pepper as needed
- 2 tbsp vegetable oil
- Lemon wedges, for serving

Instructions:

1. Over medium heat, warm the vegetable oil in a big skillet.
2. Garlic and onions Must be added to the skillet and sautéed up to transparent.
3. Slices of liver Must brown on both sides after being added to the skillet and cooking for about 5 mins.
4. Over the liver, season with salt, pepper, chili powder, cumin, and coriander. Stir thoroughly to distribute the spices throughout the liver.
5. Cook the liver for a further 5-7 mins, or up to it is cooked through but still soft.
6. Alexandrian liver Must be served hot with lemon wedges on the side after being take outd from the stove.

NUTRITION INFO: (per serving)

Cals: 240

Fat: 11g

Protein: 30g

Carbs: 5g

Fiber: 1g

283. Basbousa Bil Pistachio (Semolina Dessert with Pistachios)

Time: 1 hr

Servings: 8

Ingredients:

- 1 1/2 cups of semolina
- 1/2 cup of all-purpose flour
- 1 cup of sugar
- 1 cup of milk
- 1/2 cup of unsalted butter, dilute
- 1 tsp baking powder
- 1/2 tsp vanilla extract
- 1/2 cup of shelled pistachios, chop-up
- Syrup:
- 1 cup of water
- 1 cup of sugar
- 1 tsp lemon juice

Instructions:

1. Set the oven's temperature to 180 C (350 F).
2. Semolina, all-purpose flour, sugar, dilute butter, milk, baking soda, and vanilla extract Must all be combined in a combining dish. Blend thoroughly up to the batter is smooth.
3. Spread the batter evenly after pouring it onto a prepared baking dish.
4. The batter Must be covered with the chop-up pistachios, which you Must gently press into the batter.
5. Bake for about 30 mins, or up to the top is golden brown, in the preheated oven.
6. Make the syrup while the basbousa is baking. Lemon juice, sugar, and water Must all be combined in a pot. Stirring constantly, bring to a boil over medium heat up to the sugar dissolves completely. Simmer for a further five mins.
7. After removing the basbousa from the oven, immediately cover it with the hot syrup.
8. Before slicing the basbousa into square or diamond-shaped pieces, let it cool fully in the pan.
9. The basbousa bil pistachio Must be served at room temperature.

NUTRITION INFO: (per serving)

Cals: 340

Fat: 15g

Protein: 5g

Carbs: 48g

Fiber: 2g

284. Fiteer with Nutella (Egyptian Pastry with Nutella)

Time: 1 hr 30 mins

Servings: 6

Ingredients:

- 500 grams all-purpose flour
- 1/4 tsp salt
- 1/4 tsp sugar
- 1/2 tsp active dry yeast

- 1 1/2 cups of warm water
- 1 cup of Nutella or chocolate spread
- Powdered sugar, for dusting

Instructions:

1. Combine the all-purpose flour, salt, sugar, and yeast in a sizable combining basin.
2. Combine the dry ingredients with the warm water gradually up to a soft dough forms.
3. The dough Must be smooth and elastic after about 10 mins of kneading on a floured surface.
4. The dough Must be placed in a greased basin, covered with a moist cloth, and let to rise for about an hr, or up to it doubles in size, in a warm location.
5. Set the oven's temperature to 200 C (400 F).
6. The dough Must be slice up into 6 equal pieces, every of which Must be rolled into a thin circle.
7. Every dough circle Must have a thick layer of Nutella or chocolate spread applied to it, leaving a thin border all the way around.
8. To enclose the filling, fold the dough over and press the edges together to form a seal.
9. On a prepared baking sheet, place the filled dough, and bake in the preheated oven for 15 to 20 mins, or up to golden brown.
10. Before dusted with powdered sugar, take out the fiteer from the oven and let it to cool slightly.
11. Serve the fiteer warm or at room temperature with Nutella.

NUTRITION INFO: (per serving)
Cals: 450
Fat: 18g
Protein: 7g
Carbs: 67g
Fiber: 3g

285. Bamia Bil Dajaaj (Okra with Chicken)

Time: 1 hr 15 mins
Servings: 4

Ingredients:

- 500 grams chicken thighs, bone-in and skin-on
- 250 grams fresh okra, trimmed
- 2 onions, lightly chop-up
- 4 garlic cloves, chop-up
- 2 tomatoes, diced
- 2 tbsp tomato paste
- 1 tsp ground cumin
- 1 tsp ground coriander
- 1/2 tsp ground turmeric
- Salt and pepper as needed
- 2 tbsp vegetable oil
- 2 cups of chicken broth
- Fresh cilantro, chop-up (for garnish)

Instructions:

1. Over medium heat, warm the vegetable oil in a big pot or Dutch oven.
2. Add the chicken thighs to the pot after seasoning with salt and pepper. Cook the chicken up to golden brown on all sides. Chicken Must be taken out of the pot and placed aside.
3. Add the onions and garlic to the same pot. The onions Must be sautéed up to transparent.
4. Add the tomato paste, cumin, coriander, turmeric, salt, and pepper along with the diced tomatoes. To blend, thoroughly stir.
5. Add the chicken broth and put the chicken thighs back in the pot. Heat Must be turned down once the Mixture comes to a boil. For approximately 30 mins, simmer covered.
6. When the chicken is thoroughly cooked and the okra is tender, add the fresh okra to the saucepan and simmer for an additional 30 mins.
7. Add freshly slice cilantro as a garnish after removing from the heat.
8. Hot rice or toast Must be served with the bamia bil dajaaj.

NUTRITION INFO: (per serving)
Cals: 380
Fat: 20g
Protein: 28g
Carbs: 22g
Fiber: 5g

286. Mahshi Warak Enab (Stuffed Grape Leaves)

Time: 1 hr 30 mins
Servings: 6

Ingredients:

- 1 jar of grape leaves, drained
- 500 grams ground beef or lamb
- 1 cup of uncooked rice
- 1 onion, lightly chop-up
- 2 garlic cloves, chop-up

- 2 tomatoes, diced
- 1/4 cup of fresh parsley, chop-up
- 1/4 cup of fresh mint leaves, chop-up
- 1 tsp ground cinnamon
- 1 tsp ground allspice
- 1/2 tsp ground nutmeg
- Salt and pepper as needed
- 2 tbsp olive oil
- Lemon wedges, for serving

Instructions:

1. Ground beef or lamb, uncooked rice, diced tomatoes, parsley, mint leaves, ground cinnamon, ground allspice, ground nutmeg, salt, and pepper are all combined in a combining bowl. Blend thoroughly.
2. A grape leaf Must be placed shining side down on a spotless surface. Insert a tbsp of the meat and rice Mixture in the leaf's middle.
3. As you would with a cigar, fold the leaf's sides over the filling before securely rolling it.
4. With the remaining grape leaves and filling, repeat the procedure.
5. Over medium heat, warm the olive oil in a big pot. Place the packed grape leaves in the pot in a single layer, seam side down.
6. Fill the pot with water up to the grape leaves are submerged.
7. To stop the loaded grape leaves from unraveling while cooking, place a heatproof plate or layer of extra grape leaves on top.
8. Once the rice is done and the grape leaves are soft, cover the saucepan and let it simmer on low heat for about an hr.
9. Before serving, take the packed grape leaves from the stove and let them to cool somewhat.
10. Warm mahshi warak enab Must be served along with lemon wedges.

NUTRITION INFO: (per serving)
Cals: 310
Fat: 15g
Protein: 20g
Carbs: 25g
Fiber: 3g

288. Chicken Fatta (Layered Bread and Rice Dish with Chicken)

Time: 1 hr 30 mins
Servings: 4

Ingredients:

- 4 Big pieces of pita bread
- 2 cups of cooked rice
- 1 lb boneless chicken breasts, cooked and shredded
- 1 cup of chicken broth
- 1 cup of yogurt
- 4 cloves garlic, chop-up
- 2 tbsp vegetable oil
- 1 tbsp butter
- 1 tsp ground cumin
- Salt and pepper as needed
- Chop-up parsley for garnish

Instructions:

1. Turn on the oven to 350 °F (175 °C).
2. On a baking sheet, spread out the mini pieces of pita bread in a single layer. They Must be baked for around 10 mins to toast them up to crispy. Take out of the oven, then place aside.
3. Cooked rice and chicken shredded combined in a big bowl. Place aside.
4. The vegetable oil Must be heated in a pan over medium heat. When aromatic, add the chop-up garlic and sauté for one min.
5. To the pot, add the yogurt, butter, cumin, salt, and pepper. Up to the sauce somewhat thickens, simmer for 5 mins while stirring often.
6. Over the rice and chicken combination, drizzle half of the sauce. To coat, gently toss.
7. Place half of the toasted pita bread on the bottom of a serving plate. Spread the rice and chicken Mixture equally on top.
8. With the remaining pita bread and rice Mixture, repeat the layering.
9. Add chop-up parsley as a garnish and then drizzle the remaining sauce over the top layer.
10. Enjoy the Chicken Fatta while it's still warm!

NUTRITION INFO (per serving):
Cals: 450
Protein: 25g
Carbs: 50g
Fat: 15g
Fiber: 3g

289. Basbousa Bil Koktail (Semolina Dessert with Fruit Cocktail)

Time: 1 hr

Servings: 8

Ingredients:

- 2 cups of semolina
- 1 cup of sugar
- 1 cup of yogurt
- 1 cup of dilute butter
- 1 cup of fruit cocktail (drained)
- 1 tsp baking powder
- 1/2 tsp vanilla extract
- Split almonds for garnish

Syrup:

- 2 cups of water
- 1 1/2 cups of sugar
- 1 tbsp lemon juice

Instructions:

1. Turn on the oven to 350 °F (175 °C).
2. Semolina, sugar, yogurt, dilute butter, baking soda, and vanilla extract Must all be combined in a combining dish. All ingredients Must be thoroughly combined.
3. Butter or cooking spray Must be used to grease a baking pan. In the dish, distribute the semolina Mixture evenly.
4. Bake for 30 to 40 mins, or up to the edges are golden brown, in a preheated oven.
5. Make the syrup while the basbousa is baking. Lemon juice, sugar, and water Must all be combined in a pan. After bringing the Mixture to a boil, lower the heat and let it simmer for 10 mins or so, or up to the syrup somewhat thickens.
6. After taking the basbousa out of the oven, evenly drizzle it with the hot syrup.
7. Slice the basbousa into square or diamond shapes after letting it cool for a few mins.
8. Every square of basbousa Must have a piece of fruit cocktail on top, with split almonds for decoration.
9. Enjoy the Basbousa Bil Koktail while it's still warm!

NUTRITION INFO (per serving):

Cals: 400

Protein: 6g

Carbs: 55g

Fat: 17g

Fiber: 2g

290. Eggah (Egyptian Omelette)

Time: 20 mins

Servings: 2

Ingredients:

- 4 Big eggs
- 1 onion, lightly chop-up
- 1 tomato, diced
- 1/4 cup of chop-up fresh parsley
- 1/4 cup of chop-up fresh cilantro
- Salt and pepper as needed
- 2 tbsp vegetable oil

Instructions:

1. Beat the eggs in a combining dish up to they are well combined.
2. To the beaten eggs, add the chop-up onion, diced tomato, parsley, cilantro, salt, and pepper. Combine all the ingredients.
3. In a nonstick frying pan over medium heat, warm the vegetable oil.
4. Spread the egg Mixture evenly after adding it to the pan.
5. The omelette Must be cooked for about 5 mins, or up to the bottom is golden brown and set.
6. Flip the omelette gently and cook for an additional 3–4 mins on the second side.
7. Slice the Eggah into wedges and transfer it to a serving platter.
8. Enjoy the Eggah while it's still hot!

NUTRITION INFO (per serving):

Cals: 250

Protein: 14g

Carbs: 8g

Fat: 18g

Fiber: 1g

291. Hawawshi Sliders (Egyptian Meat Sliders)

Time: 40 mins

Servings: 4

Ingredients:

- 1 lb ground beef or lamb
- 4 mini burger buns or slider buns
- 1 onion, lightly chop-up
- 2 cloves garlic, chop-up

- 1 tomato, diced
- 1/4 cup of chop-up fresh parsley
- 1 tsp ground cumin
- 1 tsp paprika
- Salt and pepper as needed
- Vegetable oil for frying

Instructions:

1. Ground beef or lamb, diced tomato, chop-up onion, chop-up garlic, parsley, ground cumin, paprika, salt, and pepper Must all be combined in a combining dish. All ingredients Must be thoroughly combined.
2. Make 4 equal amounts of the beef Mixture into patties by dividing it into equal portions.
3. In a frying pan, warm some vegetable oil over medium heat.
4. The meat patties Must be cooked through and browned after about 5 to 6 mins of frying on every side.
5. Burger buns or slider buns Must be lightly toasted while the meat patties are cooking.
6. Place a bun over every cooked meat patty.
7. Enjoy the Hawawshi Sliders while they're still hot!

NUTRITION INFO (per serving):

Cals: 350
Protein: 20g
Carbs: 25g
Fat: 18g
Fiber: 2g

292. Ful Medames Hummus (Fava Bean Hummus)

Time: 10 mins
Servings: 4

Ingredients:

- 1 can (15 ozs) fava beans, drained and rinsed
- 2 cloves garlic
- 2 tbsp tahini (sesame paste)
- 2 tbsp lemon juice
- 1 tbsp olive oil
- 1/2 tsp ground cumin
- Salt as needed
- Chop-up fresh parsley for garnish
- Non-compulsory toppings: olive oil, paprika, chop-up tomatoes, chop-up cucumbers

Instructions:

1. Fava beans, garlic, tahini, lemon juice, olive oil, ground cumin, and salt Must all be combined in a mixer.
2. The Mixture Must be processed up to it is creamy and smooth, scraping down the bowl's sides as necessary.
3. If necessary, add extra salt or lemon juice after tasting the dish to correct the seasoning.
4. To serve, place the Ful Medames Hummus in a bowl.
5. Add fresh parsley that has been chop-up to the dish as well as any extra garnishes you choose, such as a drizzle of olive oil, a sprinkle of paprika, split tomatoes, or chop-up cucumbers.
6. Provide pita bread, tortilla chips, or raw veggies for dipping along with the Ful Medames Hummus.
7. Enjoy!

NUTRITION INFO (per serving):

Cals: 150
Protein: 6g
Carbs: 12g
Fat: 9g
Fiber: 4g

293. Basbousa with Rosewater (Semolina Dessert with Rosewater)

Time: 1 hr
Servings: 8

Ingredients:

- 2 cups of semolina
- 1 cup of sugar
- 1 cup of unsweetened shredded coconut
- 1 cup of dilute butter
- 1 cup of milk
- 1/4 cup of rosewater
- 1 tsp baking powder
- Split almonds for garnish

Syrup:

- 2 cups of water
- 1 1/2 cups of sugar
- 1 tbsp lemon juice
- 1 tbsp rosewater

Instructions:

1. Turn on the oven to 350 °F (175 °C).

2. Semolina, sugar, coconut shreds, dilute butter, milk, rosewater, and baking powder Must all be combined in a combining dish. All ingredients Must be thoroughly combined.
3. Butter or cooking spray Must be used to grease a baking pan. In the dish, distribute the semolina Mixture evenly.
4. Bake for 30 to 40 mins, or up to the edges are golden brown, in a preheated oven.
5. Make the syrup while the basbousa is baking. Water, sugar, lemon juice, and rosewater Must all be combined in a pot. After bringing the Mixture to a boil, lower the heat and let it simmer for 10 mins or so, or up to the syrup somewhat thickens.
6. After taking the basbousa out of the oven, evenly drizzle it with the hot syrup.
7. Slice the basbousa into square or diamond shapes after letting it cool for a few mins.
8. For decoration, top every piece of basbousa with a split almond.
9. Enjoy the Basbousa with Rosewater when served at room temperature!

NUTRITION INFO (per serving):
Cals: 400
Protein: 5g
Carbs: 50g
Fat: 20g
Fiber: 2g

294. Buckwheat and Vegetable Pilaf (Griby s Grechkoy)

Time: 40 mins
Servings: 4

Ingredients:

- 1 cup of buckwheat groats
- 2 cups of vegetable broth
- 1 tbsp olive oil
- 1 onion, diced
- 2 carrots, diced
- 1 red bell pepper, diced
- 1 zucchini, diced
- 2 cloves garlic, chop-up
- 1 tsp dried thyme
- Salt and pepper as needed

Instructions:

1. Buckwheat groats Must be rinsed with cold water. Add the rinsed buckwheat to the boiling vegetable stock in a saucepan. Once the buckwheat is soft and the liquid has been absorbed, reduce heat, cover, and simmer for about 15 mins.
2. Olive oil Must be heated in a sizable skillet over medium heat. Add the thyme, garlic, onion, carrots, bell pepper, zucchini, salt, and pepper. Cook for about 10 mins, or up to the vegetables are soft.
3. In the skillet with the vegetables, add the cooked buckwheat. After thoroughly combining everything, cook for a further 5 mins.
4. Serve hot as a side dish or as a main course.

295. Russian Egg Salad (Mimoza)

Time: 30 mins
Servings: 4

Ingredients:

- 4 hard-boiled eggs
- 1 mini onion, lightly chop-up
- 1 mini carrot, boiled and finely grated
- 1 mini potato, boiled and finely grated
- 1 can (7 ozs) canned peas, drained
- 1 can (7 ozs) canned corn, drained
- 1/2 cup of mayonnaise
- Salt and pepper as needed

Instructions:

1. Hard-boiled eggs Must be peel off and their yolks and whites separated. Egg whites Must be chop-up lightly and kept aside.
2. With a fork, crush the egg yolks in a big bowl. Combine the mayonnaise, chop-up onion, finely grated carrot, finely grated potato, peas, corn, and salt and pepper. Blend thoroughly.
3. On a serving dish, arrange the egg yolk Mixture in a uniform layer.
4. Over the egg yolk Mixture, evenly distribute the mashed egg whites.
5. Before serving, place in the fridge for at least one hr.

296. Buckwheat and Mushroom Stuffed Tomatoes (Griby s Grechkoy)

Time: 1 hr

Servings: 4

Ingredients:

- 4 Big tomatoes
- 1 cup of buckwheat groats
- 2 cups of vegetable broth
- 1 tbsp olive oil
- 1 onion, diced
- 2 cloves garlic, chop-up
- 8 ozs mushrooms, split
- 1 tsp dried thyme
- Salt and pepper as needed

Instructions:

1. Set the oven's temperature to 350°F (175°C). To create hollow shells, carefully scoop out the pulp and seeds from the tomatoes' tops. Tomato shells Must be set aside.
2. Buckwheat groats Must be rinsed with cold water. Add the rinsed buckwheat to the boiling vegetable stock in a saucepan. Once the buckwheat is soft and the liquid has been absorbed, reduce heat, cover, and simmer for about 15 mins.
3. The olive oil Must be heated over medium heat in a different skillet. Cook the onion and garlic after being added up to tender.
4. To the skillet, add the mushrooms, thyme, salt, and pepper. Cook the mushrooms for about 5 mins, or up to they are soft.
5. The cooked buckwheat Must be combined with the mushroom Mixture. Put the buckwheat-mushroom filling inside the hollowed-out tomato shells.
6. The tomatoes Must be soft after 30-35 mins of baking the packed tomatoes in a baking dish.

297. Mushroom and Cucumber Salad (Gribnoy Salat):

Time: 15 mins

Servings: 4

Ingredients:

- 250g mushrooms, split
- 2 cucumbers, thinly split
- 1 mini onion, lightly chop-up
- 2 tbsp fresh dill, chop-up
- 2 tbsp vegetable oil
- 2 tbsp white vinegar
- Salt and pepper as needed

Instructions:

1. Split mushrooms, cucumbers, onions, and dill Must all be combined in a sizable bowl.
2. Combine the vegetable oil, vinegar, salt, and pepper in a separate mini bowl.
3. After adding the dressing, carefully toss the salad to combine.
4. Before serving, place in the refrigerator for at least 30 mins to enable the flavors to mingle.
5. Enjoy while serving chilled!

298. Russian Potato Salad (Olivier):

Time: 1 hr

Servings: 6-8

Ingredients:

- 4 Big potatoes, boiled, peel off, and diced
- 2 carrots, boiled, peel off, and diced
- 4 hard-boiled eggs, diced
- 1 cup of pickles, diced
- 1 cup of cooked peas
- 1 cup of cooked diced ham or bologna
- 1/2 cup of mayonnaise
- Salt and pepper as needed

Instructions:

1. Combine the chop-up potatoes, carrots, eggs, pickles, peas, and ham in a big bowl.
2. Salt, pepper, and mayonnaise Must all be added to the bowl and gently combined up to everything is evenly coated.
3. If necessary, taste and adjust the seasoning.
4. Before serving, place the food in the refrigerator for at least an hr to let the flavors meld.
5. Enjoy while serving chilled!

299. Mushroom and Tomato Salad (Gribnoy Salat):

Time: 20 mins

Servings: 4

Ingredients:

- 250g mushrooms, split
- 2 Big tomatoes, diced
- 1 mini onion, lightly chop-up

- 2 tbsp fresh parsley, chop-up
- 2 tbsp vegetable oil
- 1 tbsp lemon juice
- Salt and pepper as needed

Instructions:

1. Split mushrooms, diced tomatoes, onion, and parsley Must all be combined in a sizable bowl.
2. Combine the vegetable oil, lemon juice, salt, and pepper in a separate mini bowl.
3. After adding the dressing, carefully toss the salad to combine.
4. Leting time for the flavors to mingle together will help the salad taste better.
5. Dispense and savor!

300. Buckwheat and Vegetable Pilaf (Griby s Grechkoy)

Time: 45 mins
Servings: 4

Ingredients:

- 1 cup of buckwheat
- 2 cups of vegetable broth
- 1 tbsp olive oil
- 1 onion, diced
- 2 carrots, diced
- 1 red bell pepper, diced
- 1 zucchini, diced
- 1 cup of mushrooms, split
- 2 cloves garlic, chop-up
- Salt and pepper as needed
- Fresh parsley, chop-up (for garnish)

Instructions:

Rinse the buckwheat under cold water and drain well.

1. Activate the boiling process of the vegetable broth in a medium pot. As soon as the buckwheat is added, turn the heat down to low, cover the pan, and simmer for about 20 mins, or up to the buckwheat is soft and the liquid has been absorbed.
2. Olive oil Must be heated in a sizable skillet over medium heat. Saute the onion till transparent after adding it.
3. To the skillet, add the carrots, red bell pepper, zucchini, mushrooms, and garlic. Cook the vegetables for approximately 10 mins, or up to they are soft.
4. As needed, add salt and pepper to the food.
5. Combine well after adding the cooked buckwheat to the skillet with vegetables.
6. Cook for a further five mins, stirring now and then.
7. With fresh parsley as a garnish, take out from heat.
8. Buckwheat and vegetable pilaf Must be served hot.

NUTRITION INFO (per serving):

Cals: 220
Fat: 5g
Carbs: 40g
Fiber: 6g
Protein: 8g

301. Russian Egg Salad (Mimoza)

Time: 30 mins
Servings: 6

Ingredients:

- 6 hard-boiled eggs, peel off
- 2 medium potatoes, boiled and cubed
- 2 medium carrots, boiled and finely grated
- 1 cup of canned peas, drained
- 1 cup of pickles, diced
- 1 mini onion, lightly chop-up
- 1 cup of mayonnaise
- Salt and pepper as needed
- Fresh dill (for garnish)

Instructions:

1. Four of the hard-boiled eggs Must be chop-up into mini bits and put in a sizable combining basin.
2. To the combining basin, add the cubed potatoes, finely grated carrots, canned peas, pickles, and chop-up onion. Combine thoroughly.
3. When everything is thoroughly covered, add the mayonnaise to the Mixture and toss.
4. As needed, add salt and pepper to the food.
5. Smooth the top of the egg salad before transferring it to a serving dish.
6. Place the remaining 2 hard-boiled eggs on top of the salad after slicing them into thin rounds.
7. Add some fresh dill as garnish.
8. Before serving, place in the refrigerator for at least an hr to enable the flavors to mingle.
9. Russian egg salad Must be served chilled.

NUTRITION INFO (per serving):
Cals: 320
Fat: 22g
Carbs: 22g
Fiber: 3g
Protein: 9g

Printed in Great Britain
by Amazon